DR NATHAN BROOKS

Mass Casualty

The Rise of Lone Actors

First published by Ground Proof Forensic Institute 2025

Copyright © 2025 by Dr Nathan Brooks

All rights reserved. No part of this publication may be reproduced, stored or transmitted in any form or by any means, electronic, mechanical, photocopying, recording, scanning, or otherwise without written permission from the publisher. It is illegal to copy this book, post it to a website, or distribute it by any other means without permission.

First edition

ISBN: 978-0-473-74999-6

Cover art by B. A. Brooks

This book was professionally typeset on Reedsy.
Find out more at reedsy.com

To my family – thank you for the joys, the tears, the laughter, and the love.

Most of all, the meaning you bring to my life.

Contents

Prologue 1
Introduction 8

I   The Path To Violence

1   A Troubled Childhood 21
2   A Traumatic Bond 31
3   A State Of Decline 39
4   A Modern Crisis 50
5   When Things Go Wrong 63
6   The Power Of Beliefs 69
7   When Cultures Collide 78
8   A Staircase and Bathtub 85
9   A Mind On Fire 94
10 The Many Paths To Violence 104

II   The Search For Answers

11 The Black Swan 117
12 From Reaction To Prevention 124
13 The Need For Prediction 137
14 Radical Minds 152
15 A Fight For Survival 159
16 Government Dilemmas 167
17 The Power Of Media 180
18 Creating A Good Life 190

19	Becoming A Hero	200
20	Time For Change	209

Author's Note   217
A Note On Sources   220
Bibliography   221

Prologue

'One of the issues with which I have struggled is that this accused committed a horrific crime, one of the most devastating tragedies this city has endured, for the purpose of achieving fame. And he has achieved that purpose.'

Justice J. Molloy

AT AROUND NOON on 23 April 2018, twenty-five-year-old Alek Minassian picked up the rental van he had reserved weeks earlier, carefully choosing it as the weapon for his planned attack. His goal was clear: to cause mass casualties. Earlier that morning, Minassian had posted a cryptic message on his Facebook page:

'Private (Recruit) Minassian Infantry 00010, wishing to speak to Sgt 4chan please. C23249161. The Incel Rebellion has already begun! We will overthrow all the Chads and Stacys! All hail the Supreme Gentleman Elliot Rodger!'

Once inside the vehicle, Minassian drove towards Toronto's Yonge Street. Upon reaching the traffic lights at the intersection of Yonge Street and Finch Avenue, he veered off the road onto the adjacent footpath. Accelerating, he ploughed through pedestrians along the sidewalk, continuing his rampage for more than 2.5 kilometres. The attack came to an abrupt end when a pedestrian's beverage splashed across his windscreen, obscuring his view.

Minutes later, Minassian stepped out of the van. Attempting to intimidate the sole pursuing police officer, he reached into his jacket pocket, creating the impression that he was armed. Despite his efforts to provoke the officer into shooting him, he was successfully apprehended without further incident.

During his interview with police, Minassian claimed he identified as an '**Incel**', seeking vengeance against the '*Chads*' and '*Stacys*' while asserting his superiority over the '*Normies*'. He explained, '*The Stacys [are] going for the Chads ... Chads and Stacys are above Normies ... We don't necessarily wish to kill the Normies, but we do wish to subjugate them in order to make them understand that our type is the more superior one.*'

This peculiar set of terminology might easily be mistaken for characters from a teenage science fiction magazine. The intermingling of labels, rules, and a quest for dominance blurs the line between fantasy and reality. Not only this, the social hierarchy, commands, and desire to '*win*', as articulated by Minassian, bares resemblance to the world of multiplayer video games more than the reality of everyday life. Yet, Minassian's description of his Incel identity is not a fictional tale – it is a sobering reality.

The concept of **Involuntary Celibacy** first emerged in 1993 through a university study that included a website titled *Alana's Involuntary Celibacy Project*. This platform aimed to build an inclusive community for individuals struggling with intimate relationships and to explore the causes of sexual inactivity. Alana, the project's creator, had positive intentions, stating, '*There were a lot of people who were lonely and not really sure how to start dating. They were kind of lacking those social skills, and I had a lot of sympathy for that because I had been through the same situation.*'

Over time, the notion of involuntary celibacy took a darker turn. Instead of fostering connection, as Alana had envisioned, her work was hijacked by angry men who weaponised her ideas. Involuntary celibacy evolved into an ideology espoused by Incels – men who define themselves by their perceived inability to form intimate or sexual relationships with women. This sense of rejection and isolation was a key theme in Minassian's statements following his attack. He explained, *'Celibacy means someone who never before has had sexual intercourse; involuntary celibacy means this wasn't your choice, essentially being thrown into true forced loneliness and being unable to lose your virginity.'*

The Incel movement emerged in the mid-2000s, gaining momentum through platforms such as 4chan and Reddit. With time, Incel forums and websites expanded, with the initial frustration over relationship difficulties evolving into hostility – primarily directed at women. As Incel attitudes and beliefs developed, some individuals sought retribution or resorted to acts of militant violence. The rise in hostility and violence across these platforms has led to the refinement of principles, rules, and identified enemies.

Adherents of the Incel philosophy believe their inability to attract women or establish intimate relationships stems from factors such as genetics, social structures, and evolution. A core belief is that women naturally seek out attractive and successful men, leaving those disadvantaged by physical appearance or poor socio-economic status without partners.

According to Incel principles, men with chiselled jawlines, a full head of hair, and athletic builds – labelled as Chads – are able to attract the majority of women, particularly those with large breasts, long blonde hair, and curvy bodies, who are referred to as Stacys. In contrast, Incels feel resigned to pursuing women considered unattractive or unsuccessful – known as Beckys – who themselves long for Chads but seldom succeed. Incels claim Beckys only settle for *'inferior'* men as they age and lose their youthful appeal. Even in committed relationships, Incels allege that women are prone to infidelity with Chads.

This worldview positions Chads and Stacys at the top of a perceived social hierarchy, with Normies – average people – in the middle. Incels occupy the bottom tier, viewing themselves as deprived of both social and intimate opportunities. Although Normies lack superior physical attributes, they are believed to possess greater social advantages and access to life opportunities.

Incels harbour resentment towards women, whom they blame for the failures and adversities they experience. They argue that the social and intimate hierarchy is skewed due to the unscrupulous and promiscuous nature of women. In response, Incels believe it is their mission to restore social order. This involves avenging the Stacys and Chads, oppressing the Normies, and proving that Incels are the dominant and superior group within the species.

While many Incels attempt to achieve these goals through the promotion and dissemination of their views and beliefs, some resort to violence to progress their cause.

THE EXPERIENCE OF REJECTION AND HUMILIATION ignited Alek Minassian's anger towards women and pushed him to seek companionship with other disaffected men. According to Minassian, a defining moment occurred at a Halloween party in 2013 when a group of women rejected his attempts to engage them in conversation. Instead of responding politely, they laughed at him and turned their attention to a group of *'obnoxious men'*. This incident left Minassian feeling angry and resentful, and he began sharing his frustrations in online forums and chat groups.

Minassian discovered a community of men who shared his sense of rejection and humiliation. The recognition and support he received from these groups led him to spend countless hours interacting on online platforms. Through these discussions, he claimed to have connected with Elliot Rodger in early January 2014, followed by Chris Harper-Mercer shortly afterwards.

Minassian stated that he exchanged messages with Rodger on Reddit until May 2014, when Rodger informed him of an *'important mission'* he needed to carry out. On 23 May 2014, twenty-two-year-old Elliot Rodger perpetrated a targeted attack. He began by stabbing his two roommates and a visitor at his apartment. Rodger then drove his BMW 328i Coupe to the Alpha Phi Sorority house near the University of California, armed with firearms he had purchased using savings from his family. Unable to gain access to the house, he walked to the nearby Delta Delta Delta Sorority house, where he shot three women outside, killing two.

Returning to his car, Rodger drove past the Isla Vista Deli Mart, firing his weapon and killing a male student. As he continued to drive, he shot at pedestrians who he encountered. Eventually, police confronted Rodger, leading to a brief exchange of gunfire. Cornered, Rodger turned his weapon on himself, taking his own life.

Rodger's actions were fuelled by the perceived rejection he experienced at a party in 2013. Bearing many similarities to Minassian's account, Rodger had reportedly approached a group of women at a party, only to have his advances rejected. He perceived the lack of interest as a personal slight and attempted to push one of the women off a ledge. His aggression towards the women drew the attention of a group of nearby men, who confronted him and pushed him off the ledge. Enraged by the incident, Rodger spent the following weeks and months devising a plan for revenge – purchasing weapons, writing his personal manifesto, constructing an attack plan, and recording a series of videos in which he expressed his grievances with society and women.

Rodger's attack quickly gained him notoriety on online forums. He became known as the *'founding father'* of the Incel movement after he killed and converted the *'life status'* of many, including Stacys and Chads, to *'death status'*. Rodger proved that Incels could not be oppressed.

Similarly, Chris Harper-Mercer carried out an attack in 2015 at a community college in Oregon, USA, driven by his belief that he was a virgin with *'no friends, no job, no girlfriend'*. Inspired by Elliot Rodger, Harper-Mercer callously ordered students into a classroom and shot them one by one as he asked them to plead for their lives. He left one student alive in the classroom to pass on his manifesto to the police. Like Rodger, Harper-Mercer took his own life during a shootout with police.

The actions of Rodger and Harper-Mercer served as inspiration for Minassian. He found validation, justification, and meaning in the violence of these men. Along with researching mass murders and school shootings during his high school years, Minassian spent hours immersed in Incel forums and subgroups, intently studying Rodger's manifesto.

Throughout his life, Minassian had struggled with Autism Spectrum Disorder (ASD), a developmental condition that impedes social functioning and communication, and leads to limited behavioural expression. Individuals with ASD may experience heightened sensitivity to sensory stimuli and exhibit difficulties in understanding social cues, often making it challenging for them to engage in typical social interactions. ASD is also associated with fixed interests, difficulty adjusting to change, and challenges in establishing and maintaining social connections.

Although Minassian faced significant difficulty in forming emotional bonds and was bullied during his high school years, he was highly intelligent, came from a loving family, and had been achieving success in early adulthood. He had no criminal history or prior violent behaviour, and in the days leading up to his attack, he submitted his final university assignment for his degree in computer programming. Additionally, he was about to start his first serious job working for a software development company.

On the surface, his future appeared bright and promising. However, rather than celebrating his successes and having hope for his future, Minassian was fearful about starting a proper job. Lonely and frustrated, he perceived himself as being disadvantaged by life. He was swept up in an online culture that echoed this sentiment, reinforcing the belief that women were to blame for his lack of intimacy and sex. In reality, this provided a convenient excuse and allowed him to avoid taking responsibility for his own shortcomings. Most concerningly, it gave him someone to blame and target. In his mind, women were the cause of the injustice in his life and in the world. He saw himself as a hero acting on behalf of the oppressed.

Minassian's disturbing sense of heroism and desire for significance led to catastrophic suffering. The injuries sustained by the fifteen surviving victims of his attack were horrific and reminiscent of a war zone:

Skull and spine fractures, abdominal bleeding, broken jaw, fractured ribs, bleeding in the skull, broken left ribs, collapsed left lung, kidney bleeding, brain bleeding, fractured lumbar, injuries to the arm, elbow, and left knee, dislocated shoulder, fractured ribs, fifteen stitches to the back of the head, brain trauma, broken ribs, broken scapula, broken pelvis, traumatic brain injury, surgical fracture to the lumbar spine, fractured right pelvis, twenty-four broken vertebrae, facial fractures, lacerations to the left knee, fractured pelvis, clavicle and tailbone, knocked unconscious, multiple stitches and staples to the hands, head, and forearm, numerous broken bones, both legs amputated, cervical fracture, brain bleeding, and a broken pelvis.

In addition to these horrific injuries to the surviving victims, eleven people tragically lost their lives. Altogether, the lives of twenty-six people, along with their family and friends, were changed forever on 23 April 2018.

Why?

Because Alek Minassian was angry at women and perceived himself to be a '*supreme gentleman*'.

'*I was angry that they would give their love and affection to obnoxious brutes,*' he stated.

'*I accomplished my mission.*'

Introduction

'The biggest concern we have right now is not the launching of a major terrorist operation, although that risk is always there, the risk that we're especially concerned over right now is the lone wolf terrorist, somebody with a single weapon being able to carry out wide-scale massacres ... You know, when you've got one person who is deranged or driven by a hateful ideology, they can do a lot of damage, and it's a lot harder to trace those lone wolf operators.'

Barack Obama – 2011

THEODORE BUNDY WAS RESPONSIBLE for the deaths of multiple young women across several states in the USA throughout the 1970s. Bundy targeted his victims through a combination of ruses, ploys, and prowling behaviour. In the hours prior to his execution, Bundy confessed to perpetrating thirty homicides, many of which involved rape, kidnapping, necrophilia, and decapitation. The horrific acts committed by Bundy, and other offenders who engaged in similar behaviours, led to the coining of the term '***Serial Killer***'. This form of violence was deemed to involve two or more victims being killed by an offender or offenders over a series of separate occasions. Following a murder, offenders typically had a brief period without offending before going on to kill another person for their own gratification.

Over the coming decades, serial killers emerged in high numbers across the world, particularly in the USA and Canada. Perpetrators such as Jeffrey Dahmer, John Wayne Gacy, Robert Hansen, Paul Bernardo, and Dennis

INTRODUCTION

Rader became infamous due to the heinous and cruel nature of their crimes. While at times impulsive, serial killers were typically individuals who acted with a plan, often targeting and selecting victims in a predatory and calculated manner. In response, many specialised police units were formed, often focused on serial crime or stranger-based violent offending. This included the Federal Bureau of Investigation (FBI) Behavioral Analysis Unit, which became the subject of many books and television shows, such as *Mindhunter*, *Criminal Minds*, and others. In several countries, specialised units were formed based on investigative psychology practices. Essentially, these units centred on behavioural science and analysis, bringing expert knowledge of psychology, behaviour, and crime to the apprehension of serious violent offenders. Serial killers caught police off guard across many countries, and it took the collaborative efforts of police, academics, criminologists, and mental health professionals to understand this offending and catch perpetrators promptly.

At the same time as a wave of serial killers emerged across many nations, there were occasional incidents of people killing multiple victims in a single violent act. For instance, in 1980, schoolteacher Alvin Lee King III walked into a Texas church armed with several firearms and killed five people, wounding another ten. King had been accused of raping his daughter, and after members of the church refused to support him during the trial, he sought retribution. Fortunately, acts like King's were relatively uncommon during these years, with targeted acts of violence primarily occurring due to serial offending rather than mass killing.

It's estimated that throughout the 1980s, nearly 770 serial killers were active across the USA, a number that declined to 669 in the 1990s. Throughout these years, police discovered thousands of dead bodies and were faced with many sickening crime scenes. Since then, serial killing has continued to decline sharply, with around 100 serial perpetrators believed to be operating in the last decade. The reduction in serial crime over recent decades is likely a result of the extensive resources, funding, specialised policing teams, and research focused on the apprehension and early detection of serial perpetrators. Alongside these initiatives, considerable advances have occurred in DNA technology and other forensic science methods, enabling police to solve cases promptly and identify trends across crimes with greater efficiency. Technological advances such as CCTV cameras have led to easier offender detection, and mobile phone devices have given victims quicker access to contact police and other services.

As the frequency of serial killings has declined, another form of violence has emerged, growing in both scale and severity. This shift in violent crime trends reflects broader changes in societal dynamics, where mass violence, once a rare occurrence, has become disturbingly common. Since the 1970s, there has been a steady increase in mass killings across the USA and other Western countries. In the 1960s, just four people died from this form of violence in the USA. By the early 2010s, this number had risen to 115, with an additional 160 people injured. The frequency of attacks has also increased across the USA, moving from an average of one every 180 days before 1999 to one every forty-seven days by 2015. This wave of violence has also spread to other parts of the world, particularly Europe, which has experienced a 412% increase in terrorism and mass attacks over the past three decades. Between 2019 and 2021, there were ninety-nine self-initiated terrorist attacks globally, with the majority occurring in France, Germany, Greece, the USA, the UK, and Switzerland.

Although mass attacks have been less frequent in Australia and New Zealand, several significant events have occurred in these countries, including the Sydney Lindt Café siege and the Christchurch terror attack.

THE LANDSCAPE OF VIOLENCE has shifted dramatically. While serial killers and organised terrorist groups have historically been major concerns for law enforcement agencies, the emergence of *'Lone Actors'* – individuals who self-initiate to violence – now represents a growing and significant threat. Lone actor violence typically involves a single perpetrator – but in some cases offenders operate in dyads or triads, forming connections with others who share their violent interests. Together, these individuals discreetly plan and carry out an attack. Whether it be an aggrieved school shooter or a terrorist driven by a political agenda, both attackers share similar behavioural pathways when moving towards violence.

Although often referred to as *'lone wolves'*, the term *'lone actor'* is now more commonly used. The phrase **'Lone Wolf'** was popularised by the media in the 1990s and early 2000s to describe individuals who committed mass attacks without the direct support of organised groups. However, some critics argue that the *'lone wolf'* label fails to capture the many different presentations of perpetrators. The notion of a lone wolf conjures an image of a rogue, cunning, and secretive individual, which does not always align with the reality of these perpetrators. In fact, many lone actors are not secretive about their plans. Instead, they may leave signs of their intent, and sometimes even boast of their upcoming attacks. Due to these concerns, the term lone actor has gained favour among scholars and law enforcement, as it better reflects the variety of individuals involved in these acts. While lone actor offences share many similarities, perpetrators often vary in terms of their organisation, tactics, secrecy, social isolation, motivation, and lethality.

Criminal investigative psychologist Dr Matt Logan has gone as far as to describe lone actors as *'misfits masquerading as terrorists'*. He remarks, *'many wear the jersey but few play for the team'*.

Lone actor violence typically falls into three main categories: terrorism, spree or rampage killing, and mass murder.

Terrorism is a deliberate and calculated form of violence intended to scare, intimidate, and terrorise others – often driven by political, social, racial, religious, or environmental causes. This type of violence was evident in the Manchester Arena bombing on 22 May 2017. At the conclusion of an Ariana Grande concert, twenty-two-year-old Salman Abedi detonated a bomb as patrons exited the venue, killing himself and twenty-three others. Abedi, a Libyan-born national who had immigrated to Britain as a refugee, had developed extremist Islamic beliefs and was compelled to sacrifice his life for his cause.

In contrast to terrorism, **Spree** or **Rampage Killings** are generally driven by personal crises, grievances, or extreme beliefs. These acts are characterised by the offender's geographic mobility, moving from one location to another and leaving a trail of violence. While some incidents span mere hours, others can unfold over several days. Christopher Dorner's spree killing in 2013 is an example of this type of event. A former LAPD officer, Dorner embarked on a vengeful rampage after being dismissed from the department, targeting law enforcement officers and their families. His actions, which he justified in a lengthy manifesto, stemmed from perceived injustices he faced. Over several days, Dorner killed four individuals, sparking a massive manhunt across multiple states. Cornered by San Bernardino police, Dorner ultimately took his own life.

Dorner's chaotic spree of violence stands in contrast to the calculated **Mass Murder** perpetrated by Stephen Paddock on 1 October 2017. Mass murder typically involves the killing of multiple victims in a short time frame and in a single location. In Paddock's case, he rented a room on the thirty-second floor of the Mandalay Bay hotel in Las Vegas. From the comfort of his hotel room, Paddock opened fire on thousands of patrons attending a country music festival. Armed with a small arsenal of high-caliber weapons, Paddock killed sixty people and injured more than 800 others, making it the deadliest mass shooting by a single person in US history. Despite extensive investigation, no clear motivation for his actions was identified.

Although recent mass casualty attacks have generally been perpetrated by lone actors, for decades this type of killing was predominantly associated with group actors and organised terrorists. These types of acts were typically developed and implemented by a small cell, or group of individuals, brought

INTRODUCTION

together by the shared purpose of committing terror. Their intent was to maximise casualties and cause widespread fear and mayhem. This was exemplified in the devastating events that occurred in New York on 11 September 2001, with close to 3,000 people killed through coordinated group terrorism.

Group actors have employed a variety of methods, from hijacking aeroplanes to detonating bombs, to carry out mass attacks. Often, these types of terrorists die during the commission of their attack, leading to terms such as *'suicide terrorist'* or *'suicide bomber'*. However, these individuals are not typically *'clinically suicidal'*. People experiencing suicidal ideation often feel profound depression and hopelessness, viewing suicide as a means of escaping their emotional pain. By contrast, group-based actors perceive death as the ultimate commitment to their cause. They willingly sacrifice their lives to achieve their mission, believing their actions serve a higher purpose.

For groups like Al-Qaeda and Islamic State, death is glorified as a heroic sacrifice and the highest form of devotion. Acts of martyrdom, or dying for a religious cause, are revered within these groups, often promising the individual a place in paradise in the afterlife. This ideology transforms death into a celebrated and purposeful act, rather than an escape from despair.

Lone actors, by comparison, are far more likely to have a history of mental illness. Research indicates that lone actors are over thirteen times more likely than group terrorists to have mental health conditions. One study found that 32% of lone actors had a diagnosed mental illness, compared to just 3.5% of group actors. Furthermore, lone actors tend to be older than their group-based counterparts, who are often in their twenties, though some lone attackers have been as young as thirteen. Lone actors are also more likely to be single and unemployed, with nearly 40% having a prior criminal history.

Unlike group actors, lone actors typically lack specialised training or expertise in weaponry. Instead, they tend to use weapons that are readily accessible and practical. This includes motor vehicles, which may be used to ram into crowds, as well as firearms, knives, or, less commonly, homemade explosives. Their chosen targets are often places where large numbers of people gather, such as schools, workplaces, or popular public venues.

In contrast, group actors tend to use more sophisticated weaponry and devices, reflecting greater levels of planning and skill. While they too may target public spaces, there is a stronger focus on symbolic or strategic locations, such as government buildings, transport systems, and national landmarks. These targets are often chosen to maximise the political and societal impact of an attack.

Lone actors also differ significantly from conventional homicide offenders in their methods and victim selection. A revealing study comparing these two groups found that lone actors typically attacked random victims, while homicide offenders overwhelmingly targeted family members or acquaintances. Only 10% of homicide perpetrators killed strangers, whereas 80% of lone actor offences involved stranger victims. Lone actor attacks commonly occurred in public spaces or public buildings, whereas homicide offenders committed their crimes in private settings or more ordinary public locations, such as suburban streets or vehicles. Lone actor events were significantly more lethal, with a much higher average number of victims. Among homicide offenders, the maximum number of victims killed by a single perpetrator was four. By contrast, lone actor violence has seen far higher casualty counts, with one offender killing seventy-seven people in a single event.

While there are some demographic similarities between the two groups – both are predominantly male, similar in age, and have comparable rates of unemployment and mental health issues – key distinctions remain. Nearly two-thirds of lone actors were single, and they were twice as likely to commit

INTRODUCTION

suicide following their attacks compared to homicide offenders. On the other hand, homicide perpetrators were more likely to have a history of substance abuse and prior violent behaviour.

The most striking difference between these groups lies in the nature of their violence. Lone actor attacks are typically deliberate and carefully planned, indicating a premeditated intent. In contrast, homicide offenders often act impulsively, committing murder in the heat of the moment or as a result of situational pressures.

THE RISE IN LONE ACTOR VIOLENCE over the last thirty years is enormously concerning. Despite dedicated prevention efforts, these attacks continue to occur with troubling frequency, causing substantial loss of life. For instance, in a three-week period in 2018, the United States witnessed a string of violent incidents: fifteen pipe bombs were mailed to Democratic Party offices, eleven people were killed in an anti-Semitic shooting at a Pittsburgh synagogue, and six people lost their lives in a shooting at a Tallahassee yoga studio. Similarly, in Australia during April and May 2024, three attacks occurred within just twenty-two days. These included a mass stabbing at a shopping centre, the stabbing of a priest during a sermon, and a stabbing in a hardware store car park where the perpetrator was shot by police. In late June, another attack was narrowly averted in New South Wales. The alleged attacker was armed with knives, tactical gear, and a GoPro, and had also published a 205-page manifesto before the planned incident.

Alarmingly, perpetrators are becoming younger, and their attacks increasingly more deadly. The evolving profile of lone actors reflects this troubling trend. As one expert aptly noted, *'Now it's vulnerable, young minds and contagious ideas, thrown together in a permissive environment. You don't need to be a traditional terrorist to commit an act of terror.'*

One of the greatest misconceptions about lone actors relates to **Loneness**.

Although loneness may imply that perpetrators act in secret, lone actors are often not isolated or alone. While individuals like Anders Breivik, the Norwegian attacker who killed seventy-seven people, and Theodore Kaczynski, the Unabomber, fit this stereotype, they represent exceptions rather than the norm.

Though seemingly acting in isolation, lone actors are often part of an invisible network that helps shape their ideologies and reinforces their grievances. Whether through online forums, extremist literature, or shared beliefs with close contacts, these individuals are connected to a broader social and ideological web that fosters and justifies their violent actions.

Most perpetrators have friendships or family members that they regularly have contact with. Many have had intimate partners and several have been in romantic relationships at the time of their attack. It's not a lack of social contact that is the problem, but instead a lack of social connection – a sense of not belonging, not bonding, and feeling unattached to others.

It is rare for a perpetrator to live a completely reclusive life devoid of any social engagement. Surprisingly, the social interactions of lone actors often play a central role in their offending. Through these relationships, particularly those online, many individuals gain knowledge and skills which enable them to plan and to carry out their actions.

Back in 1999, Columbine High School shooters Eric Harris and Dylan Klebold were socially active and known to many within the school and local community. On April 20 of that year, the two twelfth-graders carried out a meticulously planned attack at their school in Colorado, killing twelve students, one teacher, and injuring many more. In the months prior to the attack, the pair had cultivated an elaborate plan to harm their peers, bonding over their shared violent fantasies. Harris and Klebold connected in person and were able to cultivate their ideas and thoughts in the presence of one another – a far cry for the current digital landscape where the internet and

INTRODUCTION

social media now connects people at ease from all around the world.

With the rise of internet platforms and social media groups, many lone actors are now able to connect with others who condone violence or are disenfranchised and angry at particular sections of the population. Instead of seeking companionship and connection through face-to-face interactions, many individuals now thrive in online gaming environments or through social media and messaging platforms. In certain cases, these digital interactions can steer vulnerable individuals towards a path of violence; while for others, they provide opportunities to find like-minded individuals and exchange ideas and plans.

Every life lost to lone actor violence is a tragic and senseless loss. The challenges facing police, mental health services, correctional agencies, and other professionals working on the front lines with these individuals are immense. Lone actors are often driven by a complex mix of personal, social, and political motivations – some aim to commit acts of terrorism, while others are fuelled by grievances and a desire for retribution. Although it can be tempting to label lone actors as either calculating terrorists or mentally unstable individuals, such perspectives oversimplify the complexities of the issue.

In order to examine the underlying factors associated with lone actor violence, this book takes a broad and all-encompassing approach. While some experts and academics dedicate significant time to debating the nuances of what constitutes lone actor offending, a pragmatic and flexible approach is adopted. It incorporates a range of attacks perpetrated by individuals, from rampage killings, mass murders, school shootings, workplace attacks, hate crimes, and acts of terrorism. At its core, mass casualty events are targeted attacks designed to harm, kill, and create fear and chaos in others.

There is no single explanation for why someone decides to commit such atrocities. Lone actor violence is a profoundly complex phenomenon, layered with psychological, social, and cultural factors that demand careful exploration. Understanding this new wave of violence requires a comprehensive and considered approach.

The chapters that follow are structured into two parts: *The Path to Violence* and *The Search for Answers*.

The first part, *The Path to Violence*, delves into the psychology of violence, examining why and how individuals progress towards offending. It explores key factors such as child development, mental health, societal influences, the role of families, and the impact of technology. Alongside this, the power of ideas, beliefs, and personal experiences as catalysts for violence are investigated. The section brings together the backgrounds, mindsets, and motivations of those who commit these acts.

The second part of the book, *The Search for Answers*, shifts focus to prevention and intervention. It critically examines what works – and what doesn't – by exploring various approaches, including policing strategies, risk assessments, government influences, prison programmes, and psychological initiatives. This section also considers the delicate balance between system-wide responses and individual needs. Importantly, it offers insights into potential pathways for change and reasons for hope.

Let's begin.

I

The Path To Violence

1

A Troubled Childhood

'We may not be responsible for the world that created our minds, but we can take responsibility for the mind with which we create our world.'

Gabor Maté

ADAM WALKED INTO HIS MOTHER'S BEDROOM and shot her four times as she slept. The firearm he used was one she had purchased for him and taught him to use in an attempt to bond with her son.

Later that morning, Adam Lanza drove his mother's car to Sandy Hook Elementary School. Inside the vehicle were multiple firearms. Years earlier, he had been a student at the school.

What followed was one of the deadliest school shootings in United States history. Lanza systematically hunted down and killed twenty children, all aged between six and seven, along with six staff members who attempted to protect them. Before police could intervene, he turned the gun on himself, ending his life.

When police later searched Lanza's bedroom, they uncovered a disturbing photograph of him staring blankly into the camera, holding a gun to his head. His computer hard drive had been destroyed, erasing much of his digital footprint. However, among the items recovered was a detailed electronic spreadsheet meticulously chronicling mass murderers – an unsettling insight into his preoccupation with violence.

On 14 December 2012, the small community of Newtown, Connecticut was left devastated by the attack. Lanza not only took the lives of innocent children and dedicated teachers but also murdered his own mother before ultimately killing himself.

Sandy Hook Elementary School, the site of the attack, was closed indefinitely and eventually demolished. The removal of the school symbolised an effort to help heal the local community. Yet, the tragic day remains deeply etched in the memories of the survivors, grieving families, and the nation.

THE EARLY YEARS OF A CHILD'S life form the foundation for how they perceive themselves and understand the world around them. In the first years of life, significant brain development occurs, shaping foundational patterns of thinking, feeling, and relating to others. It is a critical window in which early experiences literally sculpt the architecture of the brain, particularly the areas responsible for emotional regulation and social behaviour.

Two key systems play a crucial role in the brain's development during the early years: the *limbic system*, often referred to as the *'emotional brain'*, and the *prefrontal cortex*, which is known as the *'thinking brain'*. The emotional brain governs all responses and reactions, from anger, fear, excitement, pleasure, and so on. It plays a central role in how individuals respond to stress and threats, particularly during the early formation of the central nervous system.

In contrast, the thinking brain – which continues to mature into adolescence and even adulthood – fosters higher-order cognitive processes such as planning, communication, impulse control, and reasoning. In a well-nurtured child, the emotional brain and the thinking brain should work together harmoniously, allowing emotional and rational responses to balance one another. However, when a child experiences disruptions in their development – such as inconsistent caregiving, an unstable environment, or difficulties in social relationships – this balance can be compromised, leading to challenges in emotional regulation and adapting or modifying behaviour.

One of the most critical factors influencing brain development is **Attachment** – the bond between a child and their caregivers. Humans, like many animals, are creatures of attachment and need the closeness and proximity of others to grow and survive the many hazards in early life. Attachment leads to survival and allows the child to feel safe and loved. A secure attachment fosters trust, predictability, and a sense of safety in the world.

The most powerful form of attachment for a child comes through their relationship with their parents or caregivers. Through these interactions, the child learns whether their cries will be met by love, or their outbursts supported through compassion. If the child feels safe and is able to have their emotional needs met, they will develop the ability to cope with stress and uncertainty. They will be able to communicate their emotions rather than acting them out. Attachment is essential for promoting brain development and forms the building blocks of social and emotional life. Conversely, when attachment is insecure – whether due to neglect, unpredictability, or emotional unavailability – a child may struggle to regulate their emotions, become disconnected from their feelings, or develop hostile and pessimistic views of the world.

A poor attachment can cause a whole array of developmental processes to go awry, and in some cases, it can lead to callous-unemotional traits, aggressive and antisocial behaviour, and emotional detachment. Importantly, not all children who experience poor attachment progress towards violence. Genetic vulnerabilities play a crucial role alongside environmental factors – it truly is an interaction between nature and nurture. Some children are born with biological predispositions that affect how their brain regulates emotions, experience empathy, and responds to fear. When these vulnerabilities are combined with a lack of love, excessive discipline, inconsistent boundaries, and other features associated with insecure or disorganised attachments, personality issues can arise, such as traits associated with narcissism or psychopathic personality. The person may come to perceive the world as hostile and uncompromising, leading to a desire for dominance and control over others.

Our genetics can be shaped by our environment, and the bonds that we establish with others early in life are critical. Attachment can strengthen or protect us against our genetic tendencies. Conversely, it can also exacerbate them. Another critical factor for brain development – particularly for ensuring harmony between the emotional and thinking parts of the brain – is **Authenticity**. Children need the freedom to be themselves, express their emotions safely, and develop their unique identities. When children feel unsafe, whether in their home, school, or social environment, they often prioritise attachment over authenticity. They alter their behaviour to please others in order to ensure that they are safe and not at risk of being harmed.

Authenticity flourishes when children are encouraged to express their natural curiosities and emotions without excessive criticism or conditional praise. A nurturing environment fosters self-acceptance, allowing children to develop confidence in their true selves. When authenticity is suppressed through factors such as rigid parental expectations, social rejection, cultural pressures, or fear of failure, children begin modifying who they are to please others. If this continues, the child begins to feel that they will only be accepted if they are someone else. As a result, they become disconnected from their true selves, leading to a deep-seated feeling of unworthiness.

A TROUBLED CHILDHOOD

A child's development is a delicate interplay between nature and nurture. Attachment and authenticity can have a critical role in shaping a child's development. If a child only receives validation when they succeed, they may equate their worth with achievement. Conversely, if they are ignored or receive little positive reinforcement, they may act out in search of recognition. The early years are a period of profound adjustment and attunement, and when disruptions occur – whether through insecure attachment, emotional suppression, or identity struggles – the effects can shape a child's trajectory for years to come.

IN THE BEST-SELLING BOOK, *The Boy Who Was Raised as a Dog,* Bruce Perry and Maia Szalavitz emphasise how violence isn't always the result of obvious factors; rather, it can stem from a series of small decisions and minor events that can shape the direction of a person's life. *'Seemingly irrelevant choices can result in tremendously different later outcomes,'* they write. *'We don't know when the smallest choice, or "stimuli," will push a developing brain onto the path of genius, or onto the highway to hell.'*

Adam Lanza's life underscores this delicate balance.

From an early age, Lanza exhibited developmental difficulties and some of the central circuitry of his brain was slow to form. He struggled with speech, had difficulties with motor coordination, was hypersensitive to sensations, and troubled by intense sounds, or unusual textures. Recognising these issues, his parents, Nancy and Peter, enrolled him in occupational therapy and speech classes. He was diagnosed with sensory integration disorder, a condition that affects how the brain processes sensory information, often leading to oversensitivity, irritation, and difficulty tolerating certain sounds, smells, tastes, or textures. The early intervention showed promise, and Lanza was able to begin primary school at Sandy Hook Elementary.

Although Peter worked long hours and was often only able to see Lanza and his older brother, Ryan, on weekends, Peter and Nancy functioned as a cohesive parenting team in Lanza's early years. He bonded with his parents and formed healthy attachments with them. Peter later described this period as the happiest and most stable time in his son's life.

However, when Lanza was nine years old, his parents separated and Peter moved out of the family home. Although Lanza continued to see his father on weekends, the structure and predictability he had relied on was disrupted. Lanza's world changed. Most significantly, he internalised the separation as abandonment. While he did not express his distress openly, he gradually withdrew from his father, and their relationship deteriorated. In turn, he became increasingly dependent on his mother, while Nancy became more preoccupied with his needs.

A year after the separation, Lanza wrote a fictional book with a peer at school titled *The Big Book of Granny*. The story depicted a grandmother who concealed a gun inside her cane and killed multiple people, including children. One character was taxidermied and displayed on her mantelpiece, while Granny carried an arsenal of weapons, including a handgun, AK-47, M16 rifle, rocket launcher, musket, and shotgun. Ultimately, she was shot in the head by her own son.

During this time, Lanza developed a deep sense of self-loathing, convinced that he was less deserving than other children. As he entered middle school, his struggles escalated. The transition from primary school, where he had remained in the same classroom for most of the day, to a more dynamic environment with multiple teachers and changing rooms, proved overwhelming. The constant shifts triggered sensory overload, and he became increasingly withdrawn – avoiding eye contact, ceasing social interactions, and adopting an awkward, hunched-over posture.

Nancy, desperate to help, began sitting in classes with him, but his anxiety persisted.

Recognising the severity of the situation, Nancy and Peter consulted a psychiatrist, who diagnosed Lanza with Asperger's Syndrome, now classified under Autism Spectrum Disorder (ASD). His parents viewed the diagnosis as a breakthrough, believing it provided a clearer understanding of his difficulties and a framework for support. However, Lanza rejected the diagnosis and resisted treatment. Despite their efforts to adjust their parenting approaches, he never received the intervention he needed.

In search of a more structured environment, Nancy and Peter enrolled him in a Catholic school, but once again, their efforts proved unsuccessful. Eventually, after further consultations with specialists, they decided to homeschool him.

By this stage, a series of seemingly small decisions had compounded into significant issues – Lanza had become increasingly isolated, his mental well-being was deteriorating, and his relationship with Nancy had evolved into a cycle of mutual dependence. He needed her, and she, in turn, became deeply enmeshed in his world.

Lanza's persistent struggles prevented him from developing a sense of identity or fostering authenticity in his life. He was unable to understand his place in the world or find enjoyment in the company of others. Isolated from peers, his mother became the sole focal point of his existence. However, homeschooling only exacerbated his difficulties rather than alleviating them.

Nancy faced an impossible task. Her son was defiant, rigid, and highly emotional. Not only did he complete his schooling at home, but he rarely left the house and remained entirely dependent on her. In response, Nancy shielded him from discomforts, walking on eggshells to maintain a fragile peace. She catered to his preferences, ensuring that everything in their home aligned with his approval. This dynamic quickly spiraled into a dysfunctional and toxic cycle. As Lanza's demands intensified, he began refusing to see his father – punishing him, it seemed, for leaving the family.

Lanza's functioning continued to decline. He became increasingly pedantic, obsessive, and socially withdrawn. He refused to touch metal objects, was intolerant of his mother's movements, reacted strongly to loud sounds, and was agitated by visitors. At times, if Nancy walked in a manner he disapproved of, he demanded she redo it. Concerned, his parents sought further psychiatric consultation, and Lanza was prescribed Lexapro, a medication used to treat anxiety. However, after just three days, he refused to continue, becoming hysterical and insisting it caused side effects. Nancy again acquiesced. He also refused therapy. His treating psychiatrist observed that Nancy was *'almost a prisoner in her own home'*.

Lanza developed a growing interest in firearms and World War II. Hoping to connect with her son, Nancy began taking him to a shooting range and even purchased firearms. Despite often refusing to touch metal objects, Lanza was comfortable holding a firearm. Unbeknownst to Nancy, Lanza was engaging with others online about mass killings, editing Wikipedia entries on murderers, and meticulously compiling a database on mass shootings.

In a 2014 article in *The New Yorker*, Andrew Solomon reflected on Nancy's missteps: *'Nancy's error seems to have been that she always focused on the day, in a ceaseless quest to keep peace in the home she shared with the hypersensitive, controlling, increasingly hostile stranger who was her son. She thought that she could keep the years at bay by making each day as good as possible, but her willingness to indulge his isolation may well have exacerbated the problems it was intended to ameliorate.'*

Lanza found solace in fantasising about violence. He spent hours researching mass killings, absorbing the intricate details of these acts. Though he was never overtly violent, his emotions grew increasingly volatile, and he became hysterical over minor frustrations. Nancy's attempts to shield him only reinforced his behaviour. His father, though concerned, remained at a distance, their relationship irreparably fractured.

Lanza withdrew from his schoolwork, frequently breaking down and claiming the curriculum was too difficult. Yet, he deceived his mother, often hiding in the library or spending hours at an arcade. His aversion to social settings and uncertainty appeared selective – when it suited him, he was able to endure loud and chaotic environments.

Despite Nancy's relentless efforts to appease her son, their relationship deteriorated further. The more she catered to his demands, the worse his behaviour became. Their bond became deeply enmeshed, lacking clear boundaries or autonomy. Lanza no longer viewed his mother as a source of support but rather as a burden – an obstacle rather than a parent desperate to make him happy.

Tragically, their relationship bore disturbing similarities to cases of *matricide* – when a child kills their mother. Such cases often involve overprotective or overbearing mothers fostering an intense, dependent, and/or conflict-ridden relationship, while the father is absent, uninvolved, or passive. In many instances, the act of killing becomes a means of severing this unhealthy dependency and reclaiming control.

By 2011, Nancy had lost all control. Lanza dictated the terms of the household. No visitors were allowed. He ceased speaking to his mother entirely. Their only form of communication was email – even though they lived under the same roof.

Nancy never revealed to Peter just how dire things had become.

Following the shooting, police recovered a document on Lanza's computer titled *'Selfish'*. In it, he detailed his hostility towards women, writing about what he perceived as their inherently selfish tendencies. Despite his mother's years of relentless accommodation and efforts to appease her son, Lanza harboured only resentment – towards her, towards his family, and towards the world. Nancy never grasped the depths of his hatred. She remained oblivious to the danger he posed, and in a tragic irony, she had unknowingly equipped him with the means to inflict mass harm.

There is no simple explanation for why Lanza carried out the massacre. As Andrew Solomon wrote, *'But the reason that no one shoots twenty random children isn't self-restraint; it's that there is no level at which that idea is attractive.'*

It is tempting to label Lanza as a *'bad seed'* or someone who was born with a predisposition to callousness and aggression. Yet, if Lanza had this type of genetic makeup, then surely his parents or brother would have exhibited similar traits. Even in relation to ASD, although autism can have a hereditary component, there is no evidence that this was the case – and importantly, ASD does not cause someone to become violent.

In reality, Lanza's path to violence was not extraordinary. It was shaped by small decisions, certain situations, and seemingly innocuous forks in the road. His trajectory was marked by troubled brain development, psychological conditions, broken attachments, stifled authenticity, and a fascination with violence.

His father, Peter, later reflected on how close he had come to being one of his son's victims.

'I know Adam would have killed me in a heartbeat, if he'd had the chance. I don't question that for a minute. The reason he shot Nancy four times was one for each of us. One for Nancy; one for him; one for Ryan, one for me.'

2

A Traumatic Bond

'The most traumatic aspects of all disasters involve the shattering of human connections. And this is especially true for children. Being harmed by the people who are supposed to love you, being abandoned by them, being robbed of the one-on-one relationships that allow you to feel safe and valued and to become humane – these are profoundly destructive experiences.'

Bruce D. Perry & Maia Szalavitz

COLT GRAY ONLY ATTENDED a couple of days of school after enrolling in Apalachee High on 14 August 2024. Despite missing most of the previous year of schooling, he was placed in Grade 9 due to his age rather than his academic ability. His transition to a new school was difficult, and he suffered a panic attack during one of his initial days. When he spoke to his grandmother about the incident, he reportedly disclosed that he had been struggling with thoughts of harming himself and others. Only three weeks earlier, he had pulled a gun on his mother when she tried to confront him in his bedroom.

On the morning of 4 September 2024, fourteen-year-old Colt Gray boarded the bus to school. He was the last student to get on, carrying a heavy bag.

Some reports suggest he had a large sports bag, while others indicate he carried a large cardboard poster tube. Gray had skipped school the previous day, but with his grandmother's encouragement, he agreed to improve his attendance.

During the first class of the morning, a teacher noticed Gray's large bag and allegedly overheard him ask another student whether Apalachee High had an active shooter plan in place. Concerned, the teacher emailed senior staff. However, due to another student having a near identical name, there was a mix-up, and staff mistakenly sought out the wrong student.

At 9.42 a.m., Gray messaged his father: *'I'm sorry. It's not your fault.'*

At 10.02 a.m., he contacted his mother: *'I'm sorry.'*

Minutes later, Gray began shooting students and staff. By the time the shooting ended, four people were dead – two teachers and two students. Nine others were wounded, leaving the small community devastated.

Gray surrendered after being surrounded by school security staff. He became the youngest mass shooter in the USA in several decades.

THE EXPERIENCE OF ADVERSITY AND TRAUMA during childhood can cause significant disruptions to emotional and psychological development.

When a child endures trauma without proper support, lasting psychological changes can occur. These experiences often cause significant stress to the nervous system, leading to intense emotions, intrusive thoughts, fear, panic, and uncertainty. Adverse Childhood Experiences (ACEs) differ from everyday life stressors as they have a lasting impact, especially when left unaddressed.

ACEs include a range of childhood and adolescent events, such as:

- Physical, sexual, or emotional abuse
- The death of a family member
- Suicide of a family member or friend
- Parental divorce or separation
- Drug use in the household
- Mental health issues within the home
- Housing instability
- Financial difficulties
- Witnessing violence
- Parental criminality or incarceration

ACEs can have a profound impact on child development and adulthood. Studies have shown that ACEs can lead to Post-Traumatic Stress Disorder (PTSD), which is characterised by reliving and re-experiencing trauma, along with fear, avoidance, flashbacks, anxiety, and heightened apprehension.

The impact of ACEs can also be more subtle, potentially leading to **Developmental Trauma Disorder (DTD)**. Dutch psychiatrist Bessel van der Kolk first proposed DTD as a condition that disrupts how children perceive themselves, regulate emotions, and view the world. DTD leads to the brain being rewired based on adversity and trauma – with the world viewed as unpredictable, unsafe, and threatening.

Childhood trauma creates a fragile foundation – one full of cracks and weaknesses, and vulnerable to the many pressures and challenges that arise in life. The exposure to adversity and trauma during childhood can also lead to changes in how genes are expressed, effectively activating underlying hereditary predispositions. In essence, trauma can act as a switch, turning certain genes on or off in ways that shape a child's physical and psychological development. For instance, early and repeated exposure to stress can trigger genetic expressions that increase inflammation in the body, alter brain development, and cause havoc to the body's stress response system. This means that while a child may carry genetic vulnerabilities, it is their environment – particularly the presence or absence of nurturing, safe, and supportive relationships – that determines whether genes are expressed in harmful ways. Ultimately, trauma does not just create maladaptive psychological responses; it also affects our health, behaviour, and emotional regulation throughout life.

Research on ACEs has found that children exposed to such experiences face a range of negative outcomes in later life: including drug use, suicide, heart disease, diabetes, and cancer. ACEs also negatively affect education and future employment opportunities. A 2019 study by the Centers for Disease Control and Prevention (CDC) found that amongst a sample of nearly 145,000 people, 60.9% of adults in the USA had experienced at least one ACE, while one in six had been exposed to four or more ACEs during their childhood.

Along with affecting health and well-being, exposure to multiple ACEs also increases the likelihood of criminal behaviour.

A child who experiences six or more ACEs before the age of ten is up to ten times more likely to engage in violent behavior by age eighteen. An analysis of more than 60,000 youth offenders in Florida, USA, identified that 67.5% had experienced four or more ACEs, and nearly 20% had endured six or more. Shockingly, studies estimate that 75–93% of youth entering the criminal justice system have experienced some form of trauma.

ACEs result in a range of concerning outcomes pertaining to criminality; including a greater likelihood of physical violence, general delinquency, bullying, weapon carrying, antisocial attitudes, and dating violence.

ACEs have also been shown to play a role in radicalisation and terrorism. Studies have found that ACEs increase a person's vulnerability to radicalisation and adoption of extreme beliefs and attitudes. Alongside this, individuals who drop out of education, hold radicalised views, and have a history of ACEs are at a higher risk of progressing towards violence and terrorism. In essence, the combination of ACEs, radical beliefs, and disengagement from education creates a dangerous pathway to violence.

COLT GRAY HAD A CHILDHOOD characterised by adverse experiences. According to Sarah Blaskey and colleagues in their comprehensive *Washington Post* article, Gray was '*adrift in a childhood ravaged by violence and addiction and overlooked by a system that failed to pull him out of it*'.

Gray's parents battled drug and alcohol addictions. His mother, Marcee, served jail time for domestic violence, while his father, Colin, reportedly developed an opioid dependency following back surgery.

The family home was chaotic, with both parents absent for extended periods. Child services were contacted multiple times due to concerns of neglect and abuse towards Gray and his siblings. In 2021, Gray's grandmother, Debbie, reported an incident where Marcee allegedly struck Gray multiple times during an argument over chicken strips. As a result, Gray temporarily moved in with his grandmother, and Marcee was required to undergo regular drug testing.

At around the same time, Gray became curious about violence. While in Grade 6, he allegedly searched online for ways to kill his father on a school computer. Staff detected the search and Gray was spoken to by two school resource officers – but no significant actions were taken. Marcee withheld this information from Gray's father for more than a year, concerned about how he would react.

In late 2021, Marcee and Colin moved their family 200 miles away to Jackson County after Colin secured a new job. However, their addictions persisted and the couple was repeatedly evicted from their homes. As a result of the constant upheaval, Gray attended six different schools over five years. Eventually, the ongoing turmoil led to Marcee and Colin separating in November 2022. The two youngest children moved away with their mother, while Gray remained with his father.

The separation was difficult on Gray, and this was compounded by relentless bullying at school. He was harassed over his unwashed appearance, and other students threw bottles of shampoo at him on the bus. Isolated and friendless, Gray became fascinated with school shootings, studying perpetrators and their methods. He studied their life histories, the number of people they had killed, and the way they carried out their attacks.

In May 2023, Gray posted on Discord, *'I'm committing a mass shooting ... I need ideas for where to shoot.'* He attached a photo of two firearms leaning against a wall.

The FBI was notified about the message and traced the email address to Gray. The local sheriff's office was alerted, and two officers visited Gray and his father. Colin, answering the door in his underwear, remained present while his son spoke with the officers. Gray denied writing the comments online, and the matter never progressed further. Unfortunately, the officers had only been briefed on the material and did not have copies of the text or photographs of the guns – which, in fact, belonged to Colin.

Gray's downward spiral continued. In August 2023, he moved back in with his mother, offering him a fresh start at a new school and the chance to rebuild their relationship. However, neither materialised. Instead, Marcee developed a methamphetamine habit, and Gray was never enrolled in school. Within months, issues emerged. During an argument with his mother, Gray slashed the household furniture with a knife. In October, Marcee failed a routine drug test conducted by child services, and all three children were returned to Colin's custody.

Alarmingly, on 3 November, Marcee arrived at her mother Debbie's home, claiming that Colin had stolen her children. Reportedly heavily intoxicated, she demanded that Debbie drive her to Colin's residence so she could kill him. When Debbie refused, Marcee allegedly bound her to a chair with tape and left her alone. As she departed, she stated, *'I'm going to kill Colt, just for you.'* Debbie remained strapped to the chair for twenty-two hours before Marcee's sister arrived and found her.

Marcee then went to Colin's home, where he was with the children. When he refused to let her inside, she carved the word *'abuse'* into the side of his vehicle. Two days later, police found her living in her car, surrounded by a series of notes detailing her plans to commit suicide. She was charged with family violence offences and remanded in jail.

For Christmas that year, Colin gifted Gray his own AR-style rifle. For his birthday in January, Debbie unknowingly contributed to his growing arsenal by purchasing ammunition. She was unaware that police had investigated Gray months earlier for his mass-shooting threat. The trips to the shooting range over the coming months taught Gray how to use the weapon and gave him confidence in handling a firearm.

By mid-2024, Gray's mental health began to deteriorate, and he turned to the internet in search of answers to his problems. Around this time, Marcee was released from prison. Despite the ongoing concerns, Colin allowed her to move back into the family home.

In August, Gray made concerning remarks to Debbie about the Parkland shooter, Nikolas Cruz, expressing admiration for him. Three weeks before the shooting, when his mother attempted to speak with him, Gray pulled a firearm on her, ordering her to leave him alone and stay out of his bedroom. Alarmed, Debbie arranged for him to visit a crisis centre for counselling, following repeated concerns. She urged Colin to support the plan, emphasising the importance of Gray attending the appointment. He never made it.

A few days later, armed with his AR-15-style rifle, Gray carried out his attack.

Gray, who was only fourteen at the time, now faces 180 years in prison on fifty-five charges, including four counts of malice murder. Despite his age, he is being charged as an adult. In September 2024, his father, Colin, was charged with second-degree murder, manslaughter, child cruelty, and reckless conduct for allegedly enabling his son's actions by providing him access to firearms.

Colt Gray's life was shaped by adversity. In and out of school, he never formed stable friendships. He was alone, isolated, and deprived of a healthy childhood.

Troublingly, Gray experienced eight significant adverse childhood experiences in his short life:

- Emotional abuse
- Parental divorce or separation
- Drug use in the family home
- Mental health issues within the household
- Housing instability
- Financial hardship
- Exposure to violence
- Parental criminality and incarceration

Gray was one of the children statistically *ten times* more likely to engage in violence before their eighteenth birthday.

3

A State Of Decline

'When the natural road towards human fulfilment is blocked, human beings retreat into themselves, become involved in themselves, and try to create inwardly that world which some evil fate has denied them.'

Isaiah Berlin

THE PURPOSE WAS SIMPLE for James Holmes: *'Human life has value. If you take lives away, that adds value to your life.'*

It was basic mathematics: every life was worth one point; the more lives he took, the more points he earned. By killing others, he believed he increased his own value and self-worth.

Although Holmes was suffering from mental health issues, his attack was meticulously planned. At midnight on 20 July 2012, the long-awaited *The Dark Knight Rises* movie premiered at Century 16 movie theatre in Colorado. Holmes had purchased a ticket to the highly anticipated screening, which had drawn a crowd of more than 400 people. Shortly after the movie began, Holmes exited the cinema through a side door and walked to his nearby vehicle, where he had stashed a small arsenal of weapons and tactical gear.

Holmes changed his clothes, equipping himself with a bulletproof neck protector, bulletproof leggings, a gas mask, and a military-style ballistic helmet. He strapped on a tactical belt holding two folding knives and several gas canisters. Just hours earlier, he had dyed his hair bright orange and rigged his apartment with enough explosives to kill anyone nearby. After suiting up for his attack, Holmes retrieved three firearms from his car and returned to the crowded cinema.

With techno music blasting through his headphones, he threw two smoke canisters into the theatre, stunning the audience and obscuring their vision. Then he opened fire. Within two minutes, twelve people were dead, and more than fifty were injured. Police arrived swiftly and apprehended Holmes, who surrendered without resistance. But in those brief moments, his high-powered firearms had already caused catastrophic loss of life.

For over a decade, Holmes had fantasised about violence. Despite what appeared to be a stable upbringing, he struggled with deep self-doubt and persistent negative thoughts throughout his teenage years. In a personal journal, he wrote about his troubled mind and intense self-loathing. He documented his perceived shortcomings – his insomnia, nightmares, social awkwardness, isolation, hyperactivity, unusual eye and ear appearance, chronic tiredness, and his unsatisfactory penis. Yet, above all, Holmes believed his greatest flaw was his *'broken mind'*.

He spent years trying to understand what was wrong with him, questioning the meaning of life and why he felt trapped in a state of doubt and uncertainty. Time and time again, his thoughts circled back to the same conclusion: *'Any problem can be solved with death.'*

In an effort to fix his mind, he pursued a doctoral programme in neuroscience after completing his undergraduate degree. However, fixing his mind *'proved insurmountable'*, and he continued to struggle with depression and inner turmoil.

In late 2011, Holmes' life took an unexpected turn when he caught the attention of a young woman at his graduate school. The pair began exchanging text messages, and a casual relationship followed. For a brief period, Holmes seemed happy – he even told his family that he had fallen in love. Although he occasionally made offhand remarks about wanting to kill people, his girlfriend never took these seriously and dismissed them as jokes.

His newfound joy was short-lived. In February 2012, after returning from the holiday period, his girlfriend told him she wanted to move on. She felt that Holmes had become too attached, and his feelings weren't reciprocated by her. The break-up sent Holmes into a downward spiral. His obsession with violence and death resurfaced.

He joined Match.com and checked his account frequently, but no women ever contacted him or responded. He went on a hike with another neuroscience student and exchanged messages with her, but he was distant and erratic – his mind consumed by dark thoughts.

Holmes began stockpiling weapons and practising at gun ranges. He considered a range of violent scenarios: suicide, a chemical attack, and building an explosive device. He even contemplated becoming a serial killer, but dismissed the idea as *'too personal, too much evidence, easily caught, few kills'*. In the end, he determined that a mass shooting was the easiest and most effective method to achieve *'maximum casualties'*.

After deciding on the attack, he explored various potential targets before settling on his final plan: *'The last escape, mass murder at the movies.'*

Within five months of his relationship ending – and just five weeks after failing his doctoral exams – Holmes executed his attack in the early hours of 20 July 2012.

IT IS ESTIMATED THAT AROUND ONE IN EIGHT CHILDREN suffer from a mental disorder. These rates are similar across genders, although emotional disorders are more prevalent among girls, while behavioural disorders are more common among boys. A large analysis of 28,160 children aged eleven to fourteen identified widespread mental health issues. Approximately one in four children reported experiencing hyperactivity and difficulties with attention, while one in five experienced conduct problems and frequent troubles with their emotions. Alongside this, around one in ten children reported having frequent concerns with their peer relationships.

The COVID-19 pandemic has further exacerbated these challenges, heightening mental health difficulties among children. Isolation from peers, coupled with increased anxiety, stress, depression, and substance use, has contributed to a marked decline in childhood well-being.

The well-being of children is on the decline, and this leads to unhappy and unwell adults. As children grow, their struggles do not simply disappear. Global studies indicate that, like children, one in eight adults also experience significant psychological distress. Alarmingly, 58 million children and 243 million adults worldwide suffer from anxiety disorders, while another 23 million children and 257 million adults battle depression. The figures are grim and sobering.

Although mental health conditions rarely lead directly to violence, they can significantly influence decision-making, coping abilities, anger regulation, and the capacity to consider alternative options.

In recent years, loneliness has surged across society, with profound implications for mental health and overall well-being. Humans are inherently social beings who rely on emotional and social connections to thrive. Even a caring and supportive home environment cannot fully mitigate the effects of isolation. When individuals feel excluded or ostracised, their sense of belonging erodes, leading to loneliness and disconnection. Shockingly, more than one billion people worldwide report being very, or fairly lonely, most of the time, and it estimated that 300 million across the globe do not have a single close friend.

This widespread social disconnection has been worsened by the rise of social media platforms and the prolonged isolation that was caused by COVID-19. Chronic loneliness carries risks comparable to smoking and is linked to increased stress, depression, and anxiety. Lonely people experience poorer immunity, increased sickness, faster aging, cardiovascular issues, and a heightened risk of dementia. Loneliness is a killer.

Men, young adults under thirty, and individuals with low incomes are particularly vulnerable to loneliness. Young adults often experience intense social pressures, with their self-worth tied to acceptance and belonging. Those with lower incomes are at a chronic disadvantage, lacking resources and opportunities to prioritise their well-being. Without adequate support, they are often left to navigate their struggles alone.

Recognising the severity of this issue, the US Surgeon General declared loneliness a public health epidemic in 2023. In his statement, Dr Vivek Murthy emphasised the need to treat social connection as a public health priority, stating, '*Given the significant health consequences of loneliness and isolation, we must prioritize building social connection the same way we have prioritized other critical public health issues such as tobacco, obesity, and substance use disorders. Together, we can build a country that's healthier, more resilient, less lonely, and more connected.*'

Loneliness manifests differently between genders. Men often externalise their distress through anger and risk-taking behaviours, whereas women tend to experience heightened insecurity and emotional distress. Disturbingly, one in seven males now report having no close friends. This lack of meaningful social connections is significant, as it affects emotional resilience and the ability to manage distress constructively. It highlights the importance of being able to turn to others for support at times of need.

Men are disproportionately responsible for violent offences – over 95% of lone actor attacks are committed by men, and studies consistently show that around 90% of homicides worldwide are perpetrated by males. This highlights just how critical attachment, authenticity, and social connection are.

It's tempting to conclude that violence is a *'male problem'*, but this oversimplifies the issue. Males are also at significantly higher risk of suicide. Statistics on suicidal deaths for 2021 and 2022 published by the CDC found nearly 80% of the suicides were by males. Despite making up around 50% of the population, males disproportionately take their own lives. Additionally, men are also more likely to consider suicide following a relationship breakdown. A 2025 study found that men were 82% more likely to experience suicidal ideation within a year of a relationship breakdown.

Somewhere, society is failing men.

Men are sensitive and vulnerable; they require validation, emotional nurturance, and healthy role models to develop healthy masculinity. Without these, unresolved distress can manifest as self-destruction or violence. Teaching boys how to express emotions, seek support, and build meaningful relationships is essential to fostering healthier men.

Boys need to be nurtured and allowed to be full emotional beings. Author Ruth Whippman highlights the importance of early emotional development, stating, '*Boys, right from babyhood, their brains are more sensitive and more emotionally vulnerable than girls' brains on average, at birth they're more immature.*' Modern-day boyhood is a lonely and uncertain experience – many boys spend more time on screens, have fewer friendships, and struggle with emotional communication. As a result, they are more likely to develop superficial relationships and feel apprehensive about expressing vulnerability.

Societal expectations pressure boys to be tough, invulnerable, and self-reliant – standards that are impossible to maintain and often lead to emotional suppression. When distress is left unaddressed, it can manifest in destructive ways. There's a lot of pressure on boys and it's destined to often go wrong.

Violence is not just a *'male problem'* – it is a societal, emotional, and developmental issue. Addressing it requires a commitment to fostering meaningful social connections, supporting emotional growth, and challenging notions of masculinity.

If we want healthier men, we must start by raising healthier boys.

JAMES HOLMES IS ANOTHER STATISTIC. Another case of childhood mental illness. Another case of adult mental illness. Another case of male violence. Another case of poor emotional development.

Holmes is also more than a statistic. The lives that he took may not have added value to his life, but they secured his notoriety, ensuring his name would be remembered for decades to come. He wanted to leave a mark, make a statement, and inflict suffering.

Holmes proclaimed: *'Terrorism isn't the message. The message here is there is no message. Most fools will misinterpret correlation for causation, namely relationship and work failure as causes. Both were expediting catalysts not the reason. The causation being my state of mind for the past fifteen years.'*

Despite a seemingly stable childhood with loving parents, Holmes retreated inward.

The first psychological marker of concern emerged following a family move from a small community in Oak Hills to San Diego when he was twelve. Holmes lost his childhood friendships and struggled with the change in schools and environment. Unlike his sister, he did not make the adjustment easily; failing to establish new friendships and shying away from social interactions. Instead, he immersed himself in video games, read in his closet, and spent time alone.

He eventually made friends, got involved in sports, and excelled academically. But his social discomfort and avoidance persisted. In October 2001, his parents sought professional help through a counsellor, yet therapy yielded little change. Holmes appeared happy and smiling, but on the inside a very different state of mind was unfolding. Holmes struggled to express his emotions and feared rejection, humiliation, and vulnerability. Although he was close with his parents, emotions were rarely spoken about in the family home. Like his father, Holmes was analytical, and rather than expressing or discussing emotions, these were internalised and intellectualised.

Holmes struggled to be his authentic self, keeping his needs hidden and concealing aspects of himself he deemed undesirable. His psychological state began to deteriorate during adolescence, leading him to see both himself and the world differently. He withdrew into an inner world of thoughts and fantasies, using this as an escape from his problems and a way to cope with his emotions. His thoughts frequently revolved around death, violence, and the meaninglessness of life. When confronted with emotional distress, Holmes retreated into fantasy to regain a sense of control. Over time, his thoughts became increasingly violent, imagining scenes of *'people getting their heads cut off'* or *'saws going against other people'*. He felt unsafe and deeply fearful of the world around him.

In his compelling book *A Dark Night in Aurora*, psychiatrist William H. Reid examined Holmes' dysfunctional coping mechanisms. He explained:

'When people are faced with great anxiety, their minds create ways to feel safer.

That means either eliminating the threat mentally or physically or moving away from it. It's like fight or flight in the jungle, but without real lions. When the person is trapped in the situation ... the mind automatically comes up with ways to eliminate the perceived threat ... being different was painful for Jimmy and those feelings intensified during his adolescence.'

Holmes studied the works of the German philosopher Friedrich Nietzsche, whose writings on nihilism and humanity are often misinterpreted. Nietzsche's concepts, such as the *Übermensch* (Overman) and the *Will to Power*, focus on individuality and self-determination – ideas that can resonate with individuals who feel alienated or inferior to society, and who seek power and a sense of superiority. At the same time, the *Übermensch* has sometimes been misconstrued as a justification for rejecting societal norms and laws, while the *Will to Power* is often misinterpreted as a licence for domination and aggression. Similarly, nihilism – the belief that life lacks inherent meaning and purpose – has been used to justify the futility of one's pursuits, when in fact, Nietzsche saw nihilism as a challenge for humanity that must be overcome.

In addition to Nietzsche's work, Holmes studied the manifesto of Unabomber Ted Kaczynski. He researched the Tylenol product-tampering murders which occurred in the early 1980s, where capsules were removed from Tylenol bottles and laced with cyanide. Seven people died and the case was never solved.

Slowly over time, Holmes' perception of himself, others, and the world began to change.

Despite his troubled mind, he managed to progress through university and commence a PhD in neuroscience. There was no doubt about his academic abilities, but his nihilistic beliefs persisted. When things were going well, he could experience enjoyment and momentary relief from his thoughts. Yet, just as quickly, he would revert back into his internal world of fantasies and detachment.

No matter what he did, Holmes couldn't escape himself – he couldn't escape his own personal inadequacy. Holmes harboured deep-seated self-loathing and thoughts of ending his life. Like Adam Lanza, rather than turning solely to suicide, Holmes fixated on violence, seeking to leave his mark on humanity and exact revenge against life itself.

The intensity and frequency of his thoughts and fantasies eventually took their toll. The dials had been turned up for too long, and his mental health began to unravel.

PEOPLE RARELY RESPOND to what has actually happened. Instead, our responses and reactions are shaped by our perceptions of a situation. Our minds create our reality, and our attributes and resources determine how we respond. Perception is influenced by our emotional capabilities, thinking patterns, self-satisfaction, and social connections. This was especially true for Holmes. He responded not to the world around him, but his own narrative – his inner dialogue. In doing so, he overlooked the opportunities, friendships, and supports that were available to him.

Holmes was sentenced to twelve consecutive life sentences without the possibility of parole, along with an additional 3,318 years in prison for 141 lesser offences – one of the longest sentences in US history.

As his case progressed through court, multiple psychiatrists were called upon to evaluate him. Across these assessments, he was diagnosed with several conditions, including schizophrenia, schizoaffective disorder, and schizotypal personality disorder. Each of these disorders involves odd and bizarre thinking, as well as difficulties with separating thoughts from reality.

The psychiatric experts agreed that at the time of the attack, Holmes was suffering mental illness. However, while his psychological state had deteriorated, neither the jury, nor some of the psychiatrists, believed this had prevented him from understanding right from wrong or absolved him of criminal responsibility.

Every juror found him guilty on all aggravation charges for the murders. He escaped the death penalty due to the refusal of a single juror.

While Holmes' mental illness did not directly cause the shooting, it played a significant role in his path to violence.

4

A Modern Crisis

'Whoever controls the flow of information dictates our perceptions and perspectives; whoever controls the news shapes our destiny.'

George Clinton

'WELL LADS IT'S TIME TO STOP SHITPOSTING and time to make a real life effort post. I will carry out and attack against the invaders, and will even live stream the attack via Facebook.

'I have provided links to my writings below, please do your part spreading my message, making memes and shitposting as you usually do. If I don't survive the attack, goodbye, godbless and I will see you all in Valhalla!'

After posting his final remarks on 8chan, Brenton Tarrant shared a link to his writings, directing users to his seventy-four-page manifesto, *The Great Replacement.* He also sent a mass email to media outlets and to the New Zealand Prime Minister. His manifesto, which soon spread across the internet, detailed his motivations for the attack and promoted his extreme right-wing beliefs. The day before, Tarrant had posted links on his Facebook page to more than forty different articles, websites, and videos promoting hate, white supremacy, and anti-immigration rhetoric.

Armed and prepared, Tarrant drove to the Al Noor Mosque in Christchurch, New Zealand. As he travelled, he filmed himself via Facebook Live, using a GoPro camera attached to his ballistic helmet. His car was stocked with firearms and an improvised explosive device. Upon arrival at the mosque, he declared, *'Let's get the party started.'*

Over the next thirty minutes, he carried out his attack at two separate mosques. At the Al Noor Mosque, he shot and killed forty-two people before driving to the Linwood Islamic Centre, where he killed another seven people. Two more victims later died in hospital, bringing the total death toll to fifty-one. Another eighty-nine people were injured, and countless lives were permanently altered.

Tarrant was apprehended by police in his car while en route to a third mosque. He was just twenty-eight years old, having spent more than two years planning and preparing for his attack.

His decision to live-stream the massacre on Facebook was unprecedented. It had never been done before and the ripple effect across the internet was staggering.

In a thought-provoking article published in 2019, researcher Graham Macklin detailed the cumulative momentum of the live-streamed attack:

'It had already been viewed 4,000 times by the time Facebook removed it, by which time it was too late to stem the flow: the video had already gone viral. Within the first 24 hours Facebook raced to remove 1.5 million videos of the attack, blocking 1.2 million of these at the point of upload and the additional 300,000 after they had been posted to its platform. YouTube's moderation systems were similarly overwhelmed as users re-cut and repackaged footage in an effort to fool the platform's automated detection systems. As a consequence, the video was shared

tens of thousands of times across the platform, at a rate of roughly one upload per second in the hours immediately after the shootings.'

Tarrant was officially branded *The Terrorist* by the New Zealand Government in the hours following the attack on 15 March 2019.

ADULTS ARE NOW AVERAGING over eleven hours a day in front of screens, while children aged eight to twelve average six hours daily. Even younger children, between two and five years old, consume around four and a half hours of screen time per day.

For decades, television was the primary source of screen exposure, but with the rapid rise of computers and smartphones, screen time has dramatically increased. On average, people touch their phones 2,617 times a day and spend approximately two and a half hours consuming content. For heavy users, these numbers soar – 5,427 times a day and anywhere from four to eight hours of daily use.

Athena Chavarria, a former executive assistant at Facebook, bluntly stated: 'I'm convinced the devil lives in our phones and is wreaking havoc on our children.'

According to Chavarria, the last – not the first – child to receive a smartphone is the real winner.

Concerns about mobile devices aren't just coming from parents and educators; they're also being voiced by the very people who created them. Some tech industry leaders actively limit or ban their own children from using smartphones. Unlike reading a book or a newspaper – where there's a natural stopping point – modern apps are designed with *infinite scrolling*, ensuring that content and the possibility for new or novel excitement never ends. The smartphone has become a *slot machine in your pocket*, offering instant gratification at the swipe of a finger. While mobile devices provide convenience, they also steal attention, hinder presence, and cause people to disengage from the world around them.

Smartphones and apps have become billion-dollar industries for tech companies and marketers. Expert teams meticulously craft strategies to keep users engaged, clicking on ads, purchasing products, and spending more time on their devices. Universities now offer courses on designing apps to be more immersive, exciting, and – above all – addictive.

As Michael Easter, the author of *The Comfort Crisis*, notes, '*If you are not paying for a digital service, you are what the company sells ... the asset is your attention which can be packed and sold to the highest bidder.*'

The services embedded in smartphones are not just designed for engagement; they are engineered for compulsion. Many apps integrate psychological principles to ensure people instinctively reach for their devices continuously throughout the day.

Stanford behavioural scientist B. J. Fogg developed the Fogg Behavioural Model, which breaks behaviour down into three key factors:

1. *Motivation* – Is there a desire to perform the behaviour?
2. *Ability* – Is the behaviour simple and effortless?
3. *Prompt* – Is there a trigger that initiates the behaviour?

Fogg originally created this model to help people break bad habits. However, the tech and marketing industries quickly hijacked it to do the opposite – to design apps that encourage repeated and habitual use.

Fogg's model shares striking similarities with research on addiction. At its core, addiction follows a simple pattern:

1. *Trigger* – A cue that sparks the behaviour.
2. *Action* – Engaging in the behaviour.

3. *Reward* – A pleasure outcome that reinforces the behaviour.

With drug addiction, the trigger is often emotional distress or withdrawal symptoms, prompting the person to seek relief. Taking the drug alleviates discomfort, triggers dopamine release, and provides a fleeting sense of pleasure – reinforcing continued use.

With smartphones, the trigger is often boredom or dissatisfaction. In search of stimulation, people instinctively reach for their phones. The endless scroll of social media, fresh content, and incoming notifications create an immediate dopamine hit, providing momentary excitement and distraction. As author Bruce Lipton puts it:

'It's far easier to be entertained by reality TV than to participate in our own reality.'

Being able to instantly pick up our phones or open a YouTube video delivers an immediate dopamine hit. This quick gratification provides an easy escape from discomfort – whether it's boredom, stress, or a lingering sense of mediocrity. By engaging in digital distractions, we divert our attention away from ourselves and temporarily silence the unpleasant emotions or sensations we might otherwise have to confront.

The time we spend on our screens – whether through television, computers, smartphones, or video games – is reshaping the social fabric of society.

Children naturally possess an incredible ability to entertain themselves, fuelled by curiosity and a desire for connection. They are also capable of sitting in silence, embracing boredom, and experiencing quiet moments without constant stimulation. Unfortunately, these qualities are being eroded in modern society, replaced by an ever-increasing dependence on digital devices. Notably, the sharp rise in mental health issues since the early 2000s has coincided with the widespread adoption of smartphones and increased screen time.

Instead of learning through exploration, trial, and error, children's developing brains are now fed by a steady stream of digital content. Of course, not all screen time is harmful, but it must be used with care. It's like fire; when used safely and with parameters it can provide warmth and comfort. But if the fire is uncontained and constantly fuelled, it can burn out of control and hurt us.

One of the most pressing concerns about screen time and social media use is the sheer volume and variety of content people are exposed to. Now more than ever, the online environment is a hotbed of strong opinions, ideas, views, and agendas. It is nearly impossible to avoid exposure to violence, prejudice, divisive political rhetoric, racism, and so on. While the internet holds endless resources to enhance learning and knowledge, it also serves as a platform for conspiracy theories, extremism, and manipulative narratives designed to provoke outrage and division.

Social media platforms have rapidly become the dominant space for shaping public opinion. Most people now read their news online and learn about key societal events through posts, comments, videos, and forums. The power of information – and the ability to control its flow – has profound implications. As George Orwell famously warned, *'Whoever controls the image and information of the past determines what and how future generations will think.'* In today's digital landscape, an information war is underway, where attention is the most valuable currency. And where attention goes, actions follow.

THE ONLINE SPACE HAS BECOME A BREEDING GROUND for bad actors, propaganda, ideologies, and emotional outrage. Countless platforms, bloggers, YouTubers, and influencers seek to spread their beliefs, often capitalising on controversy and division to gain attention. It is often the loudest and most controversial individuals who gain the most attention and views. As a result, balanced perspectives and opinions struggle to break through the noise and capture attention.

In this digital landscape, societal issues have devolved into two-sided arguments, with the many nuances and complexities overlooked. The lack of middle ground, or rationale debate, leads people to gravitate towards opinions that closely align with their own – even if they do not fully agree. The binary way of thinking – *'you are either left or right, support the cause or do not, are with us or against us'* – fuels polarisation online. Over time, as individuals repeatedly engage with like-minded content, their beliefs may shift and they may find themselves drifting towards more extreme positions. The internet, in this sense, does not just reflect opinions; it actively shapes and reshapes them.

Researcher and policy advisor Beatrice Williamson noted, *'Social media was built to learn as we use it, meaning when you view content, the algorithm will provide you with similar content and tailors your feed according to what you view and interact with.'* This algorithm-driven personalisation creates an *'echo chamber'* effect, reinforcing users' existing views while filtering out differing perspectives. Since these platforms prioritise engagement, they naturally amplify the most sensational, provocative, and controversial content – further deepening the divides.

Over time, this echo chamber of personalised content can distort reality – creating a perception of a world teetering on the brink of collapse. As technology use increases and face-to-face interactions decrease, there is a growing risk that digital experiences will define our understanding of the world. This could help explain why young adults and adolescents today report higher levels of disenchantment, anxiety, and demoralisation compared to previous generations.

The internet has also become a powerful tool for extremist groups and terrorist organisations seeking to spread propaganda and recruit followers. A 2021 study identified 198 websites operated by violent extremist or terrorist groups, with the thirty-three most popular sites receiving an estimated 1.54 million visits per month. For many lone actors, the internet serves as a source of inspiration, providing like-minded content and tactical information. Countless perpetrators have engaged with extremist websites and forums, while a simple Google search provides extensive details on past attacks and methods.

The internet has become a powerful medium for lone actors. By live-streaming attacks, releasing manifestos, or posting videos, perpetrators ensure that their actions are broadcast globally. This has contributed to a disturbing cycle of inspiration and imitation, and generations of children have grown up being exposed to this type of violence. For instance, it is estimated that the glorification of the Columbine perpetrators has inspired more than a hundred other attacks; the two offenders are often referred to online as *'gods'*, *'heroes'*, and *'martyrs'* – leading to the term *'doing a Columbine'*.

Other lone actors have dutifully researched previous attacks and methods, analysing their successes, failures, and areas for improvement. This was evident in the Parkland school shooting, where Nikolas Cruz examined mass murders, reviewing their methods, tactical choices, and kill counts. Cruz was fascinated by the Columbine attack, Virginia Tech massacre, and the actions of James Holmes, ultimately concluding that success required maintaining distance, striking quickly, having an escape plan, and completing the attack within twenty minutes – before law enforcement could intervene.

Mark Follman, author of *Trigger Points*, explained, *'It is crucial to understand that shooter-focused news coverage and social media do not cause a person to commit violence, nor is there scientific evidence that graphically violent video games, movies, or music do.'* While it is impossible to prove that media coverage or social media directly causes lone actor violence, there is little doubt that it can fuel motivation and enable individuals to become more lethal and capable. More troublingly, the media brings attention to the attackers and their causes, granting them infamy and ensuring their names live on in public consciousness. More than twenty-five years since the Columbine attack, the two perpetrators continue to be searched for and discussed by thousands on a daily basis.

Bruno Dias, who recently completed his PhD on the role of technology in targeted violence, concluded:

'Despite having decades of experience covering the topic, media outlets typically focus excessively on the attacker's appearance, the weapon(s) they used, tactics, and their grievances. The existing attacker-focused approach may impact how attackers present themselves, potentially explaining their adoption of a militarised appearance that may include tactical vests, body armour, and long guns. Offering attackers dual-purpose tools designed to deliver tactical advantages and a visual representation of what a grievance avenger warrior looks like. It represents a visual shift from being brittle and weak to warrior-like and strong.'

Some scholars have suggested that lone actor violence has become systemic – like a virus sweeping across society. It is now rare to turn on the news without hearing about a school shooting, a mass attack, or a foiled plot. Several decades ago, studies found that the widespread media coverage of suicide was contributing to increased rates of suicide. Exposure to such reports made individuals more likely to consider and, in some cases, commit suicide. As a result, news outlets collectively agreed to limit reporting on suicides due to this *'contagion effect'*.

In a 1990 study, Madelyn Gould and colleagues identified that *'suicidal behaviour is "contagious", in that it can be transmitted, directly, or indirectly, from one person to another'*. Notably, the suicide of a friend or associate significantly increases the likelihood of suicide among individuals with psychological vulnerabilities, particularly adolescents. Research by David Cutler and his co-authors found that *'teens who know friends or family members who have attempted suicide are about three times more likely to attempt suicide than are teens who do not know someone who attempted suicide'*. Exposure to suicide has also been linked to suicide clusters – cases where multiple suicides occur within a particular time frame, group, or location. Individuals at risk of being part of a suicide cluster often have pre-existing vulnerabilities such as mental illness, substance abuse problems, or recent relationship break-ups.

According to Julia Kupper and colleagues, there is strong evidence that mass attacks can also have a **Contagious Effect**, influencing others to carry out similar acts. Like suicide, in the weeks following an incident, a *'hot zone'* emerges where the likelihood of imitation rises. The contagion effect is typically driven by extensive media coverage and the viral spread of information, influencing the psychological state of at-risk individuals. Witnessing the aftermath of an attack and the media attention can reinforce the perception that violence is a justifiable solution to personal problems and a means to achieve significance. While media coverage does not cause violence, it can act as a tipping point for those already predisposed to act.

The contagious period for mass attacks typically lasts several weeks or months. However, beyond this *'hot zone'*, a more persistent **Copycat Effect** emerges. Unlike contagion, which is short-term, the copycat effect unfolds over years, with perpetrators deliberately seeking to replicate past attacks. These offenders often idolise previous attackers, incorporating their quotes into journals, manifestos, or recorded videos.

Following the Christchurch terrorist attack, multiple attackers have cited Brenton Tarrant as an inspiration. In certain online circles, he is referred to as *'Saint Tarrant'*, and his methods have been imitated. Several perpetrators have mirrored his approach – announcing intentions on online forums, live-streaming their attacks, expressing similar sentiments in manifestos, and writing the names of previous attackers on their weapons. The 2022 study by Julia Kupper and co-authors identified six subsequent attacks between 2019 and 2022 that were directly inspired by Tarrant. It's almost certain that this number will continue to rise.

The contagious and copycat effects are amplified by media coverage and social media's ability to spread content rapidly. One of the most enduring aspects of lone actor attacks is the manifesto – an increasingly common feature of their modus operandi. Many attackers send their manifestos to major news outlets, distribute them via email lists, or upload them to popular online platforms. These documents are often lengthy, detailing the perpetrator's beliefs, motivations, and justifications for their actions. In some cases, instead of a manifesto, offenders record videos where they discuss their motivations and post these online.

Manifestos serve two key purposes. First, they allow attackers to control the narrative after their attack. News reports frequently cite excerpts from the manifesto, giving the offender posthumous influence over the discourse. Second, the manifesto contributes to the perpetrator's legacy, ensuring that their name and ideology persist long after the event. This enduring visibility fuels their reputation and often inspires future offenders who seek to follow in their footsteps.

BRENTON TARRANT EMBRACED THE USE OF TECHNOLOGY in his offending, meticulously planning his attack to ensure maximum coverage. Not only did he live-stream his attack, but he also painted messages on his firearms to promote his ideology, praised and celebrated other attackers, and published a manifesto detailing his extreme beliefs. Tarrant was strongly influenced by Norwegian attacker Anders Breivik, closely studying Breivik's manifesto and adopting many of its core messages. He also followed Breivik's suggested steps to avoid detection. While Tarrant copied Breivik, he further advanced their shared extremist ideology and cause. He also took inspiration from mass shooter Dylann Roof, who in a race-based attack killed several African American churchgoers in the USA in 2015. Tarrant's strategic use of technology allowed him to have a far greater influence, making him *'viral'* online and a lasting discussion point on many extreme right-wing forums. He understood the power of *'memes'* and *'messages'* as tools to spread information and shape the opinions of others.

Tarrant's deep understanding of online influence stemmed from years immersed in gaming and the internet. His childhood was marked by Adverse Childhood Experiences (ACEs), and the internet became his refuge. He experienced parental separation, exposure to domestic violence, the death of his grandfather, the loss of the family home in a fire, his father's battle with cancer and depression, and ultimately, his father's suicide.

Like Adam Lanza, Tarrant struggled to adjust to his parents' separation and became anxious and socially avoidant. He withdrew into the online world, spending hours in his bedroom with unsupervised internet access. This continued at school, where he frequently spent his free time in the library using computers rather than socialising. He struggled to fit in and was often bullied for being overweight.

Concerns about Tarrant's behaviour surfaced during his high school years. He was disciplined twice for making racist remarks, influenced by his resentment towards his mother's partner, who was of aboriginal ancestry and had been violent in their home. During his adolescence, his father was diagnosed with lung cancer, a period when Tarrant developed an obsession with excessive weight loss, shedding over 50 kilograms. He became increasingly isolated, spending most of his time engaged in video games and online forums. In 2010, his father died by suicide, and Tarrant discovered his body. While his sister sought counselling to cope with both their father's death and trauma from their mother's abusive partner, Tarrant never recognised the need for professional support.

Following his father's death, Tarrant inherited a large sum of money and embarked on an intense period of solo travel between 2014 and 2017, moving constantly between countries. However, instead of being inspired by his experiences, he became agitated by the world he saw. His time in Europe convinced him that white European culture was under siege due to immigration. His anger was further fuelled by a series of Islamic-inspired terrorist attacks across Europe in 2017.

By late 2017, Tarrant had resolved to retaliate. He believed that the Western world was under existential threat. In his view, a *'great replacement'* was underway, in which immigrants and Muslims would ultimately displace white culture. He began donating money to far-right groups globally and actively engaged in online discussions. He joined numerous right-wing Facebook groups, frequently posting his views, and spent significant time on platforms such as 8chan and 4chan, where he shared memes, jokes, and discussions laced with racism and misogyny.

Tarrant's beliefs were shaped by his environment – an online world saturated with extreme content. To him, the internet was the sole purveyor of truth, a truth he felt was absent elsewhere. The more he sought, the more he found, and the more enraged he became. Isolated in his offline life, he immersed himself in an echo chamber that seamlessly blended racism, misogyny, and violent rhetoric. Using the remainder of his inheritance, he relocated to New Zealand and meticulously prepared for his attack.

Tarrant had a terrible childhood. His life was marked by loss, loneliness, and a search for meaning – one that ultimately ended in horrific violence. There are no justifications for his actions, yet, as one analysis noted:

'Tarrant was not radicalised in a vacuum; the internet allowed him to form social network ties and thus he was subject to group dynamics ... whereby the content he viewed became increasingly funnelled by the underlying algorithms to create a version of reality that fitted his ideological perspective. Within this environment he received positive affirmation which reinforced his perspectives and created an increasingly dark feedback loop. Tarrant's decision to act was on the basis that he identified with a group which he perceived to be under threat.'

5

When Things Go Wrong

'Gradually the unthinkable becomes tolerable, and then acceptable.'

Joni Eareckson Tada

IT HAD BEEN A DIFFICULT FEW YEARS. Andrew Joseph Stack III had experienced taxation issues, suffered a marriage breakdown, and had his rights to operate a company suspended. He felt targeted and victimised by the Internal Revenue Service (IRS), particularly after observing the widespread government bailout of conglomerate companies, financial institutions, and even some politicians during the 2008 Global Financial Crisis. There seemed to be two sets of rules: one for the elites and another for everyday people like him. He was furious at the government and the IRS.

On 18 February 2010, Stack set fire to his home in North Austin, Texas, and then drove to the nearby airbase where his small Piper Dakota plane was housed. Stack was on a mission to right a series of wrongs, having earlier penned a brief manifesto and described his reasons for what was to come.

In the final lines of his manifesto Stack wrote, *'I saw it written once that the definition of insanity is repeating the same process over and over and expecting the outcome to suddenly be different. I am finally ready to stop this insanity. Well, Mr. Big Brother IRS man, let's try something different; take my pound of flesh and sleep well.'*

After taking off in his self-piloted aircraft at 9.45 a.m. that morning, Stack flew for a short ten minutes, before descending. As the plane gradually lowered, Stack adjusted his controls and aligned the plane's trajectory to collide with the four-story IRS field office building in Austin. At full speed, Stack crashed the aircraft into the building, dying upon impact. The collision resulted in an explosion across the building, killing an IRS manager and injuring another thirteen staff. It was estimated that the attack cost the IRS close to $40 million, with the majority of expenses going towards enhancing security at offices throughout the USA.

BILLIONS OF PEOPLE ACROSS THE WORLD suffer setbacks, failures, and hardships each year. Yet, most people never proceed to pick up a knife or a firearm to avenge their difficulties. Many may feel unfairly treated or perceive that the system is rigged or unjust. Despite this, the majority of individuals understand and accept that life doesn't always work out as expected.

For a select few, injustice or mistreatment is unacceptable. To them, people must be held to account and made to pay. This can lead them to demand an apology, a pay out, or another form of recognition or validation. Unfortunately, this rarely occurs, and their anger and outrage only grow. As these feelings fester, the slippery slope towards violence begins.

The events within our lives are powerful. The experience of prejudice, humiliation, ostracism, discrimination, inequality, harassment, or trauma can alter the direction of our lives. How we perceive situations matters – events can make or break us. For many individuals, the pathway to violence begins when they experience a threat or challenge to their identity, position within society, or areas where they derive meaning or significance in their life. This trajectory is influenced by their psychological make-up, coping skills, and available support systems. The majority of people are able to find ways to resolve problems or seek out help during difficult periods. However, for some, these experiences rattle the foundations of their life, propelling them into a fight for survival and a desire to seek restoration at all costs.

A ***Grievance*** arises when a person believes they've been unfairly treated or wronged by others. This mistreatment may be real, imagined, or grossly inflated. Grievances can emerge from many situations: the perception of being slighted, a setback at work, academic failure, or difficulties in social and intimate relationships. Those experiencing a grievance often feel a sense of injustice, victimisation, injury, loss, or discrimination. They believe they have been targeted, mistreated, or ostracised without just cause. Grievances typically arise following a significant emotional event, such as the experience of shame, humiliation, or rejection. When these emotional experiences remain unresolved, anger, resentment, and persistent rumination over the perceived injustice can occur. If the issue remains unaddressed, a desire for retribution or vengeance can emerge.

Studies suggest that around 80% of lone actors harbour a grievance. Typically, around half of these grievances relate to interpersonal circumstances or perceived employment wrongdoings. One in three offenders specifically target a particular person or group. Lone actor violence does not emerge from nowhere. Many individuals who engage in such attacks experience instability, stress, and difficulties coping. On average, perpetrators face 3.6 significant life stressors in the year leading up to an attack. Additionally, a 2020 study by Karie Gibson and colleagues found that 69% of targeted violence offenders had experienced a perceived humiliating event within two years before their attack.

In a fascinating study by Emily Corner and others from 2022, grievance-fuelled violence was more likely to occur when individuals experienced instability in their living situation. In essence, a chain reaction of events was triggered by a grievance-provoking event, followed by a loss or change in living conditions. This often led to increased social rejection, which in turn, intensified feelings of anger and perceived discrimination. From here, thoughts and emotions grew more intense, resulting in shifts in attitudes and beliefs. If no support was available, the desire for revenge could solidify, eventually culminating in violence. Notably, research indicates just under one in two perpetrators experience instability with their accommodation in the months prior to their attack.

Mental health problems can also amplify a grievance, making issues seem insurmountable – as though the walls are closing in. Grievances cause a person to become stuck, fixated on perceived wrongs, and consumed by blame. More often than not, grievances lead to an overwhelming preoccupation with the perceived injustice.

Akin to a form of tunnel vision, **Fixation** occurs when a person becomes preoccupied with a particular aspect of their life. Fixations typically arise from an emotionally significant event or incidents where a person's beliefs are challenged. For instance, a fixation may develop after a relationship break-up, with an individual unable to stop thinking about their former partner. They may feel betrayed, abandoned, or angry. This anger may become more intense when they discover their ex-partner is dating someone new. As a result, they spend hours scrolling through social media, driving past their ex-partner's home, and even loitering in cafes, hoping for an encounter.

Fixations can also emerge alongside deteriorating mental health, without the presence of a grievance. For example, an individual might develop an obsession with a television reporter or local council member, despite never having met the person. In their mind, they've constructed a story: perhaps an imagined romantic relationship or the belief that the public figure is sending them secret messages. Over time, this fixation can become all-consuming, with the individual spending most of their waking hours thinking about the person and gathering information about them through news articles, online content, television appearances, and so on.

Arguably the most infamous example of fixated violence dates back to 1976 when the film *Taxi Driver*, starring Robert De Niro, premiered in cinemas. The movie depicted a lonely, obsessive, and violent man who attempts to assassinate a presidential candidate after being rejected by a woman. The film also featured a young Jodie Foster as a twelve-year-old prostitute. While the plot seemed unusual and far-fetched for most viewers, it had a profound impact on John Hinckley Jr. Hinckley became infatuated with the movie, particularly Jodie Foster, watching the film fifteen times. He believed that a special connection existed between them, developing a romantic fixation. Hinckley made phone calls to Foster, left notes in her mailbox, and even slipped letters under her dormitory room door. In response, Foster filed for a restraining order, but Hinckley remained undeterred.

In a deluded attempt to impress Foster, Hinckley decided to replicate the film and make a grand gesture. On the afternoon of 30 March 1981, he approached the front of a press line as US President Ronald Reagan exited the Washington Hilton Hotel after delivering a speech. As Reagan approached his car, Hinckley fired six shots, striking the president in the left lung and narrowly missing his heart. Other bullets hit a police officer, a secret service agent, and the president's press secretary, who was critically wounded. While Hinckley's crime does not entirely fit the profile of lone actor violence, given the evident stalking behaviour, his actions highlight the powerful impact of fixations.

ALL LONE ACTORS experience grievances and/or fixations to some degree. These are the seeds of dissatisfaction, emotional turmoil, and an inability to move forward in life. Once a grievance develops, further negative experiences can fuel thoughts of violence. Grievances often *'Push'* an individual towards violence, while beliefs, ideologies, and other perceived incentives *'Pull'* them towards action. This perception that life is unfair, and that others are responsible for their suffering, can lead an individual down a narrow path to violence.

When life is going well, it's easy to overlook minor setbacks. However, when individuals are unhappy, socially disconnected, and overwhelmed by negative thoughts, even minor difficulties can push them over the edge. Experiencing failure or setbacks can have a profound impact. Instead of viewing the situation with perspective, the person gravitates towards the most negative interpretation. They dismiss alternative explanations, automatically assuming the worst. Their reactions are shaped by past experiences, previous challenges, and recent struggles. In doing so, they lose sight of the present and, with it, the ability to address the issue in that moment. This mindset reinforces a sense of victimhood, leaving them feeling as though they are continually subjected to hardship or injustice.

Perceptions feed problems, and problems, in turn, feed perceptions. It becomes a vicious cycle – a pattern of seeing oneself under constant attack, facing one perceived threat or injustice after another. When a person feels trapped and incapable of resolving their difficulties, the situation can spiral dangerously. Violence may then emerge as the only, and ultimate, solution.

6

The Power Of Beliefs

'The mark of the immature man is that he wants to die nobly for a cause, while the mark of the mature man is that he wants to live humbly for one.'

J. D. Salinger

THEODORE KACZYNSKI MAILED or hand-delivered sixteen package bombs, killing three people and injuring twenty-three. His reign of terror lasted seventeen years, from 1978 to 1995. His early attacks targeted universities and airlines, earning him the nickname *'Unabomber'*. Kaczynski believed that industrialisation was destroying nature and eroding human freedoms. In his view, scientists, businessmen, and industries were responsible for environmental degradation and the suppression of natural born freedoms. He saw violence as the only means of effecting change, directing his attacks at those he deemed responsible for society's decline. The chaos and financial toll of Kaczynski's crimes resulted in the largest and most expensive law enforcement manhunt in US history at the time.

While developing his bombs, Kaczynski meticulously crafted his 35,000-word manifesto, *Industrial Society and Its Future*. He initially wrote it by hand before transcribing it on a typewriter. The manifesto detailed his ideological beliefs, asserting that technological progress had destabilised humanity, diminished quality of life, and stripped people of their freedoms. He warned that *'the system had to regulate human behavior in order to function'* and argued that the logical endpoint would be a society governed by technology and human genetic engineering.

In 1995, Kaczynski sent letters to multiple media outlets, demanding that his manifesto be published in full, unedited and verbatim. He claimed he would cease his bombing campaign if this demand was met. After extensive discussion between the FBI and media outlets, an agreement was reached, and on 19 September 1995, *The Washington Post* published the manifesto. Shortly after, Kaczynski's brother, David, recognised the writing style and contacted police. Approximately seven months later, Kaczynski was arrested.

Kaczynski is frequently classified as a lone actor terrorist due to the ideological motivations behind his crimes. However, aspects of his behaviour also align with serial killing, particularly his intermittent periods of inactivity, the personal nature of his mission, and the elaborate countermeasures he used to evade capture. His extensive efforts to avoid detection were documented by Clare Alley in *The Psychology of Extreme Violence*:

'When making his bombs, he would wear gloves and would soak each piece in soybean oil and salt water to remove fingerprints. He would remove the covers off the batteries because the covers contained bar codes that could aid investigators in finding out where they were purchased. In order to avoid detection, rather than purchase the materials he needed for his bombs, he would collate the majority of materials (such as the pipes for his bombs) from abandoned cars and junkyards. Kaczynski would also disguise himself when traveling to plant or mail his bombs and when searching the scrapyards for useful materials for his bomb making. For instance, he would change the colour of his hair using dyes; regularly use different types of spectacles/glasses; change the shape of his face by inserting chewing gum under his lip or would put wax or Kleenex into his nostril and use different types

of wigs and hats. He would sometimes make himself appear bigger than he was by wearing coats or jackets that were bulky underneath his raincoat. In another attempt to further mislead the authorities in their search for the "Unabomber," he used a pair of shoes that had the rubber soles of a much smaller shoe tied to the bottom. This would result in the authorities looking for someone who had a much smaller shoe size.'

Regardless of whether he is classified as a serial killer, or lone actor, Kaczynski epitomised *'loneness'*. He operated in complete isolation and had minimal social connections. Despite earning a master's and doctorate in mathematics, as well as holding a promising academic position, he abandoned his career path in favour of a reclusive life. In the early 1970s, he built a small cabin in the remote bushlands of Lincoln, Montana, living without running water or electricity. His only sources of income were occasional odd jobs and financial assistance from his family. He was secretive, socially detached, highly intelligent, practically skilled, and fuelled by his ideological beliefs.

Kaczynski's case was unique in that his crimes were not just about violence; they were a means of amplifying his ideas. His bombs and his manifesto were equally integral to his mission. At the time, it was rare for perpetrators to accompany their attacks with ideological writings, but Kaczynski's approach has since been replicated by numerous lone actors. Anders Breivik, Brenton Tarrant, and many others have all drawn inspiration from Kaczynski's manifesto – copying sections of text, mimicking his style, and adopting his strategy of coupling violent action with written advocacy. In many ways, Kaczynski pioneered the modern template for advancing an ideology through lone actor violence.

AN IDEOLOGY IS A DISTINCTIVE TYPE of human thought, rooted in particular political, philosophical, or sociocultural positions. Kaczynski's reign of violence stands as one of the most notorious examples of ideologically motivated violence by a lone individual. An ideology is built upon a set of ideas and beliefs about the future – *what ought to be*. Put simply, it is an idealised vision of life and how it should unfold.

Ideologies vary widely, ranging from commonly held societal norms to niche beliefs embraced by only a select few. For instance, Western societies tend to emphasise individual achievement, whereas many Eastern cultures prioritise the collective above the individual. Prominent ideologies include capitalism, environmentalism, nationalism, Marxism-communism, socialism, and even totalitarianism. Ideologies can be broad and acceptable, mainstream or unconventional, and deep-seated or fluid. At their core, ideologies function as guiding principles, shaping how individuals and societies believe the world should operate – often viewing opposing ideologies as inherently false or misguided.

Ideologies can either be harmless or harmful, depending on the intensity of the beliefs and the distress that arises when expectations go unmet. When ideals create emotional turmoil and social conflict, individuals may become increasingly isolated. Beliefs can shape us, make us, and break us. The weight and rigidity of an ideology determines its influence on a person's identity and actions.

In the late 1800s, German psychiatrist Carl Wernicke introduced the concept of the **Overvalued Idea** (Ueberwerthige Idee), describing how seemingly normal beliefs, when intensely held, could lead to aberrant behaviour and character changes. The notion has persisted in psychological literature for over a century. Essentially, an overvalued idea is the seed from which extreme beliefs and behaviours can grow. Ideas hold immense power – the more they are reinforced and validated, the more they take root, shaping an individual's worldview and actions.

With the rise of mass casualty attacks, psychiatrist Tahir Rahman and colleagues have examined the role of overvalued ideas in driving violence. Building upon Wernicke's work, Rahman proposed the concept of an

Extremely Overvalued Belief. Unlike an overvalued idea, which is typically unique to an individual, an extremely overvalued belief is one shared within a broader culture, subgroup, or religion. However, the intensity with which an individual embraces this belief is extreme – it becomes deeply ingrained, emotionally charged, and resistant to challenge. Over time, as a person's identity becomes increasingly tied to the belief, it dominates their thoughts and actions. In some cases, this unwavering commitment leads to violence as a means of defending or advancing the cause.

Rahman's research highlights how extremely overvalued beliefs can shape various psychological conditions, including eating disorders, body dysmorphic disorder, and gender identity struggles. While these conditions differ from violent extremism, they share a common psychological mechanism – beliefs that become so rigid and reinforced that they lead to profound behavioural changes. For instance, the early stages of anorexia may begin with doubts about body image and distortions regarding what constitutes an attractive physique. As these beliefs are reinforced through peers or online content, the individual may start restricting their diet. Over time, as their weight declines and they perceive themselves as more attractive, the belief strengthens. Eventually, starvation and excessive exercise become daily habits. The more family or friends express concern, the more resistant and defiant the individual becomes – sometimes to the point of death.

Although eating disorders predominantly affect females, mass violence is overwhelmingly perpetrated by males. Women are more likely to internalise emotional distress, whereas men tend to externalise and act upon their emotions. While both genders experience overvalued beliefs at similar rates, these beliefs often manifest in different ways. For men, overvalued beliefs frequently revolve around themes of superiority, masculinity, and significance.

Extremely overvalued beliefs are not unique to an individual but are often shared by others, even if it's only a small minority. For men, such beliefs can serve as a foundation for identity, purpose, and personal goals. Psychological needs – such as belonging, significance, and autonomy – can make individuals particularly vulnerable to ideological narratives that promise meaning and transformation. When coupled with outrage at personal or societal issues, this can create the illusion of a mission – *to right a wrong, act as a saviour, or prevent an injustice*. As seen with Kaczynski, beliefs or ideals can serve as justification and motivation to seek revenge or restore a perceived natural order. When an individual perceives their cause as righteous, they may view themselves as warriors or revolutionaries, fighting for a cause. While we all hold different views on many aspects of life, some people develop intense and rigid perspectives on specific issues.

While people hold differing opinions on issues such as abortion, gender roles, politics, climate change, and human rights, most individuals remain capable of functioning within society, even when their views are unconventional or extreme. They may be passionate and vocal about their beliefs, yet these beliefs do not dictate their lives. For some, however, the intensity escalates – the dials are turned too high, and the beliefs become all-consuming. They dedicate significant time, energy, and resources to their cause. For example, a person with extreme views on gender identity may create a website, post daily on social media, distribute flyers, and organise protests. This may consume months of their life, but there remains a limit to how far they are willing to go. They may be active and outspoken, yet they draw the line at violence. Others, however, see violence as the only true means to defend or advance their cause.

Extremely overvalued beliefs can escalate into **Violent Extremism**, where individuals use violence to support extreme or radical beliefs. Violence becomes both the mechanism and means for achieving the desired outcomes and enacting change.

For example, in October 2015, Robert Dear Jr walked into a Planned Parenthood clinic in Colorado, armed with a semi-automatic rifle, and opened fire. A staunch pro-life advocate, Dear was deeply distressed by the clinic's abortion services and the alleged sale of fetuses. He held rigid religious beliefs about God and the sanctity of life. Years earlier, he had targeted another clinic, gluing its locks shut.

Describing himself as a *'warrior for the babies'*, Dear believed he was on a mission to stop the clinic from committing further *'murders'*. His deteriorating mental health added to his sense of urgency – he was convinced the FBI was after him. In his mind, a final last stand was necessary. His attack on the clinic ended after a five-hour stand-off with police, with three people dying and another nine injured. The confrontation concluded when an armoured police vehicle breached the facility, allowing officers to rescue the hostages inside. Disturbingly, investigators later discovered that during the gunfight, Dear had been aiming at his parked vehicle, which contained several propane tanks rigged as improvised explosives.

Lone actors like Dear are often motivated by single-issue grievances. Some act in response to a specific belief, while others operate within a broader ideological framework that skews their perception of the world. **Hate-fuelled** violence is a prime example. Violence is often driven by derogatory and hostile attitudes towards those perceived as different. Perpetrators may be motivated to harm individuals based on their skin colour, gender expression, sexual orientation, religious beliefs, or racial and ethnic background. Dylann Roof's 2015 massacre of African American churchgoers in Charleston, South Carolina stemmed from his racist conviction that '*Blacks were taking over the world*' and that someone needed to stop them. At just 21 years old, Roof opened fire on a bible study class at the Emmanuel African Methodist Episcopal Church, killing nine people. Roof intended to incite a race war and believed his action would help restore white supremacy.

Violence can also stem from extreme sociopolitical ideologies and beliefs, on both the left and the right. Again, these beliefs become overvalued or idealised, with some individuals resorting to violence to accelerate their cause.

Right-wing extremists are concerned by their personal and national rights, perceiving that their rights to freedom and independence are being threatened or removed. This mindset was evident in the 6 January 2021 storming of the US Capitol Building by rioters convinced that the 2020 election had been stolen through voter fraud. While many people hold strong views about their country and may express patriotism, those with deep-seated right-wing extremist beliefs often perceive their *'way of life'* as being under attack. As a result, some individuals resort to violence in an attempt to restore what they see as a lost sense of societal balance. While others may act violently to neutralise a threat which endangers their identity or values. Many violent actors influenced by extreme right-wing ideologies hold beliefs about national sovereignty, racial supremacy, authoritarianism, and a strict allegiance to their cause. The destructive potential of such extreme ideologies has been demonstrated throughout history – most notably in the rise of Adolf Hitler and the Nazi regime, which sought to establish a fascist state built on the notion of racial and national supremacy.

Similarly, individuals with extreme **Left-wing** beliefs are also driven by concerns about rights and governmental control. However, rather than prioritising personal freedom and independence, those with far-left ideologies are often preoccupied with issues related to fairness, equality, and perceived systemic injustices. These concerns may include climate change, political or corporate corruption, institutional racism, animal rights, social equity, and even more radical issues such as population control. Those who embrace extreme left-wing beliefs may perceive that their country or community is under threat and that their right to fair treatment is being systematically removed or restricted. In response, some resort to violence, believing that it is a necessary tool to force change or spark a revolution for their cause.

Recent examples of far-left violence have been associated with groups like

Antifa (*Anti-Faschistische Aktion*), which emerged as a militant movement in the 1980s and has since spread internationally. While Antifa's stated aim is to combat fascism, corruption, and oppression, some of its members have engaged in vandalism, violent protests, and disruptive actions. High-profile incidents have included rioting following racial injustice protests (such as those linked to Black Lives Matter) and violent opposition to right-wing events, such as the destruction caused at the University of California during a scheduled appearance by controversial speaker Milo Yiannopoulos.

As author James Redfield wrote, '*Where attention goes energy flows; where intention goes energy flows.*' Thoughts are powerful – what we focus on repeatedly becomes ingrained, shaping our perceptions and actions. Ideas and beliefs hold immense power; they can inspire progress and greatness or serve as a catalyst for suffering and destruction.

Offenders rarely fit neatly into a singular ideology, form of extremism, or belief system. Instead, their pathway to violence is shaped by a combination of factors, including upbringing, personal experiences, psychological well-being, setbacks, social influences, access to resources, and individual capabilities. These elements interact to shape the beliefs that individuals develop and the degree of significance they attach to them.

Violence does not occur in isolation. It emerges when a specific set of conditions align, reinforcing the idea that violence is both necessary and justifiable. Believing in the necessity and justification of violence is a crucial component, but other elements must also align. Even among those who hold extreme or rigid beliefs, only a small fraction resort to violence. What differentiates them is often the presence of catalysts – specific events, social influences, or personal crises that pull and push them towards action. This reinforces the idea that violent extremism is not simply about ideology but about the interplay of multiple psychological and situational factors.

7

When Cultures Collide

'It is not our differences that divide us. It's our inability to recognize, accept, and celebrate those differences.'

Audre Lorde

IN THE EARLY MORNING HOURS of 9 February 2018, Momena Shoma walked into the bedroom of her homestay host and plunged a knife into his neck. As she attempted to kill him, she screamed *'Allahu Akbar'* (God is great), wrestling with him for several minutes while his terrified daughter looked on. Shoma applied such force that the knife snapped in his neck.

Shoma had arrived in Australia just eight days earlier, on 1 February. The twenty-four-year-old had travelled from Bangladesh to pursue a master's degree in Linguistics, arranging accommodation through a homestay. Within days of her arrival, her host became concerned after discovering she had stabbed her mattress with a knife. As a result, she was asked to leave and was placed with another host – who would later become her victim.

Over the coming days, Shoma's behaviour became increasingly alarming. She purchased night vision goggles and watched videos of beheadings and other Islamic State propaganda online.

Fortunately, her attack did not result in a fatality, and Shoma was arrested. In the days following the incident, police began investigating the factors motivating her violence. As part of the inquiry, authorities in Bangladesh visited her twenty-two-year-old sister, Asmaul Husna Sumona. During the visit, one of the officers was attacked by Sumona, who was armed with a knife.

In June 2019, Shoma was sentenced to forty-two years in prison, becoming the first woman in Australia to be convicted of terrorism-related offences.

Following her conviction, Shoma was incarcerated in a Victorian prison. In October 2020, she obtained a pair of gardening shears that had been concealed in the prison's laundry. Shoma approached a blonde Caucasian inmate and stabbed her with the shears before other prisoners intervened. When questioned by investigators, Shoma admitted she had hoped to attract international attention with the attack and believed that Allah would be pleased with her actions.

Shoma embraced an extreme interpretation of Islam, and her story serves as a stark illustration of how religious and cultural beliefs, when distorted, can lead to violence.

JIHADI-INSPIRED VIOLENCE HAS BEEN the subject of widespread media coverage over the last few decades, largely driven by groups such as Al-Qaeda and Islamic State (IS). These groups, led by notorious figureheads such as Osama bin Laden and Abu Bakr al-Baghdadi, believe Islam is the only path to human dignity and that the sacred scriptures of Islam are law (Sharia law). The traditional values and principles of the Muslim faith are rejected and instead violence is endorsed as the way to wage war against the corrupt and non-committed.

Jihadists argue that the West has suppressed Islam, with governments in countries like the UK and the USA corrupting the faith and promoting a hedonistic and self-indulgent lifestyle. They view citizens of the West as being complicit in their governments' actions and in the perceived moral decay of society. Consequently, Jihadists see it as their duty under Islamic doctrine to target non-believers and those they perceive as threats to the Islamic way of life.

At the heart of many cultural and religious divides is a tension between traditional values and contemporary societal norms. Issues such as freedom of expression, gender equality, sexual orientation, marriage, and abortion often ignite conflict between conservative ideals and evolving modern practices. For those deeply rooted in traditional viewpoints, these shifts can be seen as threatening or immoral, fostering a perception that core values are being undermined.

Individuals raised in tightly knit religious communities often carry specific expectations about how life should be lived. When these expectations are challenged by changing cultural practices – particularly those in Western societies – some people perceive this as an erosion of their identity or an existential threat to their way of life. In extreme cases, this perception can escalate into violence.

Across the globe, countless incidents of violence have been committed against people from different backgrounds, beliefs, and cultural practices. International events like the genocide in Rwanda, the conflict in Northern Ireland, and the ongoing Israeli-Palestinian conflict are just a few examples. Acts of terrorism and lone actor attacks have also become increasingly common. In 2005, coordinated bombings on public transport in London were carried out by four British men – three of Pakistani descent and one of Jamaican descent – driven by jihadist ideologies. These attackers targeted civilians, killing fifty-two people and injuring over 700, believing that British foreign policies oppressed Muslim countries and warranted a violent response. Similar motivations fuelled the brutal murder of British soldier Lee Rigby in May 2013. Rigby was killed in broad daylight by two men who claimed they were avenging the deaths of Muslims killed by British forces abroad, perceiving themselves as soldiers in a war between Islam and the West.

Another example of colliding cultures was the 2016 shooting at Pulse nightclub in Orlando, Florida, which had long been a haven for the LGBTQ+ community. Omar Mateen pledged allegiance to IS during the attack, killing forty-nine people and wounding more than fifty. Investigators speculated that Mateen had previously visited the nightclub prior to the attack and struggled with his own sexual identity – an identity that clashed with his religious beliefs, which condemned homosexuality as a sin punishable by death.

Those who resort to violence in defence of their cultural beliefs often feel powerless, marginalised, discriminated against, and disenfranchised. They perceive their traditions, identities, and values are being systematically ignored or dismissed by a dominant culture. In the ever-evolving digital landscape, cultural differences between the West and the East have been magnified, creating a virtual battleground for competing values. As a result, cultural disputes are no longer confined to geographical borders, but instead infiltrate people's homes and daily lives. These battles are increasingly fought in the online space where, as outlined earlier, radical beliefs can spread unchecked.

Online platforms can amplify hate and ostracise those with differing cultural or religious views, pushing individuals towards online communities that validate and reinforce their beliefs. In moments of vulnerability, this online support can come at a cost – introducing individuals to radicalised or extreme beliefs as they seek to protect their identity, faith, or sense of belonging. This gradual process of reinforcement can slowly change beliefs and become a slippery slope towards radicalisation and extremism.

Radicalisation refers to *'the actions or process of causing someone to adopt radical positions on political or social issues'*. The pathways to radicalisation vary, often emerging through a combination of internal and external influences.

For some, radicalisation is primarily self-initiated, shaped by personal experiences of discrimination, exposure to extremist content, or engagement with media that alters their beliefs. For others, it occurs through third-party influences, such as the beliefs of family members, online peer-to-peer networks, or social groups that promote alternative narratives and reinforce divisive rhetoric. The powerful influence of online communication platforms cannot be understated.

Individuals who become radicalised are often vulnerable to influence, whether due to their age, mental state, experiences of loss or injustice, or difficult social or financial circumstances. This vulnerability can create a *'cognitive opening'*, making them more susceptible to alternative beliefs. In such cases, newly adopted radical beliefs can offer a sense of purpose, hope, and belonging within a community. However, these newfound beliefs frequently promote a grievance-based mindset, reinforcing the idea they have been wronged, and that violence is a justified means to avenge injustices and demonstrate their commitment to the cause.

THE RADICALISATION OF MOMENA SHOMA and her sister, Sumona, can be traced back to a series of tragic and transformative events. In 2015, their mother lost her eyesight following a prolonged battle with diabetes and kidney disease. Desperate to find a solution, their father turned to an online platform to find a blood donor. Unbeknownst to him, the donor he connected with had ties to Jamaat-ul-Mujahideen (JMB), an extremist militant group in Bangladesh affiliated with the Islamic State.

What began as an act of medical assistance soon evolved into something far more troubling. Over the following months, Shoma and Sumona developed a close relationship with this individual, who introduced them to figures within extremist circles. After their mother's death, their bond deepened, and the sisters found solace and belonging with these individuals. Among their new connections were two of the perpetrators behind the 2016 Holey Artisan Bakery terrorist attack in Bangladesh – an incident in which diners were taken hostage and twenty-two people were killed. They were also introduced to the men responsible for the murder of blogger Ahmed Rajib Haider, as well as individuals involved in the failed attempt to detonate a 1,000-pound bomb at the Federal Reserve Bank of New York.

Through their exposure to these figures, Shoma and Sumona gradually embraced a jihadi ideology. While they were not immediately drawn to violent extremism, they found comfort in the words of those who seemed to understand their grief. The influence of these individuals, both in person and online, slowly took hold. As their radical beliefs deepened, the sisters distanced themselves from their father and severed ties with family and friends. Seeking to further immerse herself in extremist networks, Shoma attempted to study in Turkey but was denied a visa. Undeterred, she tried to travel to Tunisia – a known hub for IS recruitment – but her plans were once again thwarted.

Frustrated by these failed attempts, Shoma turned her focus online, immersing herself in IS-hosted platforms. She consumed propaganda and media that validated her radicalised beliefs, each video reinforcing her disenfranchisement with society and Western culture. Like with Tarrant and many other lone actors, she became trapped in an online echo chamber that further solidified her commitment to violent extremism. Eventually, Shoma secured approval to study in Australia. However, her intentions extended beyond academics – her goal was to enter the country and carry out an attack to further the Islamic cause.

Shoma's radicalisation was both cultural and deeply personal. It was rooted in her religious identity and a growing sense of alienation. Shoma saw herself as a warrior fighting a battle between good and evil – a defender of her faith in a world she believed had strayed from the divine teachings. To her, the attack was not just an act of violence, but a righteous mission. She viewed herself as a soldier of faith, striking back against a society that had lost its way. Just as the perpetrators of the 2005 London bombings saw themselves as avenging the wrongs done to Muslims abroad, Shoma believed her own actions were part of a global struggle. She saw herself as part of the same ideological legacy, where the West's perceived aggression towards Islam warranted acts of extreme retaliation.

Shoma and her sister were radicalised during a vulnerable period in their lives. Following their mother's death, they were in need of support and guidance. Unfortunately, rather than confiding in their father, the two women gravitated to the companionship of a charismatic blood donor who introduced them to a world that offered promises, answers, and a sense of purpose. It provided them with a way to reclaim power, assert their place in the world, and perform a holy duty by fighting back against an immoral and unjust society.

Shoma's radicalisation and descent into extremism was shaped by a complex interplay of grief, cultural uncertainty, loneliness, and personal vulnerability. What began as a search for identity and belonging ended in a commitment to violence. Her descent highlights how cultural and religious beliefs, when combined with exposure to radical networks, can deepen feelings of ostracism and disenfranchisement. As this continues, and the psychological gap widens, it can propel an individual further down the path towards violence.

Shoma was only a teenager when she lost her mother – just beginning to understand herself and the world. Less than ten years later, she would become Australia's first convicted female terrorist.

8

A Staircase and Bathtub

'Violence is the last refuge of the incompetent.'

Isaac Asimov

'SOMETIMES KILLING IS NECESSARY,' rationalised Nidal Hasan.

'The only way to stop the US is going to involve killing soldiers. They kill our soldiers, we kill theirs. They fight for "democracy", I fight for Sharia law.

'I take no pleasure in killing for the sake of unwarranted killing. But sometimes it's necessary. In war, you have to kill once you've decided to take the path of a front-line soldier.'

Armed with a pistol and revolver, Nidal Hasan strategically entered a main building at the Fort Hood military base in Texas. On confronting a group of unarmed soldiers, he shouted, *'Allahu Akbar'*, before opening fire. In his thirty-minute attack on the base, Hasan killed thirteen people and injured another thirty-two. The attack ended after a lengthy gunfire exchange with police, which resulted in Hasan being shot and injured.

Hasan grew up in Arlington, Virginia, with his parents emigrating from Palestine before he was born. Though his family followed the Islamic faith, his parents were not devoutly religious. Hasan had a largely unremarkable childhood and, after finishing school, he enlisted in the army for a three-year service. He spent his army years in California and enjoyed his time in the infantry before discharging and commencing study at Virginia Tech. Over the next few years, Hasan completed a Bachelor of Science in Biochemistry. He later applied to the military medical school,stating during his application interview that he *'loved the army'*.

Life was progressing well – until 2001, when his mother passed away after a long-term battle with cancer. Her death shook Hasan profoundly. While mourning, he began to question his loyalty to the Islamic faith. He was concerned that his mother would face an eternity burning in hell due to her lack of devotion to Islam. After reflecting on his faith and fearing for his own soul in the afterlife, Hasan became increasingly devout, believing that strict obedience to God was the only path to salvation. He convinced himself that through his actions, he could not only secure his own place in paradise but also save his mother from eternal damnation. This loss, combined with a deepening religious crisis, marked a profound emotional turning point. It was not just grief that consumed Hasan – it was an overwhelming fear of divine judgement. This fear ultimately set him on the path to religious fanaticism.

Hasan began listening to the audio sermons of Anwar al-Awlaki, who at the time was considered a Muslim leader with *'moderate'* views. However, in the coming years, al-Awlaki would become one of the most significant recruiters for Al-Qaeda, inspiring several violent actors such as Roshonara Choudhry (stabbing attack on a Member of Parliament in the UK in 2010) and Faisal Shahzad (attempted Times Square bombing in Manhattan in New York in 2010).

Over the coming years, Hasan became convinced of the importance of having absolute submission to God. He had fallouts with family members over his intense religious views, experienced difficulties with work colleagues, and began to live an isolated life centred around religion. He became increasingly intolerant of those who did not share his views. He also made efforts to bring awareness to his colleagues in the military about the plight of the war against Islam being waged by the USA. Hasan was adamant that the US military was infringing on the rights and welfare of Muslims in Afghanistan and Iraq. By 2007, he had developed a radicalised view of Islam and supported jihadism as a means to avenge the sins of the USA against the Muslim people. Between 2008 and 2009, he exchanged emails with Anwar al-Awlaki and began writing about the purpose of life and the need to submit to God.

Despite a significant shift in his religious beliefs, Hasan continued to remain in the military, and in the spring of 2009 was promoted to the rank of major. By this stage, he had completed medical school and was a qualified psychiatrist. Although he received a promotion, Hasan was already contemplating plans to carry out a violent attack against the military. In August, Hasan purchased an FN Five-Seven pistol and over the coming months frequently practised on targets at the gun range. During this time, Hasan was torn between his desire to avenge Islam and his loyalty to the US military, which had provided him with a career. However, in late October, he was informed that he was going to be deployed to Afghanistan and had orders to present for his pre-deployment training by 28 November. Hasan viewed his deployment orders as a sign from God to speed up his action, and on 5 November he launched his attack at the Fort Hood military base.

After being incarcerated, Hasan wrote a manifesto titled *The Purpose of Life: Why Were We Created?* Despite being predominantly paralysed from the chest down and causing widespread loss of life and grief, Hasan has maintained his devotion to Islam, detailing his commitment and declaring the USA as *'a nation of evil'*.

Hasan stated, *'I'm not against you for just being American, I don't hate you because of your freedoms. I hate you because every day you're supporting, funding, and committing crimes not only against Muslims but also humanity.'*

WITHIN THE RESEARCH ON TERRORISM and violent extremism, two unusually named models have been used to shed light on the underlying psychology of lone actors: *'The Staircase'* and *'The Bathtub'* models.

The Staircase: Using the metaphor of an increasing and narrowing staircase, Professor Fathali Moghaddam believes that as individuals climb the staircase, the likelihood of violence increases. With each step and each level, a person experiences fewer choices, and becomes more isolated, disconnected from others, and increasingly adamant about their cause and sense of morality.

To progress to violence, a person must ascend through five levels of the staircase, climbing each floor without stopping or turning back. To begin, an individual must experience an *'opening'* that leads them through the door of the building and onto the ground floor. At this level, a person may feel a sense of injustice and frustration, and believe they have been mistreated or deprived of certain aspects in life. For some, these difficulties are easily resolved, or the emotional intensity fades away, allowing them to exit back out the door. If this fails, the person climbs to the first floor, searching for solutions or other doors that offer hope or a means to resolve their problems. If this search is unsuccessful and solutions do not arise, the person continues to the second floor. By the time they reach the second floor, they are angry and outraged at their circumstances. If unable to find alternative options at this stage, their anger becomes directed at others, particularly anyone who fails to agree with them or take their side.

Upon climbing to the third floor, the individual begins to develop a sense of moral superiority and perceives that they are right and others are wrong. As they remain at this level, they view violence or retribution as a justified response.

At the fourth floor, a person typically begins to fuel their anger and experience more intense violent thoughts. They may engage in online forums, seek out others with similar beliefs, and consider methods and means to carry out violence. During this level, the person becomes psychologically prepared to take action, coming to believe that it is *'us vs. them'*, or a matter of *'good vs. evil'*. At the fifth, and final, floor, the individual accepts the realities and consequences that will arise from carrying out an attack. They come to terms with harming others, including themselves, and understand that there will inevitably be costs to achieving their goal or mission.

In Hasan's case, the staircase model illustrates the gradual manner in which his worldview narrowed, and his identity and purpose became intertwined with violence. The transition from a military officer and psychiatrist to a lone actor did not happen suddenly; it was the culmination of a series of emotional triggers, religious doubts, social isolation, and an evolving sense of moral superiority.

At the heart of Moghaddam's staircase model is the idea that individuals do not immediately progress to violence. Instead, the decision to commit violence is a process marked by successive stages where grievances and frustrations become more acute, and choices become more limited. By the time Hasan reached the later stages of radicalisation, his perception of the situation was reduced to a series of black-and-white beliefs: good vs. evil, Islam vs. the West. He saw himself as a soldier for his cause, with violence as the only available solution to the perceived persecution of Muslims. His preparations for violence, including purchasing weapons, practising at gun ranges, and contemplating his attack, further highlighted his narrowing of choices. By this point, he had reached the metaphorical fifth floor, where he accepted the reality and consequences of committing violence. Hasan's actions were not the product of a sudden or irrational decision but rather the result of a long, methodical climb up the staircase.

The Bathtub: Lone actor violence, according to the bathtub model, occurs due to a variety of sources, each akin to individual water faucets gradually filling up the bathtub until it is full and eventually overflows – the penultimate violent act. For some, filling the bathtub can be a slow process, while for others, there may be a sudden pouring in of water, or contributing factors, which quickly fill the tub.

The model, which was developed by Professor Boaz Ganor, identifies three main taps that fill the bath: ideology, personal, and psychological. The ideology tap may involve the development of certain ideologies, extremist views, radicalised beliefs, or even political or religious attitudes. A variety of personal factors can also fill up the tub, including relationships, failures, finances, employment, health, and family situations. The final tap filling up the bathtub is psychological influences. Some of the many psychological factors that can add to the bathtub include unresolved anger, mental illness, suicidal ideation, violent attitudes, personality traits, and poor coping or problem-solving skills.

As the bathtub fills and more taps continue to flow, the likelihood of a person progressing to violence increases. However, for some, changes in any of these three areas may slightly empty the tub, briefly pulling the plug and letting some water wash down the drain. Yet, for those who continue to add to the ever-rising water level, the closer the tub comes to overflowing. In many cases, the tub may be close to spilling over, but a final trigger or tipping point is needed for an act of violence to occur. A person may be highly motivated and have several reasons to act violently, but a final factor tips them over the edge and towards action. Often, the final tipping point may involve overcoming their inhibitions, anxieties, or conflicting morals. Like in the staircase model, although a person may be strongly motivated and have many reasons to act, it can take time to accept the significance and realities of committing violence. Once they come to terms with this, the bathtub overflows, and the desire and commitment to carry out an attack follows.

THOMAS MAIR IS THE PERFECT EXAMPLE of a slowly filling bathtub.

On a sunny afternoon in June 2016, British Labour Party Member of Parliament Jo Cox was walking towards the library in Birstall, West Yorkshire, to hold a meeting with her constituents. As she approached the library, fifty-two-year-old Thomas Mair stepped out from the shadows and shot Cox. Mair then proceeded to stab her with a knife, but was interrupted by an elderly man who tried to intervene. His efforts to assist resulted in serious injuries, as Mair also stabbed the seventy-seven-year-old. Courageously, Cox managed to scream to her two assistants to flee, shouting, *'Get away, let him hurt me, don't let him hurt you.'* Her brave words served to infuriate Mair, who shot Cox two more times. Mair then continued to stab Cox repeatedly, all the while yelling, *'Britain first, keep Britain independent, Britain will always come first.'*

Jo Cox achieved her ambition of becoming a Member of the British Parliament in 2015 when she was elected. During her short tenure, she held strong ideals and advocated for diversity in Britain. Cox campaigned for the rights of Syrian refugees and supported Britain remaining in the European Union. Cox's positions on Brexit and the rights of refugees angered Mair, who held strong nationalist views and harboured hatred for those who tried to impose limitations on Britain.

Mair had little involvement with far-right groups or organisations, but he silently held strong right-wing views for nearly twenty years. He collected material published by far-right groups in the USA and the South African Patriots, and kept an array of Nazi paraphernalia and newspaper clippings of Norwegian lone actor Anders Breivik. Mair had been a recluse for most of his adult life, with no known intimate relationships and only a small number of social acquaintances. Although he had no identifiable signs of mental illness, Mair spent many years reading and researching right-wing material, gradually becoming disenfranchised with the state of Britain and the changes in the country.

While Hasan's radicalisation followed the structured progression of the staircase model, Mair's path to violence is better understood through the bathtub model. His gradual accumulation of ideological, personal, and psychological grievances steadily filled the tub until the final trigger – the Brexit debate and Jo Cox's advocacy – caused it to overflow. His case illustrates how the slow filling of the bathtub across the ideological, personal, and psychological dimensions eventually led to the tragic attack on Jo Cox.

The ideological tap filled up over decades as Mair was exposed to and adopted far-right nationalist beliefs. His collection of Nazi memorabilia, his subscription to publications from white supremacist and far-right groups, and his admiration of individuals like Anders Breivik show that he had strong ideological beliefs. His anger towards Jo Cox's positions, especially her advocacy for refugees and Britain's involvement in the European Union, was rooted in his persistent belief in British nationalism.

The personal tap in Mair's life also steadily contributed to his violence. He lived an isolated life, with very few close relationships and limited social contact. His lack of intimate connections and withdrawal from societal norms likely fuelled his feelings of alienation and resentment towards the broader social changes in Britain. Mair had an inability to form meaningful relationships or establish a sense of identity beyond his nationalist beliefs. Although Mair did not have an identified mental illness, the psychological tap played a significant role in his offending. Mair was profoundly unhappy with his life, and instead of addressing his mental health, he withdrew from society and found solace in his obsessive focus on right-wing ideologies. Mair struggled to cope with setbacks and challenges, and he experienced increasing internal frustrations, creating a dangerous mixture of unresolved anger and distorted worldviews.

AS A PERSON BEGINS to believe that they have been mistreated, victimised, rejected, or subjected to injustice, a shift in their mindset occurs. They start to see the world through a narrow and distorted lens. This leads them to misinterpret situations and events. Initially, this may not be harmful, but over time, this continual bias and distortion comes to shape and change a person's attitudes and beliefs. The person then begins preferencing and placing greater weight on information that supports their distorted beliefs while ignoring and downplaying anything contradictory. Eventually, tunnel vision forms, and the world is seen through a highly tainted lens, causing them to feel more marginalised and disconnected from others.

Eventually, after climbing the staircase, or experiencing the rising water in the bathtub, a psychological shift occurs, and a new mindset takes over. A mindset characterised by:

- The rights to freedom and independence, or the rights to fairness and equality.
- Equality, or inequality, being laws of human nature, which should be followed.
- The perception of an imminent or existential threat.
- A *'with us or against us'* or *'good or evil'* perception of people and events.
- Rigid and fixed views of right and wrong.
- The belief that violence or force is necessary to prevail.
- The perception of being chosen, or called upon, to act.

The actions of Hasan and Mair demonstrate that lone actor violence is rarely impulsive. Instead, it is often the result of a cumulative process. The staircase and the bathtub models indicate how a combination of psychological, social, and emotional factors can narrow a person's view of the world and others overtime. As these influences gradually intensify, they become the catalysts that drive a person towards violent action.

9

A Mind On Fire

'The most dangerous thing when you have a serious mental illness, is convincing yourself that you don't have it.'

Noah Hawley

ON A BUSY SATURDAY AFTERNOON on 13 April 2024, Joel Cauchi turned the crowded Westfield Bondi Junction shopping centre in Sydney into a scene of horror. Arriving at the centre just after 3.00 p.m., the forty-year-old blended in with the other shoppers, casually dressed in a sports jersey. But within minutes, the bustling mall atmosphere was thrown into chaos. After briefly leaving the shopping centre, Cauchi returned, armed with a 30-centimetre butcher's knife, and began attacking shoppers.

Cauchi moved through the crowded shopping complex, stabbing patrons. Security cameras captured the terrifying moments as Cauchi lunged at victims, ignoring some while deliberately targeting others. As the attack continued, it became evident that Cauchi was fixated on targeting women, walking past numerous males and instead seeking out females to assault. Several brave individuals tried to confront him, preventing him from entering stores and grabbing makeshift weapons in a desperate attempt to stop his violence. However, Cauchi moved swiftly throughout the shopping mall and managed to stab eighteen people. He killed five women and a male security guard. Many other victims were seriously injured, including a nine-month-old baby girl – disturbingly, her mother was killed. Of the sixteen victims, all except two were female.

The violent spree ended when Inspector Amy Scott, a sole police officer, responded to the unfolding chaos. Hearing terrified screams throughout the shopping centre, she tracked Cauchi down on the building's fifth floor. As she confronted him, Cauchi turned and charged at her with his knife raised. Acting quickly, Inspector Scott fired, fatally wounding Cauchi and bringing the attack to an end.

IT IS ESTIMATED THAT BETWEEN 17% and 50% of lone actors are suffering from a mental illness at the time of offending. Adding to this, around two-thirds of perpetrators experience mental health concerns in the period leading up to their attack.

In an interesting analysis of 125 lone actors, several mental health diagnoses were observed. Each of these conditions causes a range of effects on a person's psychological state and the way in which they perceive the world and interact with others. The most common conditions were:

Schizophrenia and Delusional Disorders: The experience of these conditions leads to a person having thoughts and experiences that are typically out of touch with everyday life. Symptoms may include delusions, hallucinations, erratic speech, disorganised or abnormal body movements, and an array of negative symptoms (such as restricted emotions, loss of interest, or poor hygiene). Delusions relate to *'fixed beliefs that are not amenable to change in light of conflicting evidence'*. Delusions differ from extreme overvalued beliefs because they are typically unique to the individual and not shared by others. While some people may believe that the world is coming to an end (overvalued belief), a person suffering from a delusion may claim that they are Jesus reborn and here to save everyone. In addition to delusions, hallucinations are *'perception-like experiences that occur without an external stimulus. They are vivid and clear, with the full force and the impact of normal perceptions, and not under voluntary control.'* In essence, the person sees, hears, or senses things that are not there.

Autism Spectrum Disorder (ASD): Those with ASD have impairments in communication and difficulties with social interactions, along with stereotyped behaviours. ASD is a neurological and developmental disorder that impedes a person's capacity for social functioning and communication. Sufferers also have a poor ability to adjust to change, limited behavioural expression, and fixed, narrow, and rigid interests. A hallmark characteristic of ASD is the inability to take into account the mental state, feelings, or perspective of another person.

Depression: The most notable symptom of depression is the experience of a persistent low and negative mood. This state of low mood can vary in severity and intensity and can continue over several weeks or even years. Those experiencing depression often feel sad, miserable, worthless, and unhappy. In some instances, sufferers may feel irritable and struggle to complete daily life tasks, while others may have a deep and debilitating sense of despair and hopelessness. In certain people, depression can result in the experience of suicidal thoughts, self-harming behaviour, or even suicide.

Bipolar Disorder: Sufferers of this condition experience the low and negative mood states associated with depression in conjunction with periods of manic and heightened emotions and behaviour. Those with bipolar may feel depressed and sad for weeks on end, yet experience a sudden onset of high energy, excitement, and newfound motivation. In this manic state, they may struggle to sleep, have difficulties concentrating, make impulsive and reckless decisions, and act erratically. This state of excitement can last for days or even weeks, but is often followed by a psychological and emotional crash, with depression and sadness returning. Those with the condition often experience many cycles of up and down emotions, as though trapped on a rollercoaster of excitement and depression.

Personality Disorders: There are a range of different personality disorders and traits that can shape a person's behaviour and interactions with others. The different types of personality disorders can be classified into three categories, these being:

- The erratic and strange.
- The dramatic, unpredictable, and mean.
- The anxious and fearful.

Some of the prominent personality conditions include paranoid, schizotypal, narcissistic, borderline, and antisocial. Those with paranoia are distrustful and suspicious, believing that others are out to get them. People with schizotypal personality tend to be loners, distrusting, and prone to unusual and bizarre thoughts and ideas. Narcissistic individuals are entitled, self-centred, arrogant, and believe they are special and unique. People with borderline personality can also have the tendency to be entitled and self-absorbed, but are emotionally reactive, combative, and have a poor sense of identity. Lastly, antisocial individuals are willing to cheat, lie, and deceive others, and have a general disregard for societal rules and norms.

Post-traumatic Stress Disorder (PTSD) and Other Trauma: Many people experience adverse events and are exposed to tragic and confronting circumstances. These events can be traumatic and shape their views of the world and future behaviour. This can lead to anxiety, fear, uncertainty, difficulties with sleep, and even flashbacks of the event. Over time these symptoms may subside for many people, but some individuals will experience a continuation and reoccurrence of this anxiety and fear, to the extent that it can be classified as PTSD. Those with PTSD may find that in addition to having a range of difficulties, specific situations can create panic and remind them of the traumatic incidents, causing them to feel as though they are re-living the experience.

THE ROLE OF MENTAL HEALTH PROBLEMS among lone actors is a complex issue. In some cases, mental illness exacerbates stressors in a person's life or causes a spiral towards violence as symptoms worsen. In certain instances, mental health may deteriorate as an individual progresses up the staircase of violence or as the bathtub of motivation fills up. Yet, in other cases, mental health issues may play no role whatsoever in the violence.

Adding more confusion to the issue, a person may have many strong negative emotions and beliefs, but these do not meet a clinical threshold or fit a diagnostic category to be viewed as suffering from a mental illness. Some of these powerful negative emotions may include shame, envy, hatred of others, or even hatred of oneself.

The cocktail of negative emotions can result in a range of destructive and resentment-fuelled behaviours, leading a person to harm themselves, others, or a combination of both. These negative emotional states are often associated with the individual perceiving that they are a failure, inadequate, inferior, and worthless. However, rather than taking personal responsibility for their circumstances, they blame others and believe those others are responsible for their suffering. These thoughts may lead to significant anger or hatred towards others or feelings of misery and despair. Eventually, if this cycle of negative emotion continues, the person can perceive that life is pointless and has no meaning, as seen with James Holmes. In certain instances, strong feelings of envy can arise, fostering the belief that *'the game of life is rigged'* and *'it's only fair to even the score'*. This view of the world can quickly lead to a desire to see others suffer hardship and despair.

The desire to inflict suffering on others was evident in the manifesto written by Elliot Rodger. Fuelled by deep-seated inadequacy, shame, and envy of others, Rodger carried out his violent attack in the college community of Isla Vista, California. He declared:

'If humanity will not give me a worthy place among them, then I will destroy them.'

'Retribution is my way of proving my true worth to the world.'

'I must be destined to change the world, to shape it into an image that suits me.'

Causing suffering to others because of their perceived advantages and opportunities is a *'literal way to wipe tormentors' mocking smiles from their faces'* and force them to experience grief and devastation through violence. The spiral into negative emotional states and patterns of thinking can be magnified by a range of factors, such as mental health issues, trauma, a troubled upbringing, and personal setbacks. Alongside this, peer interactions, social media, and online groups play a large role in fostering these emotional beliefs. Social media promotes dissatisfaction and the sense of not being good enough, while online platforms may reaffirm negative beliefs or suggest that society is in crisis and in need of action. The widespread television and media coverage of mass shootings or mass casualty events can create the allure of attention, fame, and a lasting legacy. The fame and recognition associated with carrying out a lone actor attack offers the promise of not only retribution but also of making a mark on life.

The desire to find meaning and significance through violence has, without doubt, led numerous individuals to believe that mass violence is a suitable solution to their problems. Unfortunately, when these negative states progress to a person feeling suicidal and wanting to take revenge, they may begin to fantasise about scenarios and ways to end their pain and take others with them. Studies have shown that among mass shooters, around 90% were suicidal at the time of the attack, while other research has found that between 27% and 47% die by suicide at the scene.

In many mass attacks, suicidality is a precursor to violence. Research has found that individuals who are both suicidal and homicidal often see violence as a way to take control of their life's narrative. In this sense, violence becomes not only a form of retribution but also a way to achieve significance and control. Anders Breivik, for example, initially planned to commit suicide after his attack in Norway but ultimately chose to surrender, believing that his actions had saved his country from threats to the white race.

Death promises closure and a future. It offers an end to the anguish and emotional pain while providing the opportunity to transform one's life failures into a lasting legacy – a final act that will not be forgotten by society.

According to forensic psychiatrist James Knoll and his colleagues, mass attackers report experiencing *'a state of peacefulness and relief that arises once they have come to terms with their own death as not only inevitable and acceptable but planned, either by their own hand or as suicide by cop'*.

Those harbouring suicidal and homicidal desires believe they will experience transcendence and transformation posthumously – their life will be characterised by meaning, significance, and fame following their death. Their identity and name will live on, forever associated with that date and time in history.

Mental health can propel a person towards violence. It can alter their sense of reality, intensify their emotions, and impair reasoning. Mental health also exists on a spectrum, with some conditions more severe than others. Yet, there are many people with severe mental health conditions who never carry out violence. Mental health problems provide some explanation for why violence occurs, but this only offers part of the answer.

When mental health conditions overlap with grievances or ideological beliefs, individuals can believe that violent action is justified. Rarely does a person with mental health concerns progress to carrying out a mass casualty attack without other factors in their life pulling or pushing them towards violence.

JOEL CAUCHI HAD A LONG HISTORY of severe mental health problems. He was reportedly first diagnosed with schizophrenia at seventeen years old –experiencing episodes of psychosis, delusions, and difficulties in distinguishing between reality and his distorted perceptions.

For much of his adulthood, his mental health was adequately managed through medication and professional support. Although there were occasional issues and incidents of erratic behaviour, these were managed or resolved. His parents looked after him, and he remained living at home until he was thirty-five. However, in 2019, his psychiatrist made the decision to cease Cauchi's antipsychotic medication – this marked the first time in fifteen years where he was no longer medicated. Although this change seemed positive initially, gradually Cauchi's well-being began to decline and he disengaged from his ongoing check-ups and appointments with mental health services. In around 2023, he became fascinated by collecting knives.

Cauchi's parents were aware of his interest in knives. At one stage, when his father removed the knives, Cauchi reported his father to the police for attempting to steal them. His father disposed of six knives that Cauchi had acquired, due to concerns about his increasing preoccupation with weapons. After his knives were taken away, Cauchi purchased more.

Individuals who fixate on weapons, such as knives, often see them as symbols of power and control. To them, the weapon represents a form of security and protection, a way to combat feelings of powerlessness. Cauchi's refusal to let go of his knife collection demonstrated the importance he placed on having his knives.

After moving out of home in his mid-thirties, Cauchi lived a transient lifestyle. He struggled to form social relationships and even worked briefly as a male escort. In the months prior to the attack, Cauchi stopped talking to his parents and moved from Queensland to New South Wales around four weeks before his offence.

Despite moving to another state, Cauchi continued to experience difficulties. He was unable to find accommodation and was reportedly homeless, living in his car. In the week before the attack, he posted on social media in search of people to go surfing with – struggling with loneliness and unable to meet new people.

Cauchi's move interstate also resulted in him dropping off the radar of mental health services. Not only had he ceased his medication and medical appointments, but he moved to a new state where his presence was unknown, and he had no established mental health support. Schizophrenia, when left untreated, can result in intense delusions, paranoia, and erratic behaviour. In Cauchi's case, this decline in his well-being likely impaired his ability to think rationally and led to feelings of isolation or even persecution by others. His lack of insight into his condition – common among individuals with psychotic disorders – meant that he didn't recognise the severity of his symptoms, preventing him from seeking help at a critical time.

Cauchi's untreated mental health condition, combined with his increasing feelings of isolation and personal setbacks, created a sense of hopelessness and frustration. For several years, he had wanted an intimate relationship, but his mental health problems and lack of social skills had prevented him from finding a romantic connection. His failed attempts to form intimate relationships likely intensified his feelings of frustration and rejection. Research on violent offenders has shown that perceived social failure and romantic rejection often precipitate violent behaviour, especially among individuals already struggling with mental health issues.

Cauchi struggled to fit into society, find acceptance, and meet even the basic needs of everyday life. In a state of declining mental health, he ruthlessly attacked women inside the Westfield shopping mall with a knife.

10

The Many Paths To Violence

'Childhood constitutes the most important element in an adult's life, for it is in his early years that a man is made.'

Maria Montessori

THERE ARE MANY PATHS that can lead a person towards violence. As explored in *Part 1*, a range of psychological, social, and environmental factors can shape why and how individuals progress to perpetrating violent acts. There is no simple and singular answer to explain why mass casualty attacks occur. Yet, when everything is stripped back, it becomes clear that childhood lays the foundation for adulthood. A weak foundation leads to cracks and ruptures, especially when pressure is applied. No child is born violent. While genetic factors and family history may contribute to aggression, no one is inherently predisposed to commit mass murder. As the saying goes, *'genetics load the gun, and the environment pulls the trigger.'*

When a person's psychological foundation is unstable and riddled with problems, vulnerabilities emerge over time. Conversely, a strong foundation fosters resilience, emotional regulation, and problem-solving skills. A childhood that nurtures attachment and authenticity equips a person with the tools to navigate life's challenges.

Children need the opportunities to make mistakes and experience setbacks, challenges, and failures. Without this, they struggle to build resilience. They fail to grasp that life does not always go their way. Childhood is a crucial stage for developing character, discovering strengths, and understanding limitations. Experiencing small and manageable difficulties teaches perseverance, tolerance, and the capacity to embrace challenges. While excessive stress is harmful, moderate and controlled exposure to stress strengthens a person's ability to tackle bigger obstacles. Just as muscles grow through gradual and sustained exercise and training, psychological resilience develops through experiencing incremental stress over time. Without facing obstacles and challenges, children who are raised to believe they are special, and who are shielded from failure, struggle to cope with the complexities of life.

However, children cannot build resilience without adequate support and guidance. For centuries, the family unit was broad and interconnected, with grandparents, aunts, uncles, and extended relatives actively involved in child-rearing. This network provided continuous support, companionship, and social interaction. Today, however, children are more likely to grow up in households where both parents work, and extended family members are often thousands of kilometres away. The support networks that once surrounded children have diminished, leaving families stretched and children with fewer opportunities for close, nurturing interactions. Over the last two decades, the number of dual-income families has surged, leading to increased reliance on childcare, schools, and after-school programmes. The modern family is often exhausted, stressed, and absent during key developmental moments.

One in two children will also experience parental separation, and one in five will grow up without a father. Research consistently links parental separation to increased risks of behavioural issues, suicide attempts, difficulty forming friendships, mental health struggles, poverty, school drop-out, and even incarceration. The presence of both parents and extended family plays a crucial role in healthy development. As psychiatrist Bruce Perry notes, *'If a child grows up in a relationally "wealthy" home, with abundant opportunities for safe, stable, and nurturing interactions, they build connectedness and resilience.'*

Yet even in intact families, raising children is challenging. Parents juggle work demands, financial pressures, and the relentless pace of modern life. Then there is the internet – the ever-present intruder in the family home – demanding attention and pulling people away from meaningful interactions. Dr Perry further outlines, *'We are having far fewer family meals; our conversational skills are fading. The art of storytelling and the capacity to listen are on the decline. The result is a more self-absorbed, more anxious, more depressed – and less resilient – population.'*

A lack of resilience, parental separation, poor family cohesion, early enrolment in childcare, excessive screen time, and hours of social media use do not cause someone to become a lone actor. However, these factors can shape how a person experiences the world and lay the foundation for their emotional and social make-up. When there is harmony, connectedness, and consistency in a child's upbringing, these pillars provide a strong foundation. Yet, when uncertainty, disconnection, and inconsistency dominate, the foundation becomes fragile and prone to crumbling under the weight stressors or challenges.

Our attention, presence, and ability to connect and truly see one another is our most valuable commodity. Yet, in many ways, it has been lost and surrendered. The consequence of this loss is **Disconnection** – a disconnection with ourselves, from each other, and from the world around us. When disconnected, we lose sight of what truly matters. We become inclined towards comfort and make easy and convenient choices that may come with significant long-term costs. Disconnection causes our personal and moral compass to go awry and erodes our authenticity. It also impairs our capacity for deep and meaningful relationships. Over time, as this state of disconnection persists, **Demoralisation** can set in.

Demoralisation is marked by a fundamental shift in perception. It is the psychological tipping point where life feels meaningless, and a person's sense of identity becomes blurred. In this state, individuals may feel incompetent, incapable of meeting expectations, and overwhelmed by the challenges they face. Their ability to think critically and solve problems deteriorates, leaving them preoccupied with their own emotional state or external events that provoke strong feelings. They become easily distracted, outraged, confused, anxious, and lost. Ultimately, their biggest obstacle becomes themselves.

Modern life fosters both disconnection and demoralisation.

We live in a world where discomfort is feared and avoided, often replaced by distractions and cravings for moments of positive emotions. Yet, to grow, we need to experience the full spectrum of emotions – the joy and the sadness, the ease and the struggle. It is through experiencing and processing difficult emotions that we develop resilience and self-trust. When we continually seek comfort, we undermine our confidence in our own abilities, leaving us ill-equipped to navigate life's inevitable challenges. Navigating the complexities of life relies on connecting with ourselves, believing in our abilities, and maintaining clarity about what truly matters. Trauma is undeniably tragic, but stress and challenges are essential for growth. Without exposure to these difficulties, even minor setbacks can feel insurmountable. When people lack resilience, they find themselves unable to cope, perceiving the world as closing in around them.

Generations of traditions, practices, and knowledge that once fostered resilience and well-being are being overshadowed by urbanisation, technological advancements, and changing social structures. We must find a balance between these modern developments and the enduring values of family connection, nurturing children, and building a strong character.

Lone actor violence does not emerge in isolation. It often reflects an individual's desperate attempt to restore, salvage, or alter the inadequacies and imbalances in their life. Every person begins with a need for love, connection, and belonging. Yet, for some, these fundamental needs go unmet, leaving them profoundly disconnected. For these individuals, violence can become a misguided solution to their problems – a means to assert control, find purpose, or seek retribution.

VIOLENCE CAN ALWAYS BE JUSTIFIED. There is always someone who has wronged us, something working against us, or a setback that feels deeply unfair. It is easy to feel aggrieved, angry, and outraged. In this mindset, revenge, justice, retribution, or the restoration of a perceived natural order begin to feel not only justifiable but necessary.

Mass casualty attacks are distinct from other forms of violence. While many violent acts stem from personal conflicts, impulsivity, or general criminality, mass attacks are premeditated and coupled with an intent to inflict maximum harm in a single event.

Lone actors do not lash out in the heat of the moment, nor do they respond to immediate provocation. They are not individuals who suddenly react violently after an argument or altercation. In fact, the majority have no extensive criminal histories or prior convictions for violence, and substance abuse is rarely a defining characteristic. Instead, their attacks are calculated, deliberate, and often months or years in the making – driven by deeply entrenched grievances, ideological beliefs, or a desire for notoriety and significance. This form of violence is more than an act – it is a statement. It is designed to shock, to instil fear, and to leave an indelible mark on society. In some cases, the goal is ideological or a misguided attempt to force societal change or avenge perceived injustices. In others, it is a final act of contempt, a rejection of life itself and everything it represents.

Adam Lanza had a troubled childhood, marked by developmental difficulties, parental separation, and struggles with peer relationships and the school environment. After his parents divorced, his relationship with his father deteriorated, leaving him increasingly dependent on his mother. This dependency deepened into an enmeshed mother-child relationship, where Lanza found solace in violent fantasies and studying mass killers. His mother, who was unaware of the full extent of his psychological struggles, attempted to bond with him by purchasing a firearm – a decision that ultimately provided him with both the means and the capability to carry out his attack. For Lanza, violence was an emotional release, a means of recognition, and an act of revenge against life itself.

Colt Gray's childhood was shaped by adversity, marked by instability and uncertainty. He was exposed to violence, drug use, housing insecurity, bullying, neglect, emotional abuse, parental separation, and parental criminality. Without a stable foundation or supportive relationships, Gray struggled to find his place in the world, carrying a deep sense of anger and despair. Like Adam Lanza, he became fascinated by past violent attacks and mass killers. Equipped with a firearm purchased by a parent, Gray saw violence as his opportunity to be recognised – to finally matter – and to release years of torment and emotional pain.

James Holmes had a relatively stable childhood, but as he grew older, he struggled with self-acceptance. He often misinterpreted social situations, became trapped in his own thoughts, and found it difficult to connect with others. His fascination with violence was a persistent undercurrent in his mind, gradually intensifying as his mental health deteriorated. Over time, Holmes became consumed by feelings of self-loathing and a belief that life was meaningless. In his distorted worldview, violence became a way to free himself from his internal struggles and pursue a sense of significance in an otherwise mundane existence.

Brenton Tarrant had a lonely and traumatic childhood. Like Gray, he faced significant adversity and struggled to form lasting connections. Isolated, he spent countless hours gaming and immersing himself in online spaces. Although he travelled extensively, instead of finding inspiration in the world, he became increasingly agitated by what he saw. He withdrew further into his digital echo chamber, reinforcing his extremist beliefs and fuelling his sense of outrage. In this isolation, he found purpose – a mission rooted in violence. For Tarrant, violence was not just an expression of his anger but a calculated attempt to create social and political change, ensuring that *'foreigners'* did not infiltrate the West.

Andrew Joseph Stack III faced repeated setbacks in life, struggling with financial instability, career frustrations, and personal disappointments. Rather than acknowledging his own role in these difficulties, he externalised blame, directing his anger and resentment towards the Internal Revenue Service. Over time, his grievances grew into a deep-seated sense of injustice and persecution. Violence, for Stack, became a means of retribution – an act of defiance against a system he believed had wronged him. His attack was not just about revenge; it was an attempt to expose what he saw as mistreatment and corruption.

John Hinckley Jr was struggling in life, grappling with feelings of inadequacy, isolation, and failure. He developed an infatuation and fixation on actress Jodie Foster, believing that he could win her attention and admiration through a grand, dramatic gesture. His mental health was poor, and over months, his beliefs about Foster became amplified and overvalued, distorting his perception of reality. Violence was about proving his significance. His attack was a way to elevate himself from obscurity and garner Foster's love and admiration – harming others was a way to fulfil his desperate need for recognition and validation.

Theodore Kaczynski was unable to accept the state of the world, seeing it as a direct clash with his deeply held beliefs and ideals. He perceived that an existential crisis was transpiring – one driven by industrialisation, technological advancement, and the erosion of human autonomy. In his mind, humanity was under threat, enslaved by the very progress it had created. Violence was about the restoration of natural order, creating fear, and forcing change. For Kaczynski, each of his bombings was a statement and an attempt to disrupt the system and awaken society to what he believed was an inevitable collapse.

Momena Shoma was a vulnerable and impressionable young woman who was drawn into radical ideologies during a crucial stage of her psychological development. Influenced by extremist associations, she was exposed to a distorted interpretation of religion that reshaped her views of the world. Over time, her identity became fused with rigid beliefs about Western culture and her faith, leaving little room for alternative perspectives. Violence, for Shoma, was about proving her loyalty and unwavering commitment to her cause and advancing the ideology she had embraced.

Nidal Hasan's life took a profound turn after the death of his mother. Struggling with grief, he began to question everything – his faith, his career, and his purpose in life. His fear of death and concerns about the afterlife intensified, pushing him towards a deeper embrace of Islamic teachings. However, his growing religiosity became increasingly rigid, leading him to isolate himself from others. Unable to reconcile his beliefs with Western culture and the state of the world, he withdrew further into ideological certainty. For Hasan, violence was both an act of devotion and a means of self-preservation – an ultimate commitment to his faith in the face of existential fear.

Thomas Mair had spent his life alone – without a long-term intimate relationship, with few friends, and with limited hobbies or interests. The one constant in his life was his unwavering belief in nationalism and sovereignty. For decades, he had subscribed to far-right publications and amassed material reinforcing his ideological views. Although he had remained largely silent about his beliefs, he perceived the Brexit proposal as a direct threat to Britain's future. This perceived crisis became the catalyst for action.

For Mair, violence was about asserting power and control – an attempt to protect what he saw as his nation's rights, freedoms, and liberties.

Joel Cauchi had a long history of mental illness. During his early adult years, he was well supported by his parents, but as he grew older, he struggled to establish independence and autonomy. Living on his own proved challenging and he found it difficult to form friendships, establish romantic relationships, and maintain structure and routine in his life. Over time, he developed a fixation on knives, withdrew from mental health treatment, and relocated to another state. His violence was the tragic culmination of personal setbacks, an intense fascination with weapons, and untreated mental illness. For Cauchi, violence became a desperate means of expressing years of frustration, emotional turmoil, and perceived failings.

Those that carry out lone actor attacks do so for many reasons, and when there is a reason, there is a way. Although the causes may differ and the pathways to violence may vary, in the end the similarities across offences are striking. Violence often unfolds through a progressive climb up the narrowing confines of a staircase, where each step represents an escalation in thoughts and beliefs, or through a cocktail of the wrong ingredients being poured into a tub, combining in an unpredictable and dangerous way.

There is almost always failures and setbacks with the person's life, and there are varying degrees of mental health issues. In many cases, powerful beliefs, ideologies, or causes act as further fuel for carrying out violence. Add to this the powerful influence of social media forums and the constant media coverage of mass casualty attacks, inspiring future perpetrators.

Yet, amongst all of these factors, virtually all lone actors are driven by a grievance – a sense of being mistreated or wronged. It is the catalyst for retribution, revenge, and the need to make a lasting statement.

Across the hundreds of cases worldwide, several common features and characteristics emerge. Whether the perpetrator is a school shooter, a lone terrorist, a workplace attacker, or conducting a targeted act in a public venue, a general profile of a lone actor is evident:

- Predominately male.
- Varied in age, with no single defining demographic.
- Feels powerless or victimised, often harbouring a deep-seated grievance.
- Average to above average intelligence.
- Socially disengaged, with limited face-to-face interactions.
- Aggrieved and harbouring a perceived grievance.
- Self-absorbed, with an inward focus on personal struggles and injustices.
- Prone to identifying with causes, controversial interests, or others who share a sense of victimhood.
- Seeking revenge against an unjust or unfair world.
- Adopts ideological beliefs or causes as a justification for violence and their behaviour.
- Possesses a sense of superiority and uniqueness.
- Experienced recent instability and major life changes.
- Holds rigid, fixed, or uncompromising views and beliefs.
- Has a history of social rejection, bullying, or struggles with belonging.
- Poorly adjusts to setbacks, challenges, or adversity.
- Blames others for personal failures and struggles to take accountability.
- Harbours resentment and grudges.
- Views violence as a means to bring meaning or significance to their life.
- Struggles with feelings of misery, despair, or suicidality.
- Encounters multiple stressors in the years leading up to the attack.
- Lacks intimate relationships or experiences unfulfilling social or intimate connections.
- Distrusting and suspicious of others.
- Has a history of violent fantasies.
- Willing to die for a cause or to achieve significance.
- Unlikely to have a significant history of substance use.
- Driven by a personal narrative of being a hero, saviour, or carrying out

a mission.

This profile does not predict violence on its own, but it highlights the underlying psychological, social, and ideological patterns frequently observed in lone actor cases.

Lone actors represent a distinct type of violent offender. Understanding their backgrounds, mindsets, motivations, and characteristics is the first step towards preventing this form of violence. It provides the foundation for developing effective interventions and, ultimately, stopping these attacks before they occur.

II

The Search For Answers

11

The Black Swan

'The world is much more correlated than we give credit to ... rare events happen more often than they should because the worlds is more correlated.'

Richard Thaler

ONE EARLY SUMMER AFTERNOON in Oslo, Anders Breivik parked his white van beneath the central Norwegian government offices. Encased inside the van was a one-ton explosive device packed with ammonium nitrate. Breivik exited the vehicle and left in another car to travel to Utøya Island. At around 3.25 p.m., the device exploded, causing eight fatalities and injuring over 200 people. Over the coming hours, Breivik travelled by car and boat to Utøya Island, where a group of youths were gathered for the Young Norwegian Labour Party camp. Breivik arrived on the island dressed as a policeman and armed with an array of semi-automatic weapons. Over the next hour, he moved through the island by foot, shooting anyone that he came across. Breivik briefly ceased shooting to contact the police and report the attack, stating, *'Yes, hello, my name is Commander Anders Behring Breivik form the Norwegian anti-communist resistance movement. I'm on Utøya for the moment. I want to give myself up.'* He then ended the call. His attack on the island resulted in the death of sixty-nine people and injuries to another sixty. Breivik surrendered when he was confronted by police upon their arrival at the island.

The mass casualty attack carried out by Breivik in 2011 presented a perfect storm of factors that caught authorities off guard and led to seventy-seven dying and mass injuries among surviving victims. Breivik claimed he commenced planning his attack nine years before the incident. However, he became solely dedicated to carrying out his mission around three to four years prior to the attack. Spending his nights and days planning, preparing and developing tactical abilities. His journey to violence and his extreme right-wing beliefs were meticulously documented in his mammoth 1,600-page manifesto, *2083 – A European Declaration of Dependence*, which he emailed to 1,003 accounts on 22 July, the day of his attack.

Breivik had a clear mission and took extensive precautions to avoid detection. It was a cat and mouse game between himself and the police, and he needed to be in control and several steps ahead. The extent of his planning and precautions were extensive. He studied, trained, and equipped himself for combat. This included:

- Living alone and with limited social interaction for several years.
- Establishing a company to purchase large quantities of fertiliser and ammonium nitrate.
- Purchasing materials across several years, totalling 112 purchases from approximately ninety businesses.
- Working full-time on developing his skills, weaponry, manifesto, and technical abilities.
- Spending over eighty days grinding down fertiliser pellets to build an explosive device.
- Utilising his entire financial savings to fulfil his violent mission.
- Acquiring in excess of 8,000 email addresses to send his manifesto.
- Avoiding controversial or *'flagged'* terms on Google.
- Completing eight reconnaissance trips to surveil government agencies

and strategise his attack.
- Having packages delivered in Norway and Sweden to avoid detection from authorities.
- Burying firearms across the border in Sweden.
- Completing 15,000 hours of research and study to carry out his attack.
- Creating a special uniform and insignia, with medals that he devised.
- Using steroids to increase his energy and physical abilities.
- Training with firearms and in marksmanship for several years.

Breivik's attack was sophisticated, well-organised, and at the time was unlike any prior lone actor events. His attack showed what could be done if someone was dedicated to their mission, meticulously prepared, and willing to give their life to carrying out their attack. His commitment was unique, and his reclusiveness and preparedness comparable to Unabomber Ted Kaczynski. No one had considered the possibility of someone dedicating years of their life to preparing to carry out a mass casualty act, especially a lone individual. Breivik's dedication and tactical capabilities are now viewed as the *'gold standard'* and idealised and emulated by offenders all over the globe. Breivik inspired Brenton Tarrant, who also committed years of his life to his attack. Like Breivik, Tarrant has served as inspiration for many subsequent lone events.

IN EARLY EUROPEAN SETTLEMENT, it was well recognised amongst citizens that all swans were white. The mere suggestion of a black swan would have been scoffed at, or considered ridiculous. It was unimaginable that any other colour could exist. However, when Australia was founded in the late 1700s, the impossible suddenly became the possible, with black swans lurking across the continental land.

The *'black swan dilemma'*, or *'black swan event'*, is something which is considered rare and unimaginable. A black swan event often has a lasting impact on society, and typically defies long-held beliefs and expectations. The event is unexpected and therefore never anticipated or even imagined.

According to Nassim Nicholas Taleb, author of *The Black Swan*, there are three essential attributes of a black swan. The first is that black swans are *outliers* and beyond the realm of expectations because they are rare and uncommon. Secondly, they have an *extreme impact* on society due to the lack of preparedness and the implications from being caught off guard. Lastly, they are characterised by *retrospective distortion* whereby people concoct explanations for the event's occurrence and perceive that it was explainable and predictable.

Taleb outlined that one of the most notable black swan events was the 11 September terrorist attack in 2001. The widely coordinated group-based terrorist attack had never been seen before across the world. Although planes had previously been hijacked, they'd never been used as weapons. Adding to this, the level of coordination and training to carry out the attack was an anomaly.

The 9/11 attacks had an extreme impact on the world. An enormous number of people lost their lives. This was followed by changes to legislation and policies, along with the eventual invasion of Iraq. On top of this, there was extensive investigation into how information was missed and intelligence agencies had failed. Although the findings of these enquiries identified gaps and areas where intelligence should have been shared, the reality of the circumstances was far more complex than governments were prepared to acknowledge. As Taleb observed, *'had the risk been reasonably conceivable on 10 September, it would not have happened. If such a possibility were deemed worthy of attention, fighter planes would have circled the sky above the twin towers, airplanes would have had bulletproof doors, and the attack would not have taken place'*.

Black swan events happen.

9/11 was a black swan event.

Anders Breivik's mass attack in Norway was a black swan event.

Brenton Tarrant's targeted attack in New Zealand was a black swan event.

Events like Breivik's and Tarrant's have had an extreme impact on their respective countries and communities. Their violence has also inspired others to carry out mass attacks. The manifestos of both individuals have promoted violent beliefs and ideas, whilst providing dangerous information on tactical and technical ways to commit an attack. It is rare for an individual to dedicate their life to training and preparing for a violent event. It is also even more uncommon for someone to *'fly under the radar'* and for government agencies to be completely unaware and in the dark. The greatest fear is the unknown. Black swans are the unknown.

Yet, even when government agencies are aware of a concerning person, the threat is not always properly understood or prevented. Many mass casualty attacks have occurred when police and other services have been aware of the concerns. Despite all the tragedy resulting from lone actor events, all the inquiries, and all the research and reviews, the incidents continue to happen.

NIKOLAS CRUZ ARRIVED AT HIS FORMER SCHOOL in Parkland, Florida in an Uber and armed with a semi-automatic rifle. Upon arriving at the school, the nineteen-year-old activated a fire alarm inside the building, sending the school into chaos as students began to gradually evacuate from the buildings. As the staff and students walked towards the exits, Cruz opened fire on the crowd. He killed seventeen people and injured a further seventeen. After firing on the innocent school members, Cruz attempted to conceal his identity by blending in with the crowd and exited with the masses of students. Fortunately, within hours of the shooting, Cruz was identified as the perpetrator and was apprehended by police on 14 February 2018.

Unlike Breivik's offence, many authorities and services were aware of the concerns about Cruz's behaviour. Cruz was not a black swan. He was a missed opportunity for prevention.

In the lead-up to his attack, Cruz was expelled from Marjory Stoneman Douglas High School. Across his social media and YouTube accounts, Cruz boasted about his desire to become a school shooter. He shared images of himself engaging in self-harm and posted photos of firearms. Troublingly, Cruz also attempted to commit suicide by ingesting gasoline.

The local sheriff's office was called out to twenty-three incidents at the family home, with eighteen of these relating to Nikolas' behaviour. The FBI was notified about his actions on two occasions, and although the agency was aware of his YouTube channel, they were unable to identify the identity of the account holder. A friend of Cruz's also contacted the FBI in the week prior to the shooting due to concerns that he was escalating towards violence. Following the incident, the FBI acknowledged that it failed to sufficiently investigate the notifications that it had received pertaining to Cruz. As a result, the agency conducted a review into their response to the incident. However, the FBI was only one of the puzzle pieces and clearly did not bare the sole responsibility.

The failure to prevent the Parkland shooting was far more widespread. Across the community there were many people who didn't report concerns or share information about Cruz, including friends, family members, local law enforcement, social workers, and teachers. Some of the many notable events and incidents included:

- Shooting chickens and squirrels with a BB gun.
- Assaulting his mother.
- A diagnosis of Attention Deficit Hyperactivity Disorder (ADHD).
- Threatening to conduct a school shooting.
- Selling of knives at school.

- Talking with peers about harming animals.
- Disclosing plans for a school shooting.
- The death of his mother and instability in the family home.
- Multiple fights at school and suspensions.
- Access to knives and firearms.
- Purchasing of an AR-15 firearm.
- Conflict with foster/support family.
- Expulsion from school.

The Parkland shooting highlighted how many different people, departments, and agencies were aware of the concerns pertaining to Cruz. Yet, a coordinated response never occurred. The range of concerning behaviours exhibited by Cruz, like in many lone actor cases, indicated that he was on a pathway to violence. When these behaviours and issues are viewed together, as a whole picture, rather than in isolation, then a more concerning picture unfolds. In Cruz's case, the puzzle pieces and key information were never connected and viewed as a whole picture.

Some lone actor attacks are black swan events, but the vast majority are not. The vast majority of perpetrators leave a trail of warning behaviours. It may be threats, innocuous comments, internet searches, purchasing of weapons, disengagement from education, acquiring of military or commando attire, completing surveillance, or devising a blueprint for the attack. There will always be outliers who are able to operate in secrecy and isolation, but there is an enormous opportunity for early identification, prevention, and intervention with the remaining individuals.

This has been something that police and government agencies have had to understand. To accept that the traditional approach to policing is ineffective for lone actors and that a new method is required.

12

From Reaction To Prevention

'An ounce of prevention is better than a pound of cure.'

Benjamin Franklin

ARMED WITH A SHOTGUN and carrying a black flag bearing the Islamic Shahada, Man Haron Monis took eighteen people hostage inside Lindt Café in the city centre of Sydney, Australia on 15 December 2014. Monis, a self-proclaimed cleric, forced hostages to hold the flag against the café's window, declaring that Australia was *'under attack by the Islamic State'*. Monis claimed allegiance to IS; however, he was acting alone and had no direct association to the group. Although he identified with aspects of the jihadi Islamic doctrine, Monis was aggrieved with the Australian government and had a desire for notoriety.

Over the course of the sixteen-hour siege, Monis made several demands. He requested to have the flag of IS delivered to the café and insisted on speaking directly with the Australian Prime Minister. The situation escalated when Monis shot and killed thirty-eight-year-old hostage Tori Johnson, the café manager, who had been trying to protect others. Following the escalation, the police tactical operations unit stormed the café in the early morning hours and killed Monis. Tragically, another hostage was fatally wounded by bullet shrapnel from the police.

The siege caused a profound impact on the victims, their families, and the Australian community. As a consequence, serious questions were raised about counterterrorism policies, bail conditions (Monis was on bail at the time of the attack), and how authorities manage lone actor threats.

Monis first came to the attention of the Australian Security Intelligence Organisation (ASIO) in 1996. In 1999, ASIO assessed that his presence in Australia posed a national security risk and advised against granting him a protection visa. However, after conducting a second security assessment in 2000, ASIO revised its position and supported his application, leading to Monis being issued with a visa.

Over the following years, Monis had further interactions with ASIO and engaged in public protests in New South Wales (NSW) and Western Australia. By 2007, he had begun sending provocative letters to Members of Parliament, including the Prime Minister and Attorney General. In 2008, concerns about Monis resurfaced when the New South Wales Premier's office raised terrorism-related warnings with the Australian Federal Police (AFP). ASIO launched an investigation but ultimately took no further action.

Monis was referred to both ASIO and the AFP again in 2009, which prompted the involvement of the NSW Joint Counter Terrorism Team to review his risk. Despite this inter-agency focus, Monis continued to harass members of the public and political figures over the next two years. He was charged with intimidating his former partner in 2011, although he was acquitted in 2012. The following year, Monis's former partner was murdered, and he was charged as an accessory to the crime and granted bail. His troubling behaviour continued though, and he was convicted of menacing and harassing people by sending letters through the postal service.

In the months prior to his attack, Monis was charged with forty sexual offences dating back to 2002. Adding to this, in the week before the siege, the National Security Hotline received eighteen reports regarding alarming content on Monis's Facebook page. Despite these warnings, ASIO, the AFP, and NSW Police independently concluded that the posts did not pose an immediate threat. Days later, Monis carried out the deadly attack.

In response to the siege, an inquest was conducted to formally review the decisions and responses pertaining to the incident. The findings from the inquest identified several shortcomings and pitfalls in the New South Wales and Australian practices for terrorism and lone actors. The findings were officially released on 24 May 2017 and spanned more than 500 pages. The inquest determined that gaps existed in identifying potentially dangerous persons at the time of the siege: *'Current arrangements for identifying and assessing the risks posed by self-radicalised and isolated or fixated individuals who are not necessarily committing crimes tend to be fragmented rather than holistic, piecemeal rather than coordinated, and not presently focused on fixated persons.'*

The inquest highlighted that there were ongoing risks which were posed by individuals acting on personal grievances under the guise of extremist ideology. To address this challenge, the inquest recommended that the New South Wales Police Force, in conjunction with New South Wales Health, establish a Fixated Threat Assessment Centre (FTAC) – a practice which had been developed several years earlier in the United Kingdom.

THE UNITED KINGDOM ESTABLISHED a Fixated Threat Assessment Centre in 2006. The initial aim of FTAC was to ensure the safety and protection of Royal Family and British politicians from fixated individuals. At the time, there were over 2,000 people who were actively targeting the late Queen Elizabeth II. The majority of these matters related to unsolicited contact, harassment, and threats; although some individuals were stalking the Queen and there were constant concerns around a possible targeted assassination.

The development of FTAC arose from a review of police responses to targeted acts of violence, including harassment, stalking, and attempted assassinations. The review was commissioned by the British government in 2003 through the Fixated Research Group (FRG), which was led by psychiatrists Paul Mullen, David James, Frank Farnham, Michele Pathé, and forensic psychologist Reid Meloy.

Through a series of publications, the FRG outlined that the traditional policing approach of arresting and charging wasn't working and that a more informed and specialised response was required. Notably, individuals who were harassing and threatening members of the Royal Family were almost 100 times more likely to have severe mental illness than the general population. Whilst many of these unwanted letters or attempts at contact were harmless, there was evidence that fixated individuals were capable of planning and committing a targeted attack and that their delusions could strengthen their resolve to act. At the time, police and mental health services were typically operating in silos, and failing to work collaboratively to address individuals of concern. As a result of the pioneering research by the FRG, FTAC was born – bringing together police and mental health professionals. The centre was *'the first fully integrated, police-mental health model for preventing targeted – or planned and purposeful – violence by lone individuals'*.

Integrating mental health expertise into policing, FTAC focused on triaging cases by their level of concern, sharing information across disciplines, employing joint decision-making, and practising intervention strategies before apprehension. FTAC focused on prevention and management, and, when or if required, arresting and charging. This represented a shift from **Reaction** to **Prevention**.

The overarching goals of FTAC was to improve the outcomes for individuals that were referred to the service, whilst also reducing the risk that they posed. By triaging and classifying cases into high, moderate, and low concern, FTAC prioritises the level of urgency and level of resources. Individuals who are of high concern require an urgent response and extensive resources to support intervention and prevention. Moderate concern demands a prompt response and resources to support prevention approaches. Whilst a low concern case does not warrant any further input from FTAC.

The FTAC approach embodies a population-based solution to risk management by ensuring that any person with a moderate level of concern or greater receives intervention. In a recent review written by forensic psychiatrist Simon Wilson and others, a fascinating analogy was made contrasting the risk of a heart attack with the risk of violence:

'If one intervenes and treats the risk factors of the entire group, then adverse outcomes will be prevented without the need to know which individuals would have gone on to engage in the behaviour in question. An analogy is the risk of a heart attack. One cannot predict which individual will have a heart attack. However, one can identify factors that make a heart attack more likely, such as smoking, obesity, hypertension, and high blood cholesterol levels. One then treats everyone who possesses these risk factors – for instance, by smoking cessation therapy, weight loss, antihypertensives, and cholesterol-lowering drugs. This will prevent heart attacks, without needing to predict which individuals would have had a heart attack if they had not had treatment. Likewise, if one found that a number of individuals exhibited risk factors for violence (say, by intrusive persecutory delusions, a license to possess a firearm, substance abuse problems, poor anger control, and destitution with little left to lose), one would intervene to reduce these risks (say, by compulsory antipsychotic medication, removal of the license and firearm, treatment of substance abuse, anger management, and measures to increase social stability). This would lower the risk in the group as a whole without needing to predict which person would have become violent without such intervention.'

Although FTACs don't carry out the treatment for individuals of concern, the service works with other agencies to ensure intervention and support is provided. To ensure success, FTAC maintains accountability for the person and their risk, rather than handing this over to other departments or stakeholders and expecting them to take on the concern. Research on the effectiveness of this approach has shown that 80% of FTAC cases have been managed and reduced to a low level of concern, essentially mitigating the threat posed by the individual. In follow-up research conducted with individuals of concern over one- and two-year periods, a significant reduction in problematic communications and approaches were observed, along with a reduction in the total number of incidents of concern and number of police call outs.

Although FTAC was initially focused on fixated individuals, in time the centre expanded, and the broader model became a blueprint for preventative approaches to dealing with lone actor violence – particularly cases that were characterised by grievance or fixation. The success of FTAC led to many other countries adopting the model, each adapting this to their own needs and requirements. At the time of Man Haron Monis's siege in Sydney, the state of Queensland had established an FTAC a year earlier in 2013, having identified the importance of the joint police and mental health approach. Consequently, following the recommendations of the inquest, New South Wales established an FTAC in 2017. The other states in Australia also implemented FTACs in the proceeding years, along with New Zealand in 2019. Whilst the New Zealand FTAC is focused only on threats to politicians, the Australian services cover a breadth of concerns pertaining to violence by lone individuals. The Australian, British, and Dutch FTACs work closely alongside counterterrorism units with their respective police services, with the counterterrorism teams integrating mental health expertise and a prevention-first approach to individuals of concern.

The FTAC approach is unique, but across the US, similar centres and units have also been developed. The focus for FTACs has always been on *the causal factors* which are driving the violence (i.e., grievances and fixations), whilst in the US, specialist teams have been established around the *types of targeted violence*. For instance, back in 1990, the Los Angeles Police Department (LAPD) established a first-of-its-kind threat management unit which predominantly dealt with stalking cases – particularly the stalking of Hollywood celebrities. The unit was created following the murder of actress Rebecca Schaeffer by Robert Bardo, an obsessive fan. Since then, the unit has evolved to resemble the FTAC model, integrating a greater focus on mental health, specialist expertise, and collaboration. Many police forces across the US now have threat teams staffed by police and mental health professionals to address threats, stalking, and mass attacks.

At a national level across the US, the FBI's Behavioral Analysis Unit, specifically BAU-1[1] has led the way in examining lone attackers. In a similar vein to the BAU's work on serial killers and violent crime in the 1980s and 1990s, the BAU set out to understand the nuances of mass attackers – from their motivations, plans and preparations, target choices, methods of killing, choice of clothing and attire, and interests in violent ideologies and media. Following the mass shooting at Virginia Tech in Blacksburg, Virginia, in April 2007, George W. Bush tasked cabinet members with establishing a response to the repeat mass casualty attacks on school and college campuses. The initiative resulted in the FBI, Secret Service, and Department of Education undertaking a joint review of 272 cases of targeted violence at schooling institutions, identifying many lessons, pitfalls, and avenues for future prevention. As a result, in 2010 the FBI established the Behavioural Threat Assessment Centre, bringing together agents, psychologists, psychiatrists, and other government departments, with the aim of preventing violence and completing ongoing research on the issue. The BAU-1 has assisted local law enforcement throughout the US in evaluating and managing threat concerns, along with undertaking

---

[1] The Behavioral Analysis Unit has now expanded in five distinct units/teams. These include: BAU-1 (threats, targeted violence, and counter-terrorism), BAU-2 (cybercrime and counter-intelligence), BAU-3 (crimes against children), BAU-4 (crimes against adults and the violent criminal apprehension program), and BAU-5 (research and training unit).

extensive post-incident analyses in the aftermath of attacks. As part of building their knowledge on these incidents, members of the BAU-1 have interviewed numerous lone actors and uncovered crucial details about their progression to violence. Through these interviews and the BAU's research undertakings, the team have focused on the role of warning behaviours in the lead up to attacks, assisting local police agencies with prioritising threats and implementing prevention plans.

The BAU-1 has been essential in empowering police agencies to better understand and respond to lone actor violence. Likewise, FTACs have provided a model for police units and threat teams to adopt by ensuring that broad support and resources are provided to anyone with an elevated level of concern – in turn reducing risk.

SPECIALISED POLICE TEAMS HAVE IMPROVED the responses to lone actor concerns. However, despite better practices and approaches, the number of cases continues to remain remarkably high. As a consequence, the demands on police teams and supporting services is increasing. For instance, although twelve mass casualty attacks occurred in the UK between 2017–2019, counterterrorism teams were involved in 850 live investigations and required to make decisions on around 3,000 persons of concern. Moreover, while a gradual reduction in terrorist attacks (completed, failed, or foiled) occurred throughout Europe between 2019 and 2021, decreasing from 105 to fifteen, there were still more than 400 people convicted of terrorism offences in 2021.

Despite a brief decline, with the shifting socio-political landscape, including elections, COVID-19, and the conflict in the Middle East between Israel and Palestine, these numbers have again risen, with terrorist attacks throughout Europe jumping from twenty-eight in 2022 to 120 in 2023. Again, 358 people were also convicted of terrorism offences in 2023. Similar trends have been observed in the UK, with MI5's state threat investigations increasing by 48% throughout 2023 and 2024.

Prevention approaches are gradually working, but troublingly, there are enormous numbers of people increasingly presenting with concerns.

The shift from reaction to prevention has been crucial to managing threats and intervening before an attack. The development of specialised police teams and the embedding of mental health practitioners has changed the way many police agencies perceive offenders and has led to an improved understanding of the value and need for early intervention. However, while the policing response to lone actor violence has greatly changed, the ability of police to intervene in cases is enormously dependent on information sharing. If family, friends, professionals, or members of the public do not share their concerns with the police, then prevention efforts cannot occur.

As explained by international security expert Andrew Staniforth, *'issues which give rise to low-level crime and the development of violent extremism leading to terrorism, often begin at the most local level. Thus, national security increasingly depends upon neighbourhood security, and good intelligence to prevent terrorism.'* To successfully allow early prevention efforts to take place, information has to flow from the local community through to the police. Ultimately, an unbroken thread of information is the critical spinal cord of any endeavour to intervene and prevent violence. Ensuring that information flows to the right places is the first step in preventing lone actor attacks.

Interestingly, over the last few years, several new initiatives and approaches have been developed to send vital information upstream and through to the police and other services. In 2021, the iREPORTit app was launched in the UK, allowing citizens to anonymously and confidentially report concerning online content relating to violent extremism. Much of the content has related to Islamic State material, along with threats, and extreme far-right subjects. The app sends notifications directly through to the Counter Terrorism Internet Referral Unit, who review the incidents and determine a course of action. The app has proven to be an essential platform for connecting the public and police. Through the reporting process, thousands of violent extremist links have been removed, and in turn, the app has assisted with more than 500 counterterrorism investigations.

Another similar approach, which was established several years earlier in the wake of the Columbine shooting, is the Safe2Tell tip line. Launched initially in Colorado, USA, the app and tip line is available for all schools and educational facilities to report incidents of concern. The tip line shares information with police and school officials, who triage incidents and conduct investigations if necessary. In a review in 2011, it was identified that the app had helped prevent twenty-eight potential school attacks. More recent data from 2021–2022 noted that 19,364 reports were made to the tip line during the school year. The majority of concerns related to suicidal threats, in addition to bullying, and well-being issues. Along with allowing those within the school communities to report concerns, the tip line and app has also provided young people with the opportunity to report their own struggles – an essential tool enabling easy access to support, rather than requiring a difficult conversation.

A creative initiative has also been trialled in Sarpy County in Nebraska. Across the county, a community-wide adoption of the Awareity incident reporting platform has occurred, fostering a community approach to prevention. This has involved schools, criminal justice services, mental health providers, and other community organisations collaboratively reporting incidents and warning signs. Through the Awareity website, organisations, departments, and community members are able to report and log behavioural incidents. Like with Safe2Tell, many incidents have related to suicidal risk, concerns over well-being, intentions to harm, and threats of violence. With the community-wide approach, it has been possible for many early interventions to occur and for support plans to be developed. So far, hundreds of *red flags* have been identified and a variety of responses have occurred, including interventions for violence and suicidal ideation, along with an arrest and several police investigations.

THE FLOW OF INFORMATION is essential for early prevention. Information sharing is the first step in prevention – however, as the tragic shortcomings in the Man Haron Monis case highlighted, information sharing is only the first step of the process. Information must also be managed and actioned.

Although the development of FTACs and other specialised police teams has resulted in greater collaboration and joint decision-making, all parties must come to the table and work together. If a multi-agency approach doesn't occur, or processes and practices are lacking within certain agencies or sectors, then cracks may emerge, warning behaviours may be missed, and opportunities for early intervention may be overlooked. When things fail, it's typically due to one or more of the following factors:

Silos: In most cases of lone actor violence, someone is aware of the person's concerning behaviour, or intent, prior to the offence. Typically, family, friends, professional services, and at times police, are aware of the concerns. However, vital information is never shared, or in some instances, is filed away and never actioned. Essentially, information becomes siloed and inaccessible to others. It may be a notification by a family member that is never passed on to police, or a crucial comment concealed within a confidential psychiatric report that indicates the target of an intended attack. Other instances may involve important government intelligence being classified at a *'top secret'* level, preventing front-line police from understanding the seriousness of the threat. Another instance may be a friend who is worried about rupturing a friendship and never shares their concerns. Even restricted databases, fragmented reporting lines, or hierarchical methods of communication can create silos. Ultimately, silos occur through a variety of ways, causing information to become stuck, or lost in the abyss.

Disconnects: Across many of the inquiries into failed prevention efforts, a common theme has been the lack of collaborative multi-agency teamwork.

Although disconnects occur for a variety of reasons, they are ultimately due to a lack of harmony and collaboration. As a result of poor cohesion, intervention or prevention efforts fail. A disconnect may occur when a central office provides advice to a small local area and fails to understand the nuances and risks relevant to the region. Turf wars between departments or agencies, or even people's egos, can also create further disconnects, which prevent adequate responses from occurring. Personal biases and preconceived beliefs may result in disconnects between team members when making decisions about a person of concern, influencing judgement and the ability to analyse the threat. There may also be cultural disconnects which lead to misunderstanding, or a lack of resources which causes inadequacies in responding to risks or completing intervention.

Gaps: When gaps emerge, it is always *'due to a lack'* of something. It could be a lack of knowledge about a particular mental health condition among police officers, or insufficient training and education in relation to best practice methods. Gaps can arise from lax or inadequate approaches to assessing risk, leading to vital information being missed, or poorly informed decision-making. Similarly, a lack of oversight and accountability within teams can result in things being overlooked or neglected. Even a lack of trust within a team or between departments can create gaps which over time may lead to bigger issues and eventually disconnects.

Bunkers: Unfortunately, in some instances, prevention efforts, or attempts to intervene, can cause a negative chain reaction. This is akin to the butterfly effect, whereby an action results in a reaction. Whilst in most cases, interventions or attempts to mitigate a threat are sufficient, they can also lead a person of concern down another path. Troublingly, the act of intervening, or even engaging with the person, can cause them to change their plans and pursue a different means or method of perpetrating violence. Bunkers occur when police, or other services, mistakenly believe that their intervention approach has successfully mitigated the threat. However, rather than causing the person to cease their behaviour, it leads them to alter their target, or change their means of attack. A combination of complacency and lax threat management practices cause bunkers to occur. The threat does not simply stop once intervention is put in place. In some cases, it's simple and the plan to mitigate the threat is effective. But intervention and mitigation are rarely simple, and even great plans and processes never guarantee that everything is now okay.

Myopia: The work completed by police and other front-line agencies is demanding and often unrelenting. Preventing lone actor violence is a high stakes endeavour and over time it is easy for things to get missed. Police investigations may span many months, or a psychologist may work with a concerning person for several years. Unfortunately, this familiarity can lead to a loss of objectivity. Fatigue can set in, complacency may arise, familiarity may lead to comfort, and repeated teamwork can result in groupthink. Preventing threats of violence is messy and most professionals spend their time *'stuck in the mud'*. Over time it is easy for people to become bogged down and to miss acute or small changes. Myopia highlights that to successfully detect changes or escalations in violence, fresh eyes, and a fresh perspective may sometimes be required – in conjunction with experience.

PREVENTION IS CRUCIAL. FTACs, or units like the BAU-1, have paved the way for better practices and knowledge on lone actors. Yet, prevention is dependent on information sharing, collaboration, sound processes, and specialist expertise. Without information flow, police teams remain in the dark and unaware of an individual who may be of concern. The collection and analysis of information is the foundation of early intervention and prevention methods. From here, police and other services must ensure that collaborative and open relationships occur with adequate oversights that catch pitfalls and shortcomings early on.

The other essential piece of the puzzle is the role of threat and risk assessment – determining how concerning and dangerous a person is.

13

The Need For Prediction

'Under conditions of complexity, not only are checklists a help, they are required for success.'

Atul Gawande

AFTER SHARING A KISS with Tatiana Tarasoff on New Year's Eve, Prosenjit Poddar hoped to commence a relationship with Tatiana. He hoped the year of 1969 would be one full of love and endless possibilities. However, early into the new year, he realised that his romantic interests were not reciprocated by Tatiana, and that she only wanted a friendship. Poddar struggled to accept the rejection and actively tried to convince Tatiana to change her mind. Despite his persistence, Tatiana was not persuaded.

Over the coming months, Poddar became increasingly angry at Tatiana. He was fixated on having a romantic relationship, and unable to accept her decision. Tatiana's rejection had taken a toll on his well-being, and led to him commencing counselling with psychiatrist Dr Lawrence Moore. Poddar was a student at the University of California, Berkeley, and Dr Moore worked as the University psychiatrist.

Over the course of several sessions, Poddar spoke of his anger towards a female who had rejected him. During one appointment, he stated that he wanted to harm the woman and was considering purchasing a gun. While Poddar spoke about his anger towards the female, he never explicitly named Tatiana. Instead, he referred to her as *'the woman'* that had hurt him.

Poddar's anger and desire for retribution concerned Dr Moore, and in response, he advised Poddar that he would be obligated to admit him to hospital if he continued to make threats. Unfortunately, this perceived ultimatum led to Poddar disengaging from treatment.

As a result of Poddar ceasing treatment, Dr Moore was placed in a perilous position. After consulting with a colleague, he wrote a letter to campus security advising them of his concerns. In response to the letter, campus security visited Poddar. However, he denied the allegation and a decision was made to take no further action. Approximately two months after speaking with campus security, Poddar arrived at Tatiana's home. He shot her with a firearm and stabbed her multiple times.

In the aftermath of Tatiana's death, her parents sued Dr Moore and his psychiatric colleague. In the initial trial, the court found that the psychiatrists had followed the correct protocol and had honoured their *'duty to their patient'*, dismissing the case.

Tatiana's parents refused to accept the decision and in 1976 an appeal was heard before the Supreme Court of California. The court overruled the initial decision and ruled in favour of Tatiana's parents. The landmark ruling concluded:

'Regardless of the therapists' unsuccessful attempt to confine Poddar, since they knew that Poddar was at large and dangerous, their failure to warn Tatiana or others likely to apprise her of danger constitute a breach of the therapists' duty to exercise responsible care to protect Tatiana.'

This ruling became known as the Tarasoff law, whereby therapists were expected to have a duty to control their patients' behaviour and therefore were responsible for protecting society from dangerous cases.

The Tarasoff law changed the way psychiatrists and psychologists practiced. In the wake of the ruling, the field of psychological risk assessment flourished.

RISK ASSESSMENT IS A COMMON PRACTICE across many professions throughout the world. It is used by banks to determine whether someone is suitable for a home loan, by insurance agencies to assess the likelihood of injury or loss, and by airline companies to examine the safety of weather conditions for flying. Risk assessment involves looking at indicators or factors which increase the likelihood of harm or an adverse event occurring. Ultimately, an effective risk assessment mitigates harm and effectively predicts when things will go wrong.

When it comes to violence, risk assessments are concerned with identifying whether someone is at risk of perpetrating harm and acting violently. Although the use of risk assessments with offenders can be traced back to the early 1900s, it was not commonplace among psychologists, psychiatrists, or even within the criminal justice system until the 1970s. The Tarasoff law significantly changed risk assessment practices, and by the 1980s risk assessment was widely used in court and with offenders.

In the early days of risk assessment, the concept of risk related to dangerousness – '*How dangerous is the individual?*' Psychologists and psychiatrists used an unstructured clinical judgment approach to determine just how dangerous a person was. Clinicians used their experience and impressions of the person to reach a conclusion. Assessments typically examined whether someone was suitable to be released from prison, or whether they may pose a danger to the community. Clinicians also examined a person's state of mind and whether they should be incarcerated in prison, or instead in a psychiatric facility due to their poor state of mental health.

By the 1980s, risk assessment was a common practice within the criminal justice system. However, the process was full of faults, with predictions often wrong, or based on the assessor's own biases or prejudices. The majority overpredicted the likelihood of violence occurring, and alarmingly, those conducting the assessment were wrong twice as often as they were right.

These problems resulted in a second generation of risk assessments being created. Known as actuarial assessments, this new generation of tools comprised of *'risk factors'* that were statistically correlated with reoffending. Actuarial assessments focused on two types of crimes: the risk of violence, and the risk of sexual offending.

The assessment tools comprised of items which were identified as being associated with sexual and violent offending through research, such as the offender's age, relationship to the victim, and their criminal history. Actuarial assessments worked off the principle that past behaviour is the best predictor of future behaviour.

The second generation of risk assessments significantly advanced the field, but these tools also had limitations. Due to focusing heavily on the offender's past behaviours, the assessment tools were limited and unable to capture things such as personality, treatment progress, or the offender's level of empathy or insight.

As a result of these limitations, in the late 1990s, Structured Professional Judgement (SPJ) tools were developed as the third generation of risk assessments. SPJs incorporated statistical and research-informed risk factors, whilst also examining aspects relating to the person such as personality, individual strengths, and response to treatment. SPJs combined static (past behaviour) and dynamic (current or future behaviour) factors to broadly cover all aspects of risk and behaviour.

THE NEED FOR PREDICTION

The use of risk assessments within the criminal justice system has grown substantially over the past two decades with SPJs. When completing an SPJ assessment, mental health professionals are required to forecast the ways in which future offending may occur and assign a person to a specific risk category (such as low, moderate, or high). In addition, some of the many questions that professionals may be asked to answer through a risk assessment include:

- Is the person suitable for being granted parole and let out of custody?
- If the person offends, how severe will this offending be?
- What are the likely victims in the event that a crime occurs?
- Over a two-year period, what is the likelihood of offending occurring?
- What factors are most relevant to the person's risk of offending?
- What are the likely indicators which would suggest the individual is moving towards perpetrating an offence?
- What skills and interventions does the person need to address their behaviour?

With the rise in lone actor violence, risk assessment has become a crucial prevention tool. It is integral to informing the decision-making and the type of response required for individuals of concern. Risk assessment, along with threat assessment, is one of the primary factors which guide the decisions of specialised police and threat teams. However, the use of risk and threat assessment for lone actor violence has not come about easily.

Until recent times, lone actor attacks were novel and uncommon. There was little need for risk assessment tools as this type of offender and offending was rare. There had never been a need for a risk assessment measure for lone actors until a decade ago. As a result, in the last ten years, there has been a rapid rush to fill this void and develop new measures. This has produced a range of risk assessments to examine terrorism, violent extremism, and lone actor violence. Some of the most notable assessments which have been developed include:

- Terrorist Radicalization Assessment Protocol-18 (TRAP-18).
- Violent Extremist Risk Assessment-2-Revised (VERA-2R).
- Extremist Risk Guidance-Revised (ERG-R).
- Multi-Level Guidelines (MLG).
- Workplace Assessment of Violence Risk-21 Version 3 (WAVR-21-V3).
- North Carolina Behavioral Threat Assessment Investigation Overview-25 (NCBIO-25).

While many of these measures have been developed hurriedly to meet the urgent need, so far, they have proven to be useful and have provided valuable guidance in understanding the risk factors associated with lone actor violence. Importantly, the measures are still being studied and researched, and as findings are emerging, the tools are being revised and adjusted. Like with any risk assessment measure, there will always be gaps which are not captured by the tool, requiring clinicians or teams to identify the limitations of the assessment and consider alternative ways that risk could arise or be missed. Although it is early days, these assessments have provided professionals with a framework and map to guide their decision-making on a person's potential for mass casualty violence.

RISK IS ABOUT MAKING FORECASTS and predictions about a person over a set period of time, say one or two years. For lone actor violence, there are primarily two ways that risk assessments are used. The first is the likelihood of a person reoffending after having already committed a violent offence. The second is in cases where it's suspected that an individual may perpetrate a targeted offence. In this context, there is a concern that the person is progressing towards carrying out an act of violence.

Ultimately, **Risk** is best viewed as *'Probability x Loss'*. Essentially, it's the likelihood of something occurring and the associated consequences that may arise. In other words, what is the likelihood of the person committing a lone actor attack over the next two years, and how severe and significant may this act be if it does occur?

Because risk assessment is a prediction over a set period of time, it can be misleading. For instance, a person may have periods where they are more likely to act violently (stress, setbacks, conflicts, loss, etc.) or less likely (employed, in a relationship, participating in exercise), and a lot of change and acute issues may occur within a person's life. Due to this gap and the need to detect change, threat assessment emerged as a specific form of risk assessment. As a concept, a ***Threat*** is about progression towards action and is best thought of as '***Intent x Capability***'. For example, does the individual have the intentions (motivation) to act violently, and also the capabilities (resources and skills) to carry out the violence?

Factors associated with an increased threat have been described as warning behaviours, red flag indicators, and pre-attack signals. Warning behaviours, or threat indicators, signal a possible shift from the contemplation of violence towards mobilisation and action.

The role of threat indicators was first discussed at length in former FBI agent Mary Ellen O'Toole's analysis of school shooters. In the wake of the Columbine massacre in 1999, where students Eric Harris and Dylan Klebold killed thirteen people, O'Toole investigated the pathways and factors which lead to school shootings. Her analysis was written following an FBI-led symposium where experts gathered to discuss and examine eighteen school shootings which had occurred across the USA over previous years.

This pioneering symposium, and the publication which was produced by O'Toole, identified that in most cases, '*a student intentionally or unintentionally reveals clues to feelings, thoughts, fantasies, attitudes, or intentions that may signal an impending violent act*'. Prior to carrying out an attack, the majority of students made subtle threats, boasts, predictions, or innuendos pertaining to violence or an intended attack. Many catalogued their violent thoughts and fantasies through diary entries, stories, songs, drawings, poems, letters, or videos.

O'Toole believed that this trail of behavioural breadcrumbs was in essence a form of **Leakage** which indicated the individual's intent to act violently. For instance, 'an example of leakage could be a student who shows a recurring preoccupation with themes of violence, hopelessness, despair, hatred, isolation, loneliness, nihilism, or an "end-of-the-world" philosophy'.

Along with identifying the crucial role of warning behaviours in the lead-up to an attack, the analysis categorised threats into three categories, these being: *Low*, *Medium*, and *High*; categories that would later be adopted in one way or another by FTACs, threat teams, and numerous threat assessment tools.

A *Low Threat* was considered to be vague, indirect, and lacking in realism. A *Medium Threat* was more direct in nature and evidenced some indication of preparatory steps and thoughts about acting. Lastly, a *High Threat* was direct and specific, and demonstrated that concrete plans and steps were in place to act, such as, – *'At eight o'clock tomorrow morning, I intend to shoot the school principal. That's when he is in the office by himself. I have a 9mm. Believe me, I know what I am doing. I am sick and tired of the way he runs this school.'*

Extending on from O'Toole's foundational work, several further studies have found evidence of warning behaviours in the lead-up to mass casualty incidents. In a study of sixty-three individuals who perpetrated an active shooter attack between 2003 and 2013, nearly eighty of the offenders spent a week or longer planning the attack. Alarmingly, on average perpetrators displayed four to five red flag behaviours prior to their offence, and more than half had made threats or had a prior confrontation in the lead-up. At least one victim was specifically targeted by the offender in just under two thirds of cases, and four out of five offenders were driven by a grievance.

Offenders on average experienced 3.6 life stressors in the twelve-month period prior to their offending, indicating that their life was characterised by stress and instability – comparable to the slow dripping water faucet which eventually causes the bathtub to spill over.

In a large study of 119 lone actors, one third of perpetrators completed a dry run of the attack and around half compiled a collection of weapons in preparation. Nearly two thirds of offenders expressed extremist beliefs or wrote letters sharing their extreme views. In over half of the cases, others (such as family or friends) were aware that the individual was undertaking research, planning, and preparation for an attack.

Lone actor violence does not simply emerge from nowhere. Many individuals harbour grievances, experience stress, instability, and reduced well-being, and have difficulties with coping. A large percentage talk about their violent intentions, and the majority engage in planning and preparation. Rarely does this shift in behaviour go unnoticed, and often friends, family, or even work colleagues are aware – once again highlighting the importance of this information being shared.

Warning behaviours are especially apparent among adolescents, with nearly all teenage lone actors leaving a trail of problematic behaviour prior to the attack. For instance, a study examining thirty-one juveniles at risk of committing a mass attack found that nine out of ten displayed leakage behaviour, while over a third made direct threats. Another analysis of nine German school shooters found that all of them exhibited leakage prior to their offence.

Across a range of research studies, rates of leakage vary from 58%–100% across cases. At a conservative estimate, leakage occurs in one out of every two cases.

Forensic psychologist Reid Meloy has pioneered a framework of eight warning behaviours that signal a person may be progressing towards violence. According to Dr Meloy, the presence of these behaviours indicates an increasing concern, highlighting the need for timely intervention and support.

- *Pathway:* Evidence of activities or behaviours which relate to the planning, preparation, or implementation of an attack. This may include surveillance, stalking, cataloguing of prior attacks, practice runs, or mapping out an attack strategy.
- *Fixation:* A pathological preoccupation and obsession with a person or cause. This may involve obsessive admiration, affection, anger, or even paranoia towards an individual or broader group. A fixation may be characterised by an extremely overvalued belief, delusional thoughts, or even an obsession. In many cases, fixations can be fuelled by a perceived injustice or wrongdoing.
- *Identification:* The development of a fascination or interest in commando, military, and warrior paraphernalia and behaviour. Violence becomes associated with the person's sense of identity, and they may begin to change their appearance, collect materials, or suddenly engage in activities such as weapons training. A new-found interest in death and other violent events may also be evident.
- *Novel aggression:* The engagement in an unrelated or out-of-character act of aggression. This act of aggression, whether verbal or physical, serves as a means to test the person's ability and resolve to carry out violence. This test of character may include subtle acts of violence, such as aggression towards a spouse or a salesperson in a shop. Other examples may be an assault against a vulnerable person, such as a homeless individual, or even engaging in a fight at a bar.
- *Energy burst:* As a person commits to carrying out violence, they may display a sudden increase in energy or excitement in anticipation of the attack. Everyday behaviour may change, with the person becoming more erratic, awake for longer hours, spending days on end working on a project, travelling to multiple locations over a period of days, and even making a range of sudden new purchases.
- *Leakage:* An expressed intent to perpetrate harm through communicating this to another person or party. These remarks may be veiled

comments about wanting to carry out violence, or a direct statement about how and when they will perpetrate an attack. Leakage offers a glimpse into the person's thinking, attitudes, and even motivations pertaining to plans or intentions for violence.
- *Last resort:* The perception that violence is the only means left to resolve the issue or problem. This represents a psychological shift whereby the person accepts that violence is the only resolution. As part of the shift in the person's state of mind, they may give away property, say their goodbyes, and prepare a will.
- *Directly communicated threat:* A written or oral threat to harm a target or something of similar association. Although many people who make direct threats do not go on to carry out a lone actor attack, a direct threat can indicate an emerging focus on violence and anger towards a particular group or person, suggesting that without intervention, this could escalate.

Warning behaviours serve as a valuable guide, or goal post, to view sudden and acute changes. If there is an indication of these behaviours, then it becomes essential that police, or other relevant agencies or services, examine the concern and consider the seriousness of the matter.

Unlike risk assessment, threat assessment is about identifying warning behaviours. It is about identifying when a person has developed an intention to act violently and has commenced developing their capabilities to act on this intention. Threat assessment examines how concerning the person is at that specific moment in time – it's not about longer-term predictions. It's about determining **the Imminency of the Violence** and **the Urgency of the Response**.

THREAT ASSESSMENT AND THREAT TEAMS are essential to mitigating mass casualty attacks. However, a threat assessment isn't a panacea. It is a process which informs decision-making and guides threat teams. Completing a threat assessment doesn't mitigate the concern nor offer any guarantees that violence won't occur. The completion of a threat assessment requires due diligence and frequent monitoring and reassessment.

In December 2013, Karl Pierson arrived at his high school in Colorado with a shotgun, machete, and homemade bombs. A few months earlier in September, the school completed a threat assessment on Pierson, determining that he was *'a low risk'* for acting violently. The assessment had occurred after Pierson was overheard by a teacher stating, *'I'm going to kill that guy,'* after being demoted as captain of the debate team by a faculty member.

The threat assessment on Pierson was completed by the assistant principal and school psychologist, who had undertaken a two-hour PowerPoint training session on threat assessment. The two staff members completed the assessment alone and both were inexperienced in threat assessment. Due to insufficient record-keeping within the school and no integrated information-sharing system, the two staff were unaware of several pre-existing concerns pertaining to Pierson. They also never spoke with his parents, friends, or teachers – who all had valuable knowledge on Pierson's behaviour. The assessment was completed on face value, by interviewing Pierson and trusting his responses.

Alongside this, one of the other major failures in the case was the type of threat assessment tool which was used. The school employed a threat assessment document which spanned four pages and was a mixture of bits and pieces of information that had been pulled together to create an assessment. However, the assessment had never been validated, or studied, to ensure that an elevated score actually corresponded to a greater likelihood of violence. In reviewing the case for the Colorado Committee on School Safety and Youth in Crisis, William Woodward and Sarah Goodrum observed, *'Without a validated threat assessment tool, or a plan to validate the chosen tool, there is no way of knowing if it actually predicted violence. As an analogy, a physician would not give a child medication that was not tested and proven effective by the Federal Drug Administration. Similarly, a threat assessment tool that has not been tested and proven effective should not be used to evaluate a student's level of concern.'*

The problems did not stop there. Even though the assessment was not validated, the two staff members had failed to adequately score the assessment items. Out of the twenty-four risk factor items on the assessment, Pierson was marked on seven risk indicators. However, there was evidence to suggest that he could have been scored on another nine to ten factors, which would have substantially elevated his level of concern. These factors were missed, overlooked, or dismissed. Woodward and Goodrum highlighted, *'a properly executed threat assessment would have revealed a high level of concern, and a higher level of concern should have prompted more serious disciplinary action and more thorough monitoring and support planning'*.

The threat assessment was also never reviewed by the principal or district school board, resulting in no oversight. A range of gaps, disconnects, and silos were evident in the failure to prevent Pierson's attack. One of the most notable issues was that the two staff members who completed the assessment had treated it as though it was a risk assessment – failing to understand that threats are dynamic. Threat assessment is focused on the person's concern at the immediate moment in time and is not about making longer term predictions. Threats needs to be regularly reviewed and reassessed. Their approach was a classic example of a bunker, where the completion of the threat assessment and perceived *'low risk'* led to complacency and premature reassurance.

At around the time the threat assessment was completed, Pierson commenced writing in his diary about committing an attack. He searched mass shootings and viewed firearms on the internet in the school cafeteria, downloaded and shared the *Anarchist Cookbook* (the ultimate DIY book on preparing weapons and explosives) with a peer, showed pictures of his newly purchased shotgun to another student days before the shooting, and shared instructions on making a Molotov cocktail with a fellow student. Although a check-in was conducted with Pierson two weeks after the threat assessment, none of these details were discovered. On 6 November, Pierson settled on a date to carry out his attack, writing, *'December 13 date I chose is perfect ... 38 days.'* A few weeks later, he wrote, *'it's weird going through life knowing that in 19 days, I'm going to be dead.'*

On 6 December, Pierson purchased a firearm. He purchased shotgun shells and a belt six days later. The next day, he arrived at his school with the intention of killing the faculty mentor who he had threatened to kill a few months prior. When he was unable to locate the individual, Pierson shot a seventeen-year-old female student who was within close proximity to him at the school. A few minutes later, he turned the weapon on himself.

When used without adequate training or in ineffective ways, threat assessments can go awry. The assessment must also be validated and recognised by studies which support their use. For threat assessments to be effective, they need to be backed up by strong processes, teamwork, and support.

Back in 2002, the United States Secret Service and Department of Education published a guide to conducting threat assessments in schools. Although the principles are tailored to the school setting, they're universally relevant to any type of threat assessment. For threat assessments to be effective, the following six principles must be met:

1. There is an understandable and often discernable process of thinking and behaviour preceding targeted violence.
2. Acts of violence stem from an interaction between the person, the situation, the setting, and the target.
3. A threat assessment must be inquisitive, skeptical, and investigative.
4. An effective threat assessment must be based on facts.
5. The central question for threat assessment is whether the person poses a threat, not whether they have made a threat.
6. Threat assessment outcomes and strategies must be integrative ap-

proaches.

The six principles of threat assessment were not met in the assessment of Karl Pierson.

Threat assessment is the starting point to preventing violence. It allows assessors and teams to understand the breadth of the problem and the seriousness of it. With effective threat assessment, the focus then moves to managing the concern and implementing intervention to bring about change.

14

Radical Minds

'The best scientists are open to the possibility that they may be wrong, and they are willing to change their minds in the face of new evidence.'

Richard Feynman

IN LATE NOVEMBER 2019, twenty-eight-year-old Usman Khan stabbed two people to death and injured another three at a prisoner rehabilitation conference at Fishmongers' Hall near London Bridge. Hours earlier, Khan had spoken at the conference about his journey into and out of terrorism. After speaking, he made his way to a nearby bathroom and equipped himself with a fake suicide belt and bomb, and gathered his makeshift weapons; which included an ornamental pike and narwhal tusk. In the moments following the stabbings, Khan was killed by police as he attempted to flee from the area. He had been released from prison only eight months earlier after being convicted in 2012 of being part of a group affiliated with Al-Qaeda and conspiring to carry out attacks across the UK, including at the London Stock Exchange. During his eight years in prison, Khan completed two programmes centred on deradicalisation. Despite completing the programmes, Khan was recognised as an *'influential inmate who mixed with high-profile terrorists'* and held radical jihadi beliefs.

Following Khan's attack, another act of terrorism was perpetrated by Sudesh Amman on 2 February 2020, in Streatham, London. Amman had been released from prison on 23 January, after being convicted of terrorism-related offences in 2018.

Amman had been convicted of being in possession of extremist material and also distributing it. In messages he'd sent to his girlfriend at the time of his arrest, he remarked, *'If you can't make a bomb because family, friends or spies are watching or suspecting you, take a knife, Molotov, sound bombs or a car at night and attack ....'*

On being released from custody, the twenty-year-old was placed under active police surveillance and subject to strict parole requirements. In his attack on 2 February, Amman walked into a convenience store and stole a knife – allowing him to quickly mobilise to violence. Similar to Khan, he wore a fake suicide vest. His attack led to three people being injured and Khan was fatally shot by police. Whilst Khan had been incarcerated, he had refused to engage in deradicalisation programmes; however, sentencing legislation made him eligible for automatic release after serving half of his forty-month sentence in jail.

Like Khan and Amman, RXG, whose name is altered, had been referred to a community-based deradicalisation programme. RXG threatened to kill a teacher and claimed that Osama bin Laden was his hero. After being referred to the deradicalisation programme, RXG, who was only fourteen years old, plotted a terrorist attack in the comfort of his bedroom through his smartphone. He sent thousands of messages to eighteen-year-old Sevdet Besim, who lived in Victoria, Australia. RXG constructed a plan with Besim, for him to kill and behead police officers during Anzac Day, an Australian Memorial Day parade. Fortunately, British police discovered the communications exchange between the pair and notified Australian authorities. RXG was sentenced to life imprisonment and at the time was the youngest person convicted of terrorism offences in Britain. Besim was sentenced to ten years in prison in Australia.

IN RESPONSE TO THE MOUNTING number of lone actor and terrorism-inspired offences, deradicalisation programmes were touted as the most effective way to change an individual's proclivities towards violence. Up until around 2020, many governments and organisations promoted these programmes and courses as being critical to reducing risk and changing problematic and radicalised beliefs.

Initially, deradicalisation programmes appeared promising, and millions were spent in developing these initiatives. However, many programmes were hastily created, poorly informed, ad hoc, and lacking in evidence. For over a decade, deradicalisation programmes were the primary form of treatment for offenders. Yet, the majority of programmes were falling short and failing to produce change.

Deradicalisation programmes emerged largely to target individuals with jihadi-inspired beliefs and identifications. In essence, deradicalisation programmes were founded on the idea that violence occurred due to someone becoming radicalised and developing extremist beliefs which condoned violence. The aims were to create disengagement from these extreme beliefs and to develop solutions other than violence. The programmes aimed to provide support, a safe space, and an alternative perspective to violence. More advanced programmes, like those in prisons, focused on psychological needs, restructuring beliefs, challenging extreme attitudes, and building a healthy sense of identity.

Many programmes were rolled out in prison for offenders who had already carried out an attack, whilst other initiatives were implemented at the grass-roots level with concerning young people. Between 2012 and 2017, deradicalisation and disengagement programmes sprouted up everywhere across Western countries. They were common in prison and were widely offered by community service providers, including some schools. Eventually, there were so many different programmes, different ideas, varied methods, and outcomes. In the UK, nearly 1,700 people aged nine years old and over completed deradicalisation programmes in 2014, with this jumping to almost 4,000 in 2015.

Like with the UK, many countries were quick to adopt these programmes. Some programmes were critiqued and improved, whilst others remained poorly constructed and without clear outcomes. For example, one initiative in Western Australia had adolescents at a school plan a terrorist attack. The exercise was intended to highlight how our beliefs and values influence the type and style of attack. Although there were many benefits of the programmes, there were also many problems – and when it really mattered, the outcomes were uncertain.

In a commissioned report by the Home Office of the UK in 2018, broad issues with deradicalisation programmes across Europe were identified. Troublingly, the report concluded that 95% of programmes were *'ineffective'*. Following the tragic attacks which were perpetrated by Khan and Amman, the UK Parliament passed the Terrorist Offenders Bill, restricting the early release of individuals convicted of terrorism offences. At the time of reviewing this bill, it was identified that the role and suitability of deradicalisation programmes required continuous monitoring and review, given the uncertainty surrounding their efficacy and outcomes. Deradicalisation programmes continue to this day, but several have been terminated, and many others have now been revised and renamed as disengagement programmes.

Deradicalisation and disengagement are akin to twigs on the same branch – distinct yet interconnected. Deradicalisation focuses on untangling an individual from their commitment to violent extremist beliefs, while disengagement ensures that the behaviours and actions associated with violent extremism are halted and abandoned. In some cases, being charged with an offence or incarcerated is enough to prompt disengagement from extremist behaviour. However, disengagement does not necessarily mean a corresponding shift in attitudes and beliefs has taken place.

When deradicalisation programmes were initially developed, they were intended to address the reasons for someone progressing towards violence, but the majority of the endeavours failed to grasp the complexities of this. When many of the programmes were created, the primary focus was on jihadi-inspired violence and terrorism. However, by the time most countries had commenced using these programmes, the offending had evolved. Instead, most mass attacks were perpetrated by offenders with grievances, extremist beliefs, and mental health issues, rather than those inspired by jihad. Consequently, many programmes became unsuitable and ineffective at treating the problem.

Deradicalisation programmes were a blanket solution to a complex problem. As a result, there was overreliance and overemphasis on them. This came at a cost to other treatment and support options, with these being undervalued or ignored. Unfortunately, it required further offences and failures to occur, before different approaches were considered. Eventually, many countries have come to recognise that a toolkit of approaches is required, and *'putting all the eggs in one basket'* is not the answer. There have been many cases of success following participation in deradicalisation programmes and some programmes have proven to be effective, but they are not suitable for everyone.

A recent review of these programmes by researcher Douglas Weeks concluded:

'The reality is that there is no adoptable, singular, boilerplate program or approach that will guarantee success. Programs and approaches need to be matched to the individual, and they should be organically driven rather than ideologically or policy driven, holistic in nature, and the focus on the person, including his/her individual collective identity.'

Strangely, the dilemma around the effectiveness of deradicalisation programmes has parallels to the self-esteem movement which came to life in the 1990s.

Self-esteem, or more accurately a lack of it, was believed to be the reason for a range of adverse outcomes – from unhappiness through to criminality. Despite being heralded as the ultimate solution to all psychological problems, the relationship between self-esteem and positive outcomes *'was mixed, insignificant, or absent'*. When a range of research studies were eventually conducted, it was revealed that self-esteem was a by-product of many outcomes and processes, rather than being a direct cause. It wasn't that low self-esteem caused criminality, but instead through engaging in activities that were against social norms, harmful to others, and hurtful to oneself, low self-esteem occurred. Likewise, high self-esteem didn't directly lead to high performance, but through accomplishments and success, high self-esteem developed. Higher self-esteem seemed to emerge through greater happiness, social connection, and achievement, whilst low self-esteem coincided with failure, unhappiness, and social difficulties. Self-esteem was typically the by-product of other outcomes and factors, not the cause.

Similarly, the focus on deradicalisation assumes that someone is acting violently because they are radicalised. Perhaps, like self-esteem, radicalisation is a by-product of other factors, rather than the cause of violence. By focusing on deradicalisation, there's a danger that treatment becomes *'stuck in the weeds'* and fails to address the factors that led to an individual gradually climbing up the staircase to commit an offence. As outlined in the staircase model, it is often events within the person's life that cause them to begin climbing the staircase. Radicalisation, or the adoption of extremist beliefs, often occurs along the way, when other options and solutions fail or don't prevail.

To ensure effective change, the pathway to violence must be understood within its entirety. Violence often provides a way out. It is a dysfunctional way to resolve problems. Sometimes it's fuelled by extreme beliefs or cultural views, in other instances it's the only way to regain a sense of power and control.

In many ways, deradicalisation and disengagement programmes seem to have fallen short because they focus only on the top levels of the staircase, rather than starting at the beginning and understanding why the person commenced their journey to begin with.

The FBI's BAU-1 observed, *'For an extremist to deradicalize, he or she must discard their violent ideological identity and adopt a new identity. This identity change is, by its nature, going to be internal to the individual and may be influenced but not forged.'* Changing violently extremist beliefs requires a process of transformation, which occurs when a person begins to question themselves, their beliefs, and the world around them. It is an individualised process and not something that can be forced or compelled through a programme.

15

A Fight For Survival

'Darkness cannot drive out darkness; only light can do that. Hate cannot drive out hate; only love can do that.'

Martin Luther King Jr

AT SIXTEEN YEARS OF AGE, Aaron Stark planned to carry out a mass shooting.

His childhood had been turbulent, chaotic, and traumatic. His father had returned from the Vietnam War and took the trauma of the war out on his family. There were many violent altercations between his parents, along with frequent changes in living circumstances, interactions with the police, and regular alcohol abuse. When his parents finally separated, the violence continued, and his stepfather introduced his mother to a lifestyle of drugs and crime. Over the coming years, a lifestyle emerged where his mother and stepfather would lose their jobs, get evicted, flee the area, get a new house, get new jobs, lose those jobs, and get evicted again. This cycle continued for several years, until eventually the family settled in Denver, Colorado. Throughout his childhood, Aaron and his older brother were continually exposed to drug use, violence, and crime.

At school, Aaron struggled to fit in and was riddled by self-doubt and a lack of confidence. He was overweight, unwashed, unkept, and unappealing. He was bullied and beaten, and he had little interest in popular school activities. Instead, he found solace in reading, music, choir, and video games. Aaron made very few friends, although there was one friend, Mike, who accepted him for who he was. In his friendship with Mike, Aaron didn't need to act tough or behave like a rebel to impress him, he could just be himself.

At fourteen, following an argument with his stepfather, Aaron was kicked out of the family home. Faced with being homeless, he slept on Mike's couch for several weeks. However, eventually Mike's parents became concerned and Aaron had to leave. When he could, he would sleep on someone's couch. Often, he was left to sleep on benches, in the bush, and even on concrete paths. It was a life that no child or teenager should ever be exposed to.

As the burden of being homeless intensified, Aaron's mental health declined, and he withdrew further from others and was often isolated and alone. He eventually dropped out of school, unable to face other students and the academic demands. Aaron felt unloved and unwanted, with no home and no sense of belonging. As he reached sixteen, he was overwhelmed with anger. Anger at the world, and anger at himself. He also harboured a deep sense of sadness. Aaron turned to harming himself and knew that if he didn't seek help, he was going to end his life.

In recounting his situation during his 2018 TEDx talk, Aaron stated:

'I'm sitting there with my arm covered in blood, knowing that if I didn't do something I was going to kill myself soon. So, I did the only thing I could think of to do, I grabbed a phone book and I called social services. So, then I went to social services, sadly they didn't just bring me in, they also took my mum in there too, who happened to be one of the largest sources of my pain growing up. And since she had spent her entire life running from place to place and dealing with social workers and police officers, she knew exactly what to say to get me, to get them, to

believe that I was just making it all up. It was all just an act; I was just doing it for attention.

'Then they sent me home with her. And as they sent me home with her, she turned to me and said, "Next time you should do a better job and I'll buy you the razor blades.

'My heart just got ripped out of me at that point completely. That darkness that I had been staring at for so long, I just ran head long into it. I had nothing left to live for, I literally had nothing to lose. And when you have nothing to lose, you have everything, you can do anything, and that is a terrifying thought.

'I decided my act of doing something was I was going to express my extreme anger and rage by getting a gun.

'I was going to attack either my school or a mall food court. It really didn't matter to me which one, it wasn't about the people, it was about the largest amount of damage in the shortest amount of time, with the least amount of security. Both those places were the right targets.'

Aaron set out to purchase a gun. As he was under eighteen years of age, he was too young to buy a firearm at a store, and he was fearful of alerting others to his plan. He sought out a local gang who dealt drugs to his family and asked to purchase a gun. He was not raised around guns, so approaching the gang was the only idea he could think of to acquire a weapon. In exchange for cannabis, one of the gang members was happy to assist him and told him that they would be in touch in three days. Whilst he waited, Aaron began to get his affairs in order, as he intended to be killed during the attack. He wanted to inflict as much damage as possible and to humiliate his parents by leaving them to deal with the fallout. Aaron reached out to people that he hadn't spoken to for some time, including his ex-girlfriend and some friends. He made amends with several people, apologised for any wrongdoings, and even thanked them for any support over the years. On the third day, when he was meant to get the gun, he made his final stop at Mike's house.

When Mike opened the door, Aaron was in tears and crying. Mike took Aaron inside, fed him, and the pair watched a movie together. Mike never asked Aaron what was wrong, but he gave him unconditional support. He supported Aaron even after he had stolen from him and abused him months earlier. Mike recognised that Aaron was in trouble and struggling. He convinced his parents to let Aaron stay, and over the coming weeks Aaron had the basic necessities in life again.

Mike's actions stopped Aaron from carrying out the shooting, and he never picked up the gun. He treated Aaron like an equal and provided him with respect and compassion.

According to Aaron, *'Even when every other person in my world pushed me away – and they did – Mike never treated me like anything other than a person worthy of love and happiness.'* Mike gave Aaron the faith in humanity that he had lost.

Aaron never carried out his mass shooting. Although he was able to step back from the edge of the cliff, his mental health issues continued over the coming years.

On the night of his nineteenth birthday, he was again contemplating suicide. He no longer wanted to harm others but still was unable to accept himself. Aaron had planned to overdose on drugs to end his life.

Remarkably, Mike saved Aaron again.

On that evening, Mike contacted Aaron and invited him over to his friend's home. When Aaron arrived at the residence, he walked into a surprise birthday party for him. He was welcomed into the home with a group of friends singing happy birthday and a freshly baked blueberry peach pie.

Later in the evening, Aaron threw the drugs away that he had intended to overdose on.

He never tried to commit suicide again and over the next ten years he rebuilt his life.

AARON'S STORY HIGHLIGHTS THAT CHANGE IS POSSIBLE. Back in 1996, when Aaron was planning his attack, he fell through the cracks of government services, and his mother knew how to play the system.

He needed someone to step in and recognise the situation for what it had become. Aaron was in and out of programmes, services, schools, and homes. No one stopped to examine his circumstances, or to see him as a person that was desperate for love and acceptance. The agencies that were meant to support him failed. It took acts of kindness and compassion to prevent Aaron from harming himself and others.

A plan to carry out a mass attack wasn't formed by Aaron because he was a violent person, or because he was radicalised and held extreme beliefs or ideologies. His plans to carry out violence arose because he was suffering and lacked the resources, support, skills, and abilities to change his life. He was powerless to change his circumstances and ultimately at the mercy of others. Fortunately, Mike recognised just how vulnerable and distressed Aaron had become.

Aaron perceived that his livelihood and well-being were at threat and he was unable to find a way out. To him, violence was the only option to regain some control over his life and make others recognise his distress.

In 2018, the Power Threat Meaning Framework was proposed by psychologists Lucy Johnstone and Mary Boyle to explain *'why'* and *'how'* people like Aaron may resort to violence. According to the authors, people are hardwired to live meaningful and connected lives; yet, along the way, these basic needs get impacted or hindered. Some people are able to adjust and have the resources and skills to respond to the setbacks – others are trapped, stuck, and lost.

When basic needs are thwarted, people can respond in a range of maladaptive and harmful ways, with violence one of the many possibilities.

Some of the many destructive ways may include drug use, avoidance, gambling, infidelity, risk taking, aggression, defiance, overworking, berating a spouse, lashing out at others, and so on. All of these problematic responses are common ways that people try to cope with setbacks and hardships in life. Violence is just another option, and another path that a person can choose to take.

As explained by the staircase and bathtub models, violence begins as a thought and potential solution. Only over time does this become the ultimate answer.

According to forensic and clinical psychologist Caroline Logan, once violence becomes the solution and answer, *'a person decides that a harmful act is an acceptable, necessary and proportionate response ... they decide that a violent act will achieve what is required – it is the right response for the situation – and the negative consequences of using violence are ones they can live with'.*

Johnstone and Boyle believe that a set of questions help explain why someone chooses violence over other solutions:

- What has happened to you? How have you lost your power and independence?
- How did it affect you? What threats have you been exposed to and in what way?
- What sense did you make of it? What meaning did you derive from these experiences?

- What did you have to do to survive it? What kind of threat response did you need to use?

Aaron Stark was exposed to endless uncertainty and threats throughout his childhood. His upbringing shared many similarities to that of fourteen-year-old Colt Gray, who also experienced constant instability, uncertainty, and trauma in his childhood. Like Gray, Aaron was desperate for recognition and to feel as though he mattered. He was also desperate to change his external environment and to find a way out of the life he was living. Despite Aaron's efforts to improve his circumstances, he was defeated, angry and distraught. His plans to carry out a shooting were intended to make people stop and recognise him – to recognise his suffering and distress.

The threat framework suggests that violence often emerges as a last resort response. It is a last resort response because other alternative options have failed – or at least are perceived to have failed. Last resort thinking and behaviour suggests a person has reached a point of no return and is willing to accept the consequences of acting violently.

The path to violence has a starting point which is typically a loss of power and autonomy following a humiliation, loss, or experience of ostracism. It also has an end point – when a person perceives that there are no other options to resolve their current situation and violence is the last resort.

The starting point and the end point matter.

While there are many steps in between, such as planning and preparation, these two points can serve as crucial guideposts for police and threat teams. When someone starts on the pathway to violence and experiences a loss of power and independence, there is ample opportunity for early intervention and prevention to occur. In contrast, when someone is at the end and has reached a point of last resort, then an urgent and immediate response is required to prevent harm from occurring. When police receive information on a person of concern, it's essential to determine where the individual is placed on the pathway to violence. When police or other teams are able to identify the presence of a *'starting event'* coupled up with *'last resort'* tendencies, this should signal an immediate concern. Not only should this be concerning for police and threat teams, but it also may prove to be a vital warning signal for family, friends, or other bystanders who are acquainted with the person.

Evidence of last resort thinking and behaviour following a loss, humiliation, or setback, highlights that prevention and intervention are required regardless of whether other warning behaviors are present. It shows the person has suffered and that they perceive that there are no solutions to resolve their circumstances.

Lone actor attacks occur because of an inability or unwillingness to pursue alternatives. The threat framework highlights that there are universal ways to understand the *'how'* and *'why'* of violence.

It's idealistic to think that every concerning person can be adequately supported to find better solutions and strategies to their problems, but it does raise questions of what can be done to solve this dilemma. What can be done to improve the capabilities of people to choose prosocial options, to overcome obstacles, and to assist them in a time of crisis?

Maybe the answer lies with government. Maybe it's solvable through the media and big tech. Maybe it's about helping people to live better lives.

16

Government Dilemmas

'Government exists to protect us from each other. Where government has gone beyond its limits is in deciding to protect us from ourselves.'

Ronald Reagan

MARTIN BRYANT WALKED INTO the Broad Arrow Café at the historical Port Arthur site in Tasmania carrying a large sports bag on 28 April 1996. The café was crowded and Bryant ordered a meal and sat down to eat his lunch. Shortly after finishing his food, he pulled his Colt AR-15 semi-automatic rifle out of his sports bag and pointed it at a nearby couple who were seated at a table across from him. Bryant commenced firing. He killed multiple people inside the café within minutes. Bryant then exited the café and began hunting down other people at the site, shooting at anyone who crossed paths with him.

Despite arriving to Port Arthur in his own vehicle, Bryant car-jacked a BMW 7 Series, shooting the owners. He transferred the items from his car into the new vehicle, including additional ammunition, rope, two sets of handcuffs, and several fuel containers. As Bryant drove away from the site, he encountered a couple in their car near a local service station. Bryant confronted the couple at gunpoint and whilst holding his firearm at the male driver, Glenn Pears, Bryant pulled the female passenger, Zoe Hall, from the car and forced her into his vehicle. When Glenn tried to intervene, Bryant pushed him over and then demanded that he get into the boot of the BMW. During this saga, Zoe tried to escape, resulting in Bryant shooting her.

Bryant returned to his stolen vehicle, with Glenn locked inside the boot, and resumed his journey. He fired at several cars as he continued to drive, before arriving at the Seascape guesthouse. Earlier that morning, before travelling to the Port Arthur historical site, Bryant had killed the elderly owners of the guesthouse where he was staying. On arriving back at his accommodation, Bryant dragged Glenn inside the apartment and handcuffed him to the stairs. He then set the car on fire and bunkered down inside the property. Over the next eighteen hours, Bryant remained in a stand-off with police, using his hostage as bargaining power. He made numerous demands, including requesting a helicopter, and repeatedly discharged multiple firearms during the negotiation period, with it being estimated that he discharged in excess of 150 shots in various directions. Eventually, Bryant set the building on fire and attempted to escape amongst the commotion; however, police observed him fleeing and apprehended him. Sometime during the stand-off, Bryant killed Glenn.

Bryant's ruthless and callous attack resulted in the deaths of thirty-five people and injuries to another twenty-three.

The aftermath of the Port Arthur massacre was marked by shock and grief. Amongst the Australian public and also politicians, there was a determination to prevent such a tragedy from ever happening again. Within days of the attack, the Australian Prime Minister at the time, John Howard, spearheaded a push for sweeping gun reforms. In a rare show of unity, all Australian states and territories agreed to the National Firearms Agreement (NFA). This landmark legislation introduced some of the strictest gun control measures in the world.

Under the NFA, automatic and semi-automatic firearms were banned, and all firearms had to be registered. A strict licensing system was implemented, requiring owners to demonstrate a genuine reason for gun ownership and undergo thorough background checks, including mental health evaluations. The reforms were accompanied by a gun buyback programme funded by the Australian government, which saw over 650,000 firearms surrendered and destroyed.

The impact of the gun reforms was profound. Gun-related deaths in Australia, including homicides and suicides, declined significantly in the years following the massacre. Importantly, there have been no mass shootings of the same scale since the NFA was introduced. The tragedy of Port Arthur demonstrated the power of collective action in response to a horrendous event – it showed that governments can have an effective role in preventing mass violence.

GOVERNMENTS ARE ABLE TO SHAPE society, culture, and people for the better or worse. They can empower, enable, prohibit, and restrict people. The responses of countries and their governments to terrorism and lone actor violence are often highly emotive and political. Governments need to be seen to be doing something, yet sometimes these responses are ill-conceived and inadequate. In other instances, responses can be intrusive, extreme, and disproportionate to the situation.

In recent decades, the events of 11 September 2001 undoubtedly resulted in one of the most significant government responses in history. The terrorist attacks in the USA, particularly the devastating attack on the Twin Towers in New York, resulted in fundamental changes across society in response to the event. This included significant military responses in Iraq and Afghanistan, thousands of extra lives being lost, changes to airline protocols, the establishment of counterterrorism policing units across multiple countries, changes to immigration policies, collaborative intelligence relationships, financing of new departments and positions, and an increase in data collection and surveillance of citizens. The response to the attacks changed the foundation for much of Western society, and caused conflict, devastation, and unrest in much of the Middle East.

Many states and countries collaborated and coordinated in policies and law-ratifications post 9/11, with considerable international pressure pushing changes to police powers, criminal law, and the prioritisation of national security over civilian rights. Some of the changes that were adopted included, *'sharpened penalties for terrorist acts, prohibiting financing of terrorist activities, banning preparation of terrorist acts by conspiring with others, further criminalization of providing training methods that could be used in terrorist acts, and, lastly, increased leeway for the usage of surveillance methods'*. The response to 9/11 was drastic. It led to figureheads such as Osama bin Laden, Saddam Hussein, and Abu Bakr al-Baghdadi eventually being killed, but hundreds of US soldiers lost their lives. The US dismantled Al-Qaeda and to some extent IS; however, *The Washington Post* recently remarked, *'Rather than exemplify the nation's highest values, the official response to 9/11 unleashed some of its worst qualities ...'*

Like the US, New Zealand employed widespread changes in the wake of Brenton Tarrant's attacks in Christchurch. Following the attack, the government placed heavy restrictions on firearm access, with semi-automatic weapons restricted, and new licencing conditions for weapon ownership established. The changes to firearms access mirrored the Australian response following Bryant's attack in 1996. Alongside this, as mentioned, government officials refused to report Tarrant's name, referring to him only as *'The Terrorist'*. The government also classified his manifesto as an illegal document within New Zealand, making it a criminal offence to possess a copy.

An inquest into the Christchurch attack was also undertaken to comprehensively review the response of the police, government agencies, and other departments, ultimately generating a series of findings and recommendations which spanned over 900 pages. As a result, a new firearms agency was established, a new prison facility was developed, mandatory reporting processes for firearm incidents were implemented, policies were changed, funding to some departments increased (arguably at a cost to others), aspects of the terrorism legislation were amended, and multiple changes occurred across the counterterrorism infrastructure, including funding for early prevention.

The response to the Christchurch attack focused on restrictive and concerted measures to create change. In contrast, the response to 9/11 was on a far greater scale, intent on achieving international order and control. Inevitably, no matter which path is taken, some citizens will be pleased by governmental decision-making, and others outraged.

MANY COUNTRIES HAVE NOW DEVELOPED succinct and marketable strategies to explain their approaches to preventing mass casualty attacks. In the UK, the **PREVENT** model has been widely publicised and promoted. Consisting of four pillars, the model promotes the objectives of **Prevent**, **Pursue**, **Protect**, and **Prepare**. The first pillar, *Prevent*, emphasises the importance of reducing intent and safeguarding people from becoming involved in violence. The next step, *Pursue*, aims to reduce the capability of those who intend to offend, ultimately stopping attacks before they happen. *Protect* focuses on reducing the vulnerabilities across the UK for attacks to occur, through a variety of means such as target hardening, or making access to highly frequented locations more difficult. Lastly, the fourth pillar, *Prepare*, seeks to reduce the impact of an attack when it occurs, ensuring that strategies, resources, and methods of mitigation are ready and available when required.

Likewise in Australia, a similar four-step model has been implemented by the government through the **Safeguarding Our Community Together** strategy. The model is founded on four principles, **Prevent**, **Prepare**, **Respond**, and **Recover**. Bearing many resemblances to the four UK pillars, *Prevent* works to divert and disengage those with intent or extreme views, and ensures that intelligence and police resources are used to investigate and disrupt individuals or groups. *Prepare* centres on empowering communities, law enforcement, and other agencies to have greater awareness, capabilities, and capacity to service concerns when they arise. The third step, *Respond*, focuses on timely and efficient responses immediately following an attack, with this ranging from adequate police staffing through to providing accurate and frequent communication to the public. The final step, *Recover*, emphasises the need for readily available services and support options to assist affected people, to ensure that communities are able to function, and that learnings and lessons are reviewed in the wake of an attack.

The strategies and initiatives developed by governments determine how countries or states allocate their resources, funding, and services. Put crudely, these are typically *'a bang for the buck'* approach, intended to reduce the likelihood of harm and to ensure that most citizens are protected. It's impossible for governments to protect everyone, to finance and fund everything, and to establish endless services and agencies dedicated to addressing problems.

In recent decades, there have been widespread changes to the counterterrorism policies across countries. Generally speaking, most governments have expanded their powers through enhanced legislations, laws, and police capabilities. These changes have occurred in the interest of protecting national security and creating a safer society. Although governments provide no guarantee of citizens being entirely safe, they are unwilling to accept acts of terrorism or other similar attacks being perpetrated. Therefore, to ensure the safety of the community and to prevent attacks, increased security measures and greater governmental control have emerged as the solution.

Unfortunately, the pursuit of safety and reduction in violence comes at a cost to the civil rights of citizens.

Terrorism is typically viewed as an attack on society as a whole and therefore represents a threat to the way of life as we know it. To combat this, governments have introduced extraordinary measures to stop attackers in their tracks and to intervene before they are able to mobilise to violence. Although democracy relies on a state or country being governed by its people, terrorism typically provides governments with the ability to act outside of the traditional regulations and principles of democracy – security and safety trumps personal rights.

For more than two centuries, the **Old Protective Paradigm** has functioned as the sole model for criminal law. In essence, crimes were only punished after they'd been committed or attempted. A crime had to be perpetrated, or at least attempted for a person to be charged with an offence. In line with this approach, police investigations only commenced after the crime or incident. If an individual was attempting a crime, there was an onus on police to prove that the offence would have occurred. An example of this would be finding a person parked outside a bank, with a firearm, balaclava, and sketches of the bank layout. Although the robbery may not have occurred, there is ample evidence to suggest that the person was conspiring or attempting a robbery.

Following 9/11, the **New Protective Paradigm** emerged. The new paradigm was no longer about waiting for a crime to occur, it was about preventing it before it happened. In many ways, this approach embodied the idea of pre-active criminality, with the aim of identifying, responding, or apprehending before harm occurs. The pre-active approach to mass casualty attacks is to stop the individual before the crime. Although the intention is to provide prevention and support, as part of the new protective paradigm, several changes have been made to criminal laws. These changes now allow police to charge someone with preparing to carry out an attack. The challenge, however, lies in determining the intent behind the behaviour. For instance, buying fertiliser is a normal everyday activity, yet, on the rare occasion, it may be purchased to build a bomb rather than to nourish the vegetable garden. Working out this distinction is tricky and requires considerable investigative efforts to ensure that the person is intending to act, and not just curious, experimenting, or fantasising.

Criminal law has ventured into future-oriented predictions and probabilities, where suspecting intent is enough to apprehend and convict. As the saying goes, *'it's better to be safe than sorry'*.

Like many other countries, Norway made broad changes to their policies and criminal laws on terrorism in the aftermath of 9/11. Some of the changes included the adoption of the United Nations recommendations on terrorist financing, and modifications to the Norwegian Terrorist Act to criminalise the planning and preparation of terrorist acts through conspiring with others. This allowed for people to be charged with sharing ideas, information, or assisting in the preparation or organisation of an attack. Yet, the charge could only occur when an individual was conspiring or consorting with others. In the early 2000s, it was unimaginable that someone would carry out a solo, or lone actor attack. This all changed in 2011 when Anders Breivik carried out the attack which he had been meticulously planning for several years.

Despite stringent laws and legislation, Breivik fell through the cracks.

In the fallout from Breivik's attack, a Commission was established to examine how the attack was able to occur. The Commission outlined that even if Breivik was identified, he would have never been charged, due to operating in isolation, and never conspiring with others to carry out a terrorist attack. Consequently, in 2013, the law was again revised, stipulating that *'any person, with the intent to commit a terrorism offence and who undertakes actions that assist to facilitate the attack to the point of implementation will be punishable'*. Further changes were made over the coming years, and in 2016, Proposition 68L was passed into Norwegian law, granting expanded access to coercive measures for investigating, deterring, and preventing serious offences. The changes to the law allowed the police to utilise more intrusive methods, including communication control, searches, surveillance, camera monitoring, and technical tracking for preventive and protective purposes. Police and other intelligence services were granted unrestricted access to covert methods and techniques when there was suspicion that a serious offence might occur.

Ensuring the security of countries and states is high stakes and a controversial conundrum. The proactive approach to stop attackers in the preparation stage is a well-intentioned endeavour. But the effectiveness of this approach is reliant on governments making informed and critical decisions. As French author Voltaire wrote, *'with great power comes great responsibility'*. Unfortunately, governments often make decisions based on **Retrospective Predictability**, rather than **Prospective Predictability**.

In his book *The Black Swan*, Nassim Taleb spoke about retrospective predictability occurring when decisions about the future are made based on the past. Rather than viewing a situation as an anomaly and something that could not be controlled, this form of decision-making is prone to bias and overestimates the perceived predictability and patterns. Retrospective distortions lead decision-makers to perceive the future as being of greater certainty, where the same patterns and opportunities for intervention will emerge.

Based on the retrospective thinking, the answer to preventing the next lone actor or terrorist attack lies in addressing the shortcomings and failures arising from the last attack. At first glance, this approach sounds effective and worthwhile, yet, as Marianne Angvik observed in her dissertation, *'Continuously trying to prevent the last attack from occurring, in reality, makes one badly prepared for a new attack.'*

In contrast, prospective predictability seeks to understand the broader patterns and trends which may shape future attacks, and therefore influence future predictions. Prospective decisions require considerable data and well-defined parameters to ensure that any predictions and plans are based on evidence, rather than bias and assumptions. For instance, going back to the scenario of purchasing fertiliser, *'at an early stage of preparing for a terrorist attack, the terrorist's activities may not differentiate that much from normal activities. There may be many people doing similar activities without intending to do something criminal. There can be a lot of threats to look into when trying to establish who is intending to do something criminal, and who is not.'*

A prospective approach would seek to understand the role of the fertiliser specifically for a given individual, rather than having all fertiliser purchases tracked and monitored in the hope of identifying someone who is purchasing it for harmful reasons. The prospective approach is similar to that embraced by threat assessment, where research and evidence informs the development of the threat assessment tool, while careful analysis and inquiry is used to complete the assessment. It is a process of making finely attuned adjustments when required, rather than using broad and blanketed approaches.

The tendency of governments to favour retrospective responses typically results in more restrictions, policies, laws, and legislation. These increase governmental powers under the promise of making future offending more difficult. These approaches are typically targeted at the masses and rarely account for outliers – such as those that may use a different method of offending for a future attack.

Retrospective approaches of course can be beneficial, such as the decisions to restrict firearm access in countries like Australia and New Zealand. While controversial, these decisions have prevented many further incidents of gun violence. When compared to the USA, per capita these measures have been remarkably effective at reducing attacks which are perpetrated with firearms.

Governments also allocate funding to the police and other organisations who are able to facilitate preventative efforts focused on early intervention and psychological change. Although some police forces across countries still continue to employ an enforcement approach, the development and funding of specialised threat and police teams has resulted in prospective practices. As spoken about, many teams utilise threat assessment tools and information-sharing systems, which have been carefully designed to identify the warning behaviours or red flag indicators. Through bringing this practice to policing, it has become possible to separate the wheat from the chaff and identify who may actually be of concern.

Governments have also enabled other endeavours such as reporting hotlines, the development of treatment programmes, training and education for professionals, research, internet moderation of extreme content, and public space protection through barriers and bollards. These are great initiatives – yet scrutiny and reviews still remain important.

In late 2023, the Australian government announced the Healthy Masculinities Project, funding a three-year trial to reshape the attitudes of young males. The project was touted as an innovation to *'tackle the insidious impact of social media messaging targeting young men and boys, with the primary aim of eradicating gender stereotypes perpetuated online and promoting a culture of respect and supportive relationships among peers'*. Any endeavour that intends to reduce violence and provide greater education and understanding to young people is positive. However, rolling out a masculinities project offers no guarantee of changing men or their attitudes. Funding programmes and initiatives is great, but without careful oversight and refinement, these can fall short and have little to no impact. In many ways, one of the biggest challenges for governments is in the execution, specifically how well any initiative or approach is executed and conducted.

Governments are the archetypal example of a **System**. System-level responses are typically targeted at the masses and seek to control or limit the extent of the problem. It takes a lot to change a system, and this level of response often occurs in reaction to significant events, or when there is a need to keep structure, order, and processes in place. The most recent example of a system-level response was the range of measures implemented during the COVID-19 pandemic, from lockdowns, mask wearing, vaccinations, and other prohibiting orders. These measures were carried out by governments and other agencies at a mass societal level, targeted at populations, and intended to have a widespread response. System responses are broad and universal, seeking to maximise outcomes by affecting change at a societal or sub-population level.

The system often does not account for individual needs or requirements, and works on the principle *'what is good for everyone is good for you'*. In contrast, the **Individual** level is focused on identifying the root causes, attributes, or characteristics associated with the problem and targeting these to produce change. This type of response seeks to understand the issue, solve the problem, and make change. It's about what will work for the individual, what is required to intervene, and tailoring the response to the unique circumstances. For instance, much of medicine is based on a systems approach to illness, whereby widespread interventions are utilised to treat disease. However, specialist surgeons will tailor their operation and treatment plan to the patient. Some doctors and medical clinics also strive to enhance the health of their patients in the absence of disease, by focusing on improving their health and developing their individual capabilities to function optimally, in lieu of waiting for illness to strike.

To adequately respond to problems and create change, a continual interaction and feedback process needs to occur between the individual and system levels. In essence, the individual level should inform the system, and in turn, the system should effectively support the individual. Through this cycle, a gradual refinement and adjustment should occur, whereby gaps, challenges, and shortcomings at the individual level filter through to changes at the system level. In a perfect world, a harmonious relationship exists between both levels, like a yin and yang, adjusting and changing to ensure balance and equilibrium. However, in reality, the interaction between the system and the individual is often fragmented, disjointed, and reactive.

Governments will always face dilemmas with their responses and decisions. It's often about costs and benefits. The governments put frameworks in place, but each person has different needs, challenges, and vulnerabilities. There are many factors that can influence violence, and societal efforts to control these – while well intentioned – often fail to understand there are many layers to behaviour. You can make it harder to offend, but ultimately, you want to get to the cause – to the very origin of *'why'* and *'how'* the behaviour developed.

Marianne Angvik articulately summed up the need for governments to critically question their role in preventing mass attacks, proclaiming, *'one can never create an entirely safe society and that humans must accept that they have to live with some degree of threat and uncertainty. We have an illusion that we can protect ourselves 100 percent from terrorism when reality proves otherwise ... More security measures and governmental control are thus not necessarily the answer to all threats ... it becomes paramount to look at the larger picture of already implemented measures to determine whether new measures will, in fact, be effective, and not undermine society's liberal values and principles in the process, due to political pressures of urgency. In short, one must be careful not to overestimate one's ability to predict the future.'*

There's a danger that by implementing extensive measures to combat terrorism and other attacks, governments actually destabilise a democracy. Governments can create the exact problem they're trying to prevent.

Many governments have made considerable advances in their response to mass attacks, but there are still many challenges ahead.

Of course, then there's the media and big tech.

17

The Power Of Media

'The media's the most powerful entity on earth. They have the power to make the innocent guilty and to make the guilty innocent, and that's power.'

Malcolm X

OVER TWENTY-FIVE YEARS HAS PASSED since the Columbine High School attack on 20 April 1999. Since then, the infamy of Eric Harris and Dylan Klebold has proven remarkably enduring, fuelled by a potent combination of sensationalist media coverage and an endless range of material circulating on the internet. Notably, *'Columbine'* has become a byword for school shootings, and the digital age has further cemented the attackers' legacy – providing a platform for their writings, videos, and other materials to reach audiences far beyond what was possible in 1999. Certain corners of the internet have provided Harris and Klebold with cult-like status, portraying them as anti-heroes or martyrs.

The mainstream media's periodic revisiting of Columbine – whether in the context of anniversaries, comparisons to other attacks, or broader discussions on gun violence, continues to further the infamy of Harris and Klebold. Adding to this, documentaries, books, and movies have further perpetuated their notoriety, with each retelling exposing new generations to their violence.

Harris and Klebold are searched by thousands of people daily on the internet. The pair are viewed as anti-heroes and rebels who fought back against society. As a result, a whole array of online subculture on the individuals is spread across numerous platforms. There are artistic tributes, drawings, memes, and photographs of the two shooters. Common symbols include black trench coats, firearms, Harris's *'Natural Selection'* T-shirt which he wore during the attack, and references to the shooters' writings. These communities thrive on platforms like Tumblr, Reddit, and Discord, where extensive archives of Columbine-related materials, from journal excerpts to crime scene photos, are shared and discussed.

Author Mark Follman believes the legacy of the perpetrators has inspired more than a hundred further mass attacks.

SINCE THE COLUMBINE ATTACK, mass casualty events, particularly mass shootings, have become commonplace in the media. These tragedies consume days of media coverage, and endless hours each day are devoted to the attack. For instance, with the frequency of mass shootings in the USA, the constant stream of media has led to mass attacks becoming normalised – another day, another attack.

In a recent article, journalist Abené Clayton remarked, *'News coverage of high-profile mass shootings on American cable news has adopted near clockwork patterns: first comes shock and the scramble for information, followed by calls from communities and legislators for new gun restrictions, then reporting and speculation about the motives of the shooter ("Is evil or mental illness to blame?"). The remainder of the time is spent toggling between analysis of why the US sees these shootings so regularly, how the shooter got their gun and which signs of violence could have been noticed earlier. Rinse and repeat.'*

In addition to the mainstream media coverage, there are a barrage of articles, videos, photos, and opinions which circulate online and through social media. It is virtually impossible to escape the frequent content on mass attacks. While some research has found that the media reporting does not increase the prevalence of mass attacks, other studies have shown that media coverage has significantly enhanced the notoriety of perpetrators and propagated their grievances or ideologies across the domestic and international landscape. Certainly, the majority of people are not being influenced to commit an attack after viewing this through the media – but it only takes one person to be inspired by this content for an attack to transpire. There are currently no international policies or agreements between media outlets on the reporting of mass attacks and lone actors, meaning that no consensus or uniformed approach can be undertaken to change the way that these incidents are covered.

Of course, media outlets can't control the myriad of content that circulates online, which is an entirely different echo system to news-related content. Like the media-based news, content that is sensational, glorified, and divisive typically garners the most views and captures attention.

Following the Christchurch terrorist attack, the then New Zealand Prime Minister Jacinda Ardern established the Christchurch Call in conjunction with French President Emmanuel Macron. The New Zealand government was able to work alongside some social media companies in the immediate hours following the attack, resulting in an estimated 1.5 million copies of Tarrant's attack video being removed online – highlighting what could be achieved through coordinated efforts.

In late 2019, Ardern and Macron hosted a summit in Paris, bringing together world leaders and the heads of major technology companies. The mission of the summit was to eliminate extreme online content and to prevent this from being used by groups or individuals to prolongate violence. The collaborative approach sought to have governments and technology companies work alongside each other to moderate content, establish policies and laws for social media companies, and develop algorithms to detect extreme material.

Recently, the endeavour has spanned to include over fifty governments, the European Commission, an advisory board of academics, two major international organisations, and ten technology companies. Since governments and tech companies have commenced working together, several algorithms have been implemented to detect and remove extreme content more promptly, whilst various extreme material has been moderated or suppressed in certain countries, making it harder to view and locate. While the exact mechanisms of content moderation remain unclear, the initiative demonstrates that, through combined partnerships, there is now the capacity to respond to the online repercussions arising from an attack, shaping how material is distributed and shared online. Reading between the lines, this material can be quickly suppressed and the distribution reduced.

The relationship between governments and tech companies is complex and contentious. In recent years, technology and social media companies have developed increasing powers and capabilities to influence citizens – perhaps more so than governments. Although not wielding the same authority as governments, social media platforms and technology services have an unrivalled influence on the masses. Tech giants have enormous control over their platforms and are able to influence what information people view, hence the echo chamber effect. Algorithms are designed to preference controversial material, which grabs the attention of users and often results in strong reactions and engagements.

For years, social media companies have been a law unto themselves. Platforms have had their own guidelines on the appropriateness of content. It has even been found that some platforms have swayed content to preference and favour certain political parties and social agendas – biasing the information that people are able to view and presenting only one side of the argument.

Tech companies are powerful organisations and this has led to governments seeking to regulate this industry and encourage content moderation. Incredibly, *The Wall Street Journal* recently examined *'an almost dystopian scenario in which governments and tech firms coordinated to suppress unpopular views'*. The review uncovered that some organisations were pressured by the US government to monitor and suppress information which contradicted their agenda, proclaiming, *'government officials were essentially taking a hands-on role in silencing opinions they disagreed with'*. In a recent federal court ruling on the matter, the presiding judge concluded that the Biden administration and the US government likely violated the First Amendment throughout 2020 to 2023. Judge Terry. A. Doughty stated, *'During the COVID-19 pandemic, a period perhaps best characterised by widespread doubt and uncertainty, the United States Government seems to have assumed a role similar to an Orwellian Ministry of Truth.'*

The relationship truly is complex. Where government influence and content moderation should start and stop is a political minefield.

The Australian government has recently introduced landmark laws to ban social media use for people under sixteen years of age. The Online Safety Amendment (Social Media Minimum Age) Act 2024 prohibits individuals under sixteen from creating accounts on major social media platforms such as Facebook, Instagram, TikTok, Snapchat, Reddit, and X. The legislation requires social media companies to implement age verification measures to enforce this restriction, with non-compliance resulting in multi-million-dollar fines.

This legislative move was driven by escalating concerns over the mental health and safety of young Australians. The government cited studies linking social media use to increased anxiety, depression, and cyberbullying among teenagers. There have also been several tragic deaths of teenagers due to suicide over recent years, such as the December 2024 death of a twelve-year-old boy due to online bullying.

Florida, USA, has followed suit and recently implemented a new law restricting those under fourteen years accessing social media. In China, a *'youth mode'* was introduced on TikTok in 2021, limiting users under fourteen years of age to just forty minutes of daily use. The time restriction was intended to curb excessive screen time and promote healthier online habits. Likewise, South Korea enacted the *'Cinderella Law'* several years earlier in 2011, which prohibited online gaming for individuals under sixteen between 12.00 a.m. and 6.00 a.m.

While the Parliament of Australia has approved the new law, it will not come into place until late 2025. Although many have welcomed the change, others have vehemently argued against the restrictions. Somewhat surprisingly, Christopher Stone, the executive director of Suicide Prevention Australia, a large non-profit organisation, has argued that the legislation risks placing more young Australians at harm. Stone described the new laws as being rushed and reckless and approved without sufficient evidence-based research to support the policy. *'Social media provides vital connections for many young Australians, allowing them to access mental health resources, peer support networks, and a sense of community. Cutting off this access risks exacerbating feelings of loneliness and isolation,'* said Stone.

Implementing such a policy without research and evidence begins to sound like a retrospective response rather than a prospective response. Of course, the Australian government may end up using research and evidence to guide the implementation of the law, given that a year has been allowed before it becomes official – offering the promise of a prospective approach. As the saying goes, the devil is in the details.

Children and adolescents are vulnerable and require safeguards. There are laws around the age of alcohol consumption and when it is safe to drive a car.

Surely, social media is no different. Learning how to safely use social media and to make discerning decisions about content seems important. There's clearly an upside to protecting children. Limiting the use of social media will no doubt help many adolescents with their mental health, but it's unclear whether this will do anything to reduce violent extremism. Whilst social media certainly promotes extremist material, there is nothing stopping teenagers from accessing Discord, Reddit, 4chan, and many of the other platforms where this material is widely available. It may create some minor barriers, but the internet is a wide web of content that exists beyond just social media. This also won't stop adults.

Bruno Dias points out that if you Google *'I want to be a school shooter'*, a range of websites and Wikipedia entries immediately pop up with details about perpetrators, previous attacks, and much more. Interestingly, though, as Dias notes, when you search *'I want to shoot myself'*, instantly various Lifeline support services and contact details appear at the top of the search list, redirecting the person towards help. Those same support options occur for other search terms such as *'I want to hit my wife'* and *'I am thinking about sex abuse'*. In this instance, it's clear content moderation around searching for school shootings and other lone actor violence would benefit.

It is evident that there needs to be clear guidelines governing search engines, social media, and other platforms. Violent content moderation is essential on social media platforms. Without these, attack videos such as Brenton Tarrant's spread virally within hours. There are many bad actors and angry individuals that strive to create controversy and upset others online. Tech companies must develop functions and algorithms to identify violent material within minutes, something which has been a focus of the Christchurch Call. In addition to this, threats to kill on social media platforms or forums should be flagged and referred through to the police or relevant threat teams within technology organisations, so that they may be able to further investigate the comments. There is already widespread monitoring and surveillance of user comments on social media platforms for marketing purposes, so it can be done. Extending these algorithms to threats would assist in capturing a cohort of individuals who are victimising others or experiencing grievances which require support.

There is no place for threats of violence, regardless of whether this occurs online or offline.

In summing up the role of tech firms in preventing violence, Bruno Dias recommended '*a framework should be created for users to appeal content removal decisions, balancing free speech with safeguarding against misinformation and harmful material. This multifaceted approach could help create a safer, more accountable online ecosystem while preserving essential free thinking and expression elements*'. People need to be able to freely express their views, but they cannot be threatening or encourage violence.

So far, technology companies have implemented various measures to combat the spread of extremist content online. For instance, Facebook has utilised artificial intelligence to detect and remove terrorist propaganda, claiming to have achieved a 99% success rate in removing flagged content. Similarly, the European Union introduced the Digital Services Act in 2022, mandating platforms to remove illegal content, including extremist material, within twenty-four hours or face substantial fines. YouTube also made significant changes in 2019, adjusting its algorithms to limit the recommendation of conspiracy theories and harmful content. This reform led to a reported 70% reduction in views of extremist material, demonstrating the impact of algorithmic interventions in curbing the spread of such content.

Another dimension of the online content issue lies in the growing ubiquity of screens in our lives. The constant use of smartphones and social media has created environments where boredom, isolation, and anger can be easily channelled into increased use and reliance on devices and screens. Promoting healthier screen habits is essential to address this trend. Families, schools, and workplaces need to encourage screen-free zones, periods without technology use, and alternative activities that promote face-to-face interactions. Our lives are now set up around our devices, and by reducing the reliance on these, it's less likely that adverse outcomes will arise. Australian Prime Minister Anthony Albanese, who pushed for the social media age restriction, proclaimed, *'I want people to spend more time on the footy field or the netball court than they're spending on their phones.'*

Combatting technology is one thing, but media networks must also change. Clearly defined parameters need to exist for the media. By minimising sensationalist reporting, avoiding the publication of attackers' manifestos, and focusing instead on the victims and community impacts, the media can reduce the risk of copycat attacks and the contagion effect. Many media outlets are now able to reach wider audiences than ever before with the internet. Unfortunately, this has resulted in sensationalised headlines in an effort to go *'viral'* and grab people's attention.

Following the Parkland shooting at Marjory Stoneman Douglas High School by Nikolas Cruz, the families of the victims launched the *'No Notoriety'* campaign, urging news outlets to change the ways they reported attacks. The campaign argued for media organisations to not name perpetrators or show images of them. Advocates have reached out directly to media outlets, urging them to adopt policies that minimise attention on the perpetrators, instead requesting that the narratives focus on the victims, their families, and the impact of the violence.

Media organisations play a crucial role in giving attackers infamy. There needs to be agreed upon guidelines and principles for covering lone actor and mass attacks. These should ensure that the focus is on the victims and include a range of steps for reducing notoriety. It's tempting to believe that this can't be achieved, but it has been done before for suicide. The established guidelines for suicide reporting offer a valuable framework for achieving a shift in the narrative. Media reporting needs to be consistent with public messaging campaigns and government initiatives around mass violence. Government can't say one thing and then media do another. The end goal should be to build the awareness of the public and prevent this form of violence.

As already discussed in the chapter on Adam Lanza, in his *New Yorker* article, Andrew Solomon remarked, *'the reason that no one shoots twenty random children isn't self-restraint, it's that there is no level at which that idea is attractive'*.

Taking this a step further, at no level should the idea to murder multiple people ever be attractive.

It is time for more responsible media coverage and time to change the way technology is used in our lives. By reducing the reliance on devices, overcoming excessive social media use, and by shifting the narrative of media companies, then it becomes possible to help people live better lives.

18

Creating A Good Life

'The good life is a process, not a state of being. It's a direction not a destination.'

Carl Rogers

AARON STARK WAS IN A DARK PLACE throughout his childhood and into his early adulthood. Although he was moments away from carrying out a mass attack, his journey has been one of redemption, transformation, and empowerment. It took him several years, numerous challenges, and many more difficult moments. He is now married and a father to four children. Remarkably, Aaron now gives talks to audiences throughout America, sharing his story and educating others about the pathways to violence. After publicly sharing his story in 2018, his TEDx talk has been viewed more than 15 million times.

Redemption is a matter of determination and self-commitment. Aaron succeeded where many others have failed. His story shows that it's possible to live a good life. It's possible to change and it's possible to develop the missing ingredients to a good life.

Trying to prevent violence is not a new problem in society. Nor are the concepts of rehabilitation and change.

For decades, psychologists, psychiatrists, social workers, and other professionals have worked tirelessly to help people change their behaviour. Although lone actor violence is a new phenomenon sweeping across society, there are many lessons that can be learnt from the well-established approaches to treating and preventing sexual and violent offending.

Back in 1996, a landmark research project, titled the Liverpool Desistance Study, commenced in the UK. Over the course of two years, Professor Shadd Maruna interviewed sixty-five offenders aiming to understand why some were able to cease their offending, whilst others continued to perpetrate crimes. The study was focused on understanding the process of going straight and staying straight.

The research focused on two key concepts, **Desistance** and **Persistence**. Desistance from offending was defined as *'the long-term abstinence from crime among individuals who had previously engaged in persistent patterns of criminal offending'*. At the other end, persistence described those who were *'actively persisting with criminal pursuits'*.

To understand why offenders changed or remained the same, Professor Maruna explored the differences between thirty individuals who had desisted from crime and twenty offenders who continued to persist with breaking the law. All offenders had at one stage or another been considered as persistent offenders, committing crimes on a daily or weekly basis. However, those that had desisted from crime had been able to achieve two to three years *'clean'* without further offences.

Through interviews which spanned several hours, Professor Maruna found that change only occurred when offenders were able to make sense of their lives. Surprisingly, offenders made sense of their lives by constructing a new narrative, which allowed them to see the relationship between their crimes and their experiences of adversity in life. For most, criminality had emerged as a response to their undesirable life; yet, those who desisted were able to reframe their life story and form a redemption-oriented narrative. This in turn created a new sense of identity and motivation for change. In contrast, those that persisted with offending remained burdened by their experiences and were captive to a narrative and life story that centred on condemnation and being the victim of forces beyond their control.

Although those that desisted from offending had similar antisocial traits and a dislike for rules and regulations as the persistent offenders, they were able to develop greater control over their lives. While personality traits can often remain relatively stable throughout a person's life, the stories and narratives that they tell themselves are malleable and changeable. Professor Maruna found that desisting offenders were able to reinterpret and reshape their experiences. Rather than being defined by their crimes, they perceived themselves as being essentially a good person who through bad influences, unfortunate circumstances, and poor decisions, perpetrated criminal offences.

Despite many of the desisting offenders making excuses and justifications for their offending, they didn't fall into the trap of believing they were a victim. Instead, they came to believe that they were in control of their lives and had the power to change their circumstances and future. This sense of empowerment was characterised by the belief of *'making good'* and achieving purpose and meaning in life. Through this change in narrative, desisting offenders were able to develop a reshaped sense of identity, whereby they sought to learn new skills, seek positive relationships, act according to values, and contribute to the community.

However, this psychological shift was not found in those who continued to persist with offending. The persistent individuals were unable to develop a positive outlook for the future. Instead, they believed that their circumstances had been imposed on them and there was no way to break free. The idea of *'making good'* was a distant and fanciful dream. Many persistent offenders claimed they had already attempted their best life under the circumstances and it didn't work.

The Liverpool Desistance Study showed that change is possible and that people have a powerful role to play in shaping their future. The *medical model* suggests that through treatment, programmes, and rehabilitation, people's problems can be fixed and overcome, thereby resulting in desistance. In contrast, the *specific deterrence theory* proposes that incarceration results in lessons and learning, causing the person to choose a different life course to avoid returning to prison. It is likely that desistance may occur for both reasons. There are also other factors that may explain desistance, such as an older age, attaining stable employment, forming prosocial friendships, undertaking education, and finding supportive intimate relationships. Improved life conditions may help a person to make different choices and protect them from choosing bad ones.

The late sociologist Walter Gove suggested that for long-term change, a shift must occur in a person's thinking patterns. People must change their psychological make-up and become less self-absorbed and more aware of others and their place in the larger community. Gove described five key changes which needed to occur:

- A shift from self-absorption to concern for others.
- Increasing acceptance of societal values and behaving in socially appropriate ways.
- Increasing comfort with social relations.
- Increasing concern for others in the community.
- Increasing concern with the issue of meaning of life.

In a New Zealand-based study which also explored why offenders desisted from a life of crime, remarkably similar findings to Walter Gove's comments and Professor Maruna's findings were found. Julia Leibrich who authored the research, said, '*Although there do seem to be some differences between people who are going straight and those who are not, the differences do not lie in simple facts of life, but rather in the way that people interpret their lives.*' Leibrich went on to say, '*individuals exposed to the same environment experience it, interpret it, and react to it differently*'.

Change comes down to the individual. Professor Maruna explained, '*People construct stories to account for what they do and why they did it. These narratives impose an order on people's actions and explain people's behavior with a sequence of events that connect up to explanatory goals, motivations, and feelings. These self-narratives then act to shape and guide future behavior, as people act in ways that agree with the stories or myths they have created about themselves.*'

ONE OF THE BIGGEST REASONS that people fall into the trap of creating negative stories about themselves is due to failure. Often, a failure to achieve the basic needs of life. According to Professor Tony Ward, there are three basic needs which people require to live meaningful lives. The first, *Body Needs*, are physiological needs, things to help keep the body healthy and regulated. This includes food, water, warmth, sleep, and sex. The second, *Self Needs*, relate to emotional and psychological well-being, requiring the development of autonomy, competence, and relatedness. In other words, being able to have independence and freedom, the resolve to take on new challenges and undertakings, and the attributes to form connected and reciprocal relationships. The third and final need, *Social Life Needs*, concerns the opportunities and support that are available. This may involve having a supportive family or friendship group, or being able to pursue education, work, or other accomplishments. In essence, there must be an equal opportunity to pursue endeavours, rather than being restricted or deprived.

Pioneering the *Good Lives Model*, Professor Ward has proposed that a fulfilling life require ten primary ingredients, or primary goods, which ultimately satisfy the Body, Self, and Social Life needs. The Good Lives

Model suggests that when people have meaning and purpose in their life, along with an array of skills and resources, they are unlikely to commit crime, instead being happy and fulfilled. The key ingredients are:

- Life – Staying alive, safe, and physically healthy.
- Knowledge – Learning about one's self, others, and the world.
- Excellence in work and play – Seeking mastery across endeavours.
- Excellence in agency – Striving for independence and freedom.
- Inner peace – Achieving emotional stability and mitigating stress.
- Relatedness – Forming close and connected bonds with others.
- Community – Finding belonging and being a part of something.
- Spirituality – Pursuing interests which produce meaning.
- Happiness – Experiencing frequent states of positive emotion.
- Creativity – Trying new things and exploring different means.

These ingredients, which Professor Ward calls *Primary Goods*, are innate states, experiences, activities, and outcomes that people seek in life. Although somewhat confusing at first glance, Ward suggests that primary goods are in fact the outcomes or experiences which are attained through pursuing *Secondary Goods*. In essence, secondary goods are the choices, undertakings, and means through which primary goods are achieved. Let's say a person spends an enjoyable day with friends and family at a birthday party – this would likely foster relatedness and provide happiness. The secondary good in this instance would be the decision to spend time with family and attend the birthday party, rather than going to a bar and trying to find social connection. To achieve primary goods, a person must act in a manner that is consistent with the values and goals that relate to their primary goods. It's all about knowing what is important and acting in a way that is consistent with this. When someone takes shortcuts, fails to prioritise, avoids problems, or acts in other unhealthy ways, suddenly things can start to crumble.

There are four types of obstacles and barriers that typically prevent someone from being able to attain a primary good.

The first is when an individual uses *inappropriate or ineffective means* to achieve the good, such as frequenting a strip club in the hope of finding a wife. The next obstacle, a *lack of coherence*, relates to a person being inconsistent in the pursuit of primary good. For example, an individual may place emphasis on being a *'family man'* and also a good friend, parent, and partner. Yet, by trying to please everyone, they end up failing. Because of excessive socialising with friends, they're unable to meet their needs on the home front with their family. The next issue that can arise is a *lack of scope*, when certain primary goods dominate over others. Let's say someone values their fitness and health to the point of excess, neglecting other primary goods such as their personal relationships or enhancing their knowledge. Finally, some people are unable to attain key primary goods because of a *lack of capacity* to overcome the barriers or obstacles that may be in the way. This may be due to lower cognitive abilities, troubles with managing emotional states, poor problems solving skills, limited finances, and many other scenarios.

So, what does all this have to do with lone actors? Well, the Good Lives approach suggests that offending occurs because a person is unable to attain the basic things in life and resorts to problematic ways to achieve their primary goods. It is the secondary goods, as in the actions and choices that the person pursues, which are the problem. Offending is a dysfunctional and maladaptive solution to their problems – much like the threat framework. This may involve theft or drug selling as a means to get by and survive, or more serious crimes such as sexual or violent offending to satisfy other needs. Take for example sexual offending; from the Good Lives perspective, many sexual offences are the result of failed efforts to attain intimacy, connection, significance, and sexual gratification. Through factors such as a lack of capacity (e.g., poor social skills, tendency to become aggressive, and sense of entitlement) or even limited scope in needs (e.g., fixated on sexual and intimate needs at a cost to other primary goods), the person commits the offence.

To change behaviour and rehabilitate someone, the Good Lives approach focuses on increasing a person's capacity and enabling them to overcome their obstacles, rather than concentrating on their failures and shortcomings. It's a glass half full, rather than a glass half empty approach.

People have many strengths, qualities, and attributes which can be drawn on to help them overcome their obstacles and challenges. It is often the means and methods that the person has undertaken to satisfy their needs which are problematic and maladaptive. As Professor Ward points out, *'a violent man may seek the goods of intimacy and support through destructive and aggressive relationships. Moreover, the goods associated with positive self-regard may be sought through intimidation and aggressive actions.'*

The answer lies in helping people to enhance their strengths, capabilities, and skills, so that they are able to achieve their needs and goods in a prosocial and legal way. People do not need to deradicalise, they need to find better means and methods to live a good life. When this occurs, extreme beliefs will gradually fade away as other values and priorities take over.

If primary goods are the ingredients of life, then the recipe to create change among offenders, or those on the pathway to violence, is as follows:

1. Identify the risks relevant to the person and put support and strategies in place to reduce the exposure to these.
2. Determine the obstacles within the person's life (whether these be internal and/or external) which have prevented them from living a prosocial and fulfilling life.
3. Develop a comprehensive plan to equip the individual with the skills and capabilities to pursue primary goods in a different way.
4. Review and revise.

It sounds simple, maybe too simple.

Changing behaviour can be complex and straightforward. The first challenge lies in achieving clarity – identifying what needs to change and determining the best approach. When the problem is clearly understood, it becomes easier to apply the right methods and strategies to facilitate effective change.

The second challenge involves motivation and acceptance. Change is almost impossible when someone denies there is a problem or refuses to accept their role in creating it. For meaningful progress, the individual must desire a different life or, at the very least, want to alter their current circumstances.

The Liverpool Desistance Study highlights that change often begins with a shift in narrative. This occurs when a person acknowledges the need for change and believes in their ability to lead a different, better life. From this foundation, change transitions into action. It involves learning, skill development, problem-solving, and planning. It requires seeking prosocial opportunities, building new support networks, fostering resilience, and leveraging existing strengths to create a path forward. As the FBI's BAU-1 suggest, change is about working with the person to create guiding billboards and exit ramps – enhancing their awareness and helping them to navigate the many potholes that arise in life.

Change is not about fancy treatment programmes or targeting a particular belief system, it's about ensuring that things are practical and achievable for the person. It's about helping them identify the obstacles and barriers that are in their way and developing strategies to overcome these. There will always be the occasional bad egg that is unable to change, but for most, change is attainable. That doesn't mean that change is easy or comes quickly, but through courage, perseverance, ownership, and self-belief, it is possible to live a good life.

The final step is to rewrite the stories we tell ourselves – reshaping the lens through which we view ourselves and our lives.

19

Becoming A Hero

'I am not what happened to me. I am what I choose to become.'

Carl Jung

IMAGINE FOR A MOMENT that individuals like James Holmes, Adam Lanza, Alek Minassian, or any of the hundreds of other lone actors had found a way to overcome their struggles and discover meaning and purpose in their lives. Had they been able to access support, guidance, and healthier coping mechanisms, not only would thousands of lives have been spared, but these individuals might have gone on to lead lives of significance. They could have built families, contributed positively to their communities, and made valuable contributions to society. In this alternate reality, the lives lost to violence would have been replaced by potential contributions – individuals who, once lost in despair and anger, could have been the ones to inspire, build, and create a better world.

Aaron Stark achieved this – his story is one of redemption that demonstrates what is possible. Unfortunately, stories like his remain all too rare.

What we tell ourselves matters. How we think about people, situations, and events is powerful, powerful enough to cause violence.

We make sense of life by constructing stories and narratives. The world as we know it, or perceive it, revolves around us. Although most people do not consciously view their life like a movie where they are the main character in the plot, the reality is that we centre everything in our lives around us.

We tell ourselves stories and create narratives in order to make sense of the world and our place within it. Over time, these stories form a narrative, like a movie, which comes to function as the overall theme for our lives. Narratives place us as the main character, where we are faced with successes, failures, setbacks, tribulations, losses, despair, and other experiences.

Our beliefs, values, morals, goals, and sense of purpose are shaped by the narrative and stories we tell ourselves.

JOSEPH CAMPBELL PUBLISHED HIS BOOK, *The Hero with a Thousand Faces*, in 1949. Drawing on mythology, religion, and psychoanalysis, Professor Campbell, who taught literature at Sarah Lawrence College, Bronxville, New York, argued that recurring tales, myths, and stories have emerged throughout human history. These narratives feature universal characters: victims, villains, gods, martyrs, fools, and the unscrupulous, among others. Among these archetypes, **The Hero's Journey** stood out as the quintessential representation of success.

Professor Campbell coined this concept as The Hero's Quest, later popularised as The Hero's Journey. He proposed that a *'master narrative'* could define those who succeed and triumph in life.

According to Professor Campbell, The Hero's Journey represents the central pursuit of a meaningful life, with other life stories and narratives emerging when individuals fall short of achieving this quest. By embarking on this journey, people can find meaning, establish significance, and move beyond the allure of instant gratification. Moreover, The Hero's Journey serves as a shield against adversity, offering purpose and resilience in the face of suffering. For example, many soldiers have overcome the trauma of war by framing their experiences within narratives of patriotism, fraternity, and service to the *'greater good'*. Similarly, doctors navigate the immense stress, pressure, and exposure to death by focusing on their ability to save lives and improve the well-being of their patients.

The Hero's Journey is characterised by the protagonist, or central character, *'who is called to adventure, faces challenges, and – with the help of others – overcomes adversity before ultimately returning home triumphant and transformed to make a positive and lasting impact on their community'*. The Hollywood film industry has created thousands of movies which depict the Hero's Journey. Iconic examples include *Star Wars*, *The Wizard of Oz*, *Rocky*, *The Lion King*, *Batman*, *The Matrix*, *Citizen Kane*, *Gladiator*, and *Braveheart*.

At the heart of The Hero's Journey lies redemption, empowerment, transformation, and self-mastery. Heroes may stumble, make mistakes, or feel lost along the way, but they ultimately take charge of their destiny, overcoming obstacles and challenges to achieve what's important.

Filmmaker Patrick Solomon said, *'Humans, whether living in the pyramids three thousand year ago, or in the trailer park right now, we all fear and desire the same thing. We all fear judgement, pain, and death. We all desire love and happiness. What you see when you watch a movie is your own hopes, dreams, and fears chasing each other around in the form of good guys and bad guys; causing drama, resolving conflict, just like life ... If it's all one journey then that makes you a hero. You are the hero of your own journey.'*

Recent research published in the *Journal of Personality and Social Psychology* by Benjamin Rogers and colleagues outlines that The Hero's Journey can be broken down into seven stages:

1. Protagonist – The individual recognises that they are in control of their own life and capable of defining their future.
2. Shift – A turning point arises as the circumstances or situation in their life becomes untenable, compelling them to take action and make a change.
3. Quest – They set a clear goal to achieve and begin mapping out a path for their journey.
4. Allies – Along the way, they often receive support from others, relying on their trust, knowledge, loyalty, or encouragement to move forward.
5. Challenge – They encounter numerous obstacles and must overcome them to progress. Each success strengthens their purpose, belief, and determination.
6. Transformation – By overcoming challenges, they undergo significant personal and moral growth, becoming wiser, selfless, knowledgeable, and increasingly capable.
7. Legacy – Their actions create a lasting and positive impact on others, earning them respect, admiration, and a meaningful place in their community.

The Hero's Journey can take many forms and doesn't have to involve a death-defying endeavour or a battle with an extreme enemy. The journey, and its success, can be self-defined and deeply personal to the individual. It might be the story of a struggling young woman who rises to become the CEO of a business, or a man who endures bullying throughout his school years and later becomes a school counsellor, changing the lives of other teenagers. A Hero's Journey could also be as profound as finding a partner, getting married, and building a family together.

Remarkably, the essence of The Hero's Journey lies in our perception and the way we frame events in our lives. When we see ourselves as being in control of our destiny and capable of facing challenges and overcoming failures, we can begin to view our lives as a quest or journey. On the surface, the idea of The Hero's Journey may seem almost too simple to be true or effective.

However, a series of new studies have demonstrated that embracing this narrative can have profound and transformative implications.

The research by Rogers and his co-authors found that viewing life as a journey filled with challenges and triumphs is strongly associated with greater meaning and purpose. Intriguingly, individuals who perceive their lives as akin to a Hero's Journey are more likely to see obstacles as challenges to overcome rather than as limitations that define them.

As a result, their inner dialogue and narrative reinforce the belief that they are in control of their lives and capable of conquering challenges. This mindset not only increases the likelihood of flourishing across various areas of life but also reduces the risk of depression, ultimately leading to greater overall life satisfaction.

Moreover, when connecting and interacting with others, these individuals often share stories that highlight how they have overcome challenges and obstacles. Their narratives embrace change and focus on transformation, which becomes a central theme in their stories and conversations.

The Hero's Journey has proven to be a powerful framework for shifting how people perceive their lives. It is so effective that it can function as both an intervention and a treatment approach to inspire change. In one experiment, participants were asked to write about their life. Those prompted to structure their life story around the seven stages of The Hero's Journey were significantly more likely to view themselves as heroes undertaking a meaningful journey or mission. In contrast, participants in the control group, who simply wrote about their lives without the Hero's framework, were far less likely to see their life as a journey. This experiment highlighted the malleability of our inner narratives and demonstrated that they can be reshaped and rewritten.

The benefits don't stop there. Writing one's life story using The Hero's

Journey framework fosters a deeper sense of meaning and improves overall well-being. This process enhances psychological resilience and hardiness, enabling individuals to better cope with stress and challenges. By reimagining themselves as heroes, people suddenly become more equipped to handle stress, adjust to setbacks, and persevere in the face of adversity.

The Hero's Journey provides meaning, purpose, significance, and resilience. Pursuing goals and accomplishments is a vital part of life, and these endeavours create focus, instill a sense of purpose, and guide our decisions and actions.

If The Hero's Journey is considered to be the *'master narrative'* which leads to meaning and purpose, it would seem that by reframing adverse events, situations, and occurrences, it may be possible to change the stories and overall narrative that we tell ourselves. The lens through which we see ourselves and the world matters, and as people we are drawn towards goals, achievements, and personal triumph.

Lone actor attacks resemble an **Inverted Hero's Journey** – or **Villain's Journey** – where the individual embarks on a quest or mission to avenge perceived wrongs or harm. Instead of viewing obstacles as challenges to overcome and opportunities for personal growth, these individuals allow the obstacles to define their identity and path. For them, overcoming setbacks is not about triumph, progress, or altruism, but about retribution, revenge, and a distorted sense of justice.

Many lone actors perceive themselves as the *Central Character* in their narrative, embarking on a mission or quest. Typically, a *Shift* in their circumstances makes their situation untenable, prompting a need for change. In response, they develop a focus or objective, and identify a target that fuels their *Quest*. At this stage, they often seek out allies – whether ideologically aligned individuals, online communities, or resources – that provide knowledge, skills, and support. Through preparing and planning for the attack, they become physically and psychologically ready to take on the perceived challenge. In carrying out the attack, many believe that they will undergo a *Transformation*, whether through death or the act itself. The final stage of their journey is their *Legacy*, often proliferated through the media coverage, manifestos, videos, or the lasting impact of the attack on the victims and society.

Lone actor violence is a dysfunctional and destructive form of The Hero's Journey – a version gone tragically wrong. It lacks structure, reframing, and any positive means of finding meaning or significance, instead leading to devastation and harm.

The Hero's Journey is not the sole answer to preventing lone actor violence, but it's an important piece of the puzzle. It demonstrates the power of the stories we tell ourselves and emphasises that these narratives can be reshaped to provide purpose, meaning, and a sense of accomplishment.

It's an algorithm and antidote for life, yet it remains largely untaught in schools, unused in prisons, and unfamiliar to many mental health professionals.

Imagine if The Hero's Journey was taught in schools or used to rewrite and rescript the stories of individuals presenting with concerns? The introduction of this into educational settings could provide people with the knowledge and means to change their lives through stories. If every school taught students this psychological framework, young people would have more purpose, meaning, and resilience within their lives.

Teaching children to swim is a vital life skill that helps prevent drownings. Similarly, learning to change the way we see ourselves is an essential life skill – one that safeguards our welfare and protects our well-being.

If violence emerges as a maladaptive or dysfunctional response to a perceived threat, equipping individuals with the ability to reframe their challenges as part of a broader journey and bigger picture could be immensely beneficial. It would encourage them to see obstacles as opportunities for growth, rather than triggers for destructive behaviour.

At present, only a fortunate few may stumble upon The Hero's Journey. However, it has yet to be widely adopted as a preventative strategy or a method to facilitate meaningful change. Expanding its reach could represent a significant step forward in fostering healthier, more constructive responses to life's challenges.

The Hero's Journey is a free and accessible intervention method. All it requires is spending time with the person of concern and guiding them to write out their life story – helping them rescript and reshape it into a hero's narrative. By reframing barriers and obstacles as challenges to overcome, rather than as defining features of their identity, we can provide individuals with a path forward.

The responses of governments, media companies, and technology organisations are often political, complicated, and slow. While these larger systems have a role to play, we cannot afford to wait for them to create the much-needed change.

For those working on the front line – whether in threat assessment teams, psychology, social work, or support services – helping individuals build a meaningful life and rewrite their story can be a powerful antidote to violence. This approach hinges on listening, understanding, supporting, and guiding the individual towards a healthier narrative.

By embracing the Hero's Journey, we can help individuals find purpose, resilience, and connection, ultimately steering them away from their path to violence. The Hero's Journey is not just a tool for change – it's a crucial piece in the broader effort to prevent lone actor violence and foster hope in even the most challenging circumstances.

20

Time For Change

'We cannot solve our problems with the same thinking we used when we created them.'

Albert Einstein

In 2022, Myles Sanderson committed a brutal stabbing spree across multiple locations in Saskatchewan, Canada. The attacks, which spanned several communities, were a harrowing mix of targeted and random violence. Initially planned with his brother Damien, the attacks ultimately became a solo rampage after Sanderson stabbed his brother shortly before commencing his violent spree. At the time, Sanderson was on parole. He had a history of violent behaviour and multiple prior convictions. Over the course of his rampage, Sanderson stabbed nearly thirty people and claimed the lives of eleven individuals.

Following the tragic attack, criminal investigative psychologist and member of the Royal Canadian Mounted Police, Dr Matt Logan, completed a post-incident behavioural analysis of the mass casualty event with his colleagues. The review established that Sanderson had a childhood that was characterised by trauma, abuse, and instability, which had paved the way for his life of crime and violence.

In discussing the tragedy, Dr Logan urged society to stop *'fishing downstream'* and relying on convenient or misguided solutions. To illustrate his point, he shared a story popularised by Dan Heath in his novel *Upstream*.

The story goes as follows:

A group of friends are enjoying a picnic by the river when their day is suddenly interrupted by shouting and the sound of splashing in the water. Rushing to investigate, they see a child being swept downstream. Acting quickly, they manage to pull the child to safety.

Relieved, the friends return to their picnic. But a short while later, the same thing happens again – another person is in the water, shouting for help. The group rushes to rescue them. Then it happens yet again, and yet again, until the group is overwhelmed, struggling to keep up with the constant rescues.

Finally, one woman from the group breaks away and starts running upstream. Frustrated, another group member shouts after her, *'Where are you going? We need you here!'*

She replies, *'I'm going to fix the hole in the bridge.'*

UPSTREAM EFFORTS FOCUS ON preventing problems before they happen. They represent proactive and prospective decision-making at its finest, addressing the causes rather than merely reacting to consequences. Similar to retrospective or reactive efforts, downstream actions focus on addressing immediate problems as they arise – fixing the symptoms rather than solving the underlying issue. Downstream thinking can be effective and can reduce the extent of a problem, but it's like a hamster on a wheel that never stops. At some point, something has to give.

Lone actor violence is not something that can be simply resolved or fixed with a one-size-fits-all approach. It requires a toolkit of approaches, where results may not be seen for several years. Downstream approaches are popular because they produce an immediate response and offer the promise of fixing the problem. On the other hand, upstream initiatives are often slow to bring about change, and the effectiveness cannot always be quickly and easily measured. They take time and the rewards do not emerge immediately.

In his book, Dan Heath discussed the scenario of two police officers who are trying to prevent road accidents.

'The first officer spends half a shift standing on a street corner where many accidents happen; her visible presence makes drivers more careful and might prevent collisions. The second officer hides around the corner, nabbing cars for prohibited-turn violations. It's the first officer who did more to help public safety ... but it's the second officer who will be rewarded, because she has a stack full of tickets to show for her efforts.'

People like to see results – whether they're true results or not.

Downstream work is easy. Easy to see and easy to measure. Upstream work is more ambiguous. It's like a red wine that gets better with time.

As Dan Heath points out, *'How do you prove what did not happen?'* This question underscores the challenges of trying to demonstrate success for preventative measures. The FTAC practice of putting prevention measures in place for all individuals who present as a moderate or above level of concern, mirrors the medical approach to prescribing cholesterol-lowering medication to those with high blood pressure and other heart disease indicators. Just as it remains unknown which patients would have suffered a heart attack without intervention, we cannot determine with certainty who would have gone on to commit a mass attack. However, the value lies in reducing the overall likelihood of harm through preventative measures.

The answer to mass casualty attacks by lone actors lies in prevention. It's not something that control and restrictions are ever going to resolve – it's a Band-Aid over a gaping wound.

Dan Heath aptly observed, 'Most of us would agree that "an ounce of prevention is better than a pound of cure," but our actions don't match these words. In most of our efforts in society, we've optimized ourselves to deliver pounds of cure. Speedy, efficient pounds of cure. We celebrate the response, the recovery, the rescue. But we're capable of greater things: less Undo and more Outdo. What the world needs now is a quieter breed of hero, one actively fighting for a world in which rescues are no longer required.'

PREVENTION STARTS IN CHILDHOOD. The first part of this book, *The Path to Violence*, delved into how a poor childhood creates a fragile psychological foundation, predisposing a person to vulnerabilities as they age. Children need safety and stability in their upbringing. They also need to experience setbacks, failures, and challenges. Childhood is all about balance and ensuring that there are appropriate boundaries, safeguards, and supports in a child's life.

Children need their parents and the care of extended family members. The breakdown of families, the decline of family meals, and the ever-increasing presence of technology in our lives has changed modern childhood. There are less face-to-face interactions, more lonely people, and greater mental health issues than ever before. There's less play, less conversations, and less connection.

Trauma has a profound impact on a person's development. Adversity leads to numerous poor life outcomes, of which violence is one. But among many lone actors, the problems are not all trauma related; instead, there's a marked lack of resilience and an inability to cope with hardships and setbacks. There is no ability to tolerate stress or unmet expectations. Add to this excessive screen time, hours of social media use, poor family cohesion, and unfulfilling social relationships, and a clear problem emerges – a problem characterised by disconnection and demoralisation. What fundamentally matters in life is gradually becoming lost.

As Bruce Perry concluded, we now have *'a more self-absorbed, more anxious, more depressed – and less resilient – population'*.

The first section of this book also explored how thoughts and ideas can take on a problematic and harmful turn. Our thinking and our perceptions can drive violence – especially when feeling wronged, mistreated, or ostracised. Grievances are powerful emotional catalysts and the more these are fed and reinforced, the greater the problem becomes. Whether it's a staircase or a bathtub, over time our thinking can become more intense, narrow, and fixated – to the point that violence is viewed as the last or ultimate response.

Thoughts, ideas, and beliefs can take many forms. However, the more that we value an idea and the more that we ignore alternative perspectives, the greater the chance that our objectivity may wane and we may come to overvalue the belief. There are many topics and issues that divide people throughout society, whether this is culture, rights, freedoms, and so on. There are always things that are unfair, tragic, or outrageous. There is also always a choice in how to respond to these issues.

Lone actor violence doesn't just occur, it is a gradual process of change, and a gradual process towards violence. Sometimes, declining mental health serves as a final tipping point, while in other cases, it may be a series of events that build up over time and eventually become too much. Then there are factors which occur in the social and political landscape, such as COVID-19, various government policies, or the increasing powers of corporations. In the end, all lone actors have different reasons and justifications for their violence, but their intended outcomes are all the same – revenge, justice, retribution, or the restoration of natural order.

The second part of the book, **The Search for Answers**, covered a wide range of endeavours and responses that are needed to solve the crisis of mass attacks. This included the problems of constantly trying to prevent previous attacks, the development of specialised police units, the importance of information sharing, the traps for police and threat teams to avoid, the need for risk and threat assessment, the danger of misguided treatment programmes, the dilemmas facing government agencies, and the questionable role of media and technology companies.

The task of preventing lone actor violence is not simple, nor is it solely the role of police, the government, or the media. It is a combined effort encompassing considered approaches at a systems level and extensive support and resources at an individual level. Better policies by governments or uniform media reporting practices will help greatly, but there also needs to be psychologists, social workers, and educators who can work with at-risk individuals and provide the much-needed support and intervention.

The various initiatives and approaches discussed are all vital components of the solution – but building a good life and rewriting our own story stand out as being particularly crucial. These concepts serve as both the recipe and the ingredients for meaningful change. When children, or even adults, learn to view themselves as being in control of their lives, their sense of well-being and purpose improve significantly. Just as swimming is a crucial life skill taught early on to safeguard against drowning, so too should we prioritise teaching frameworks like the Good Lives Model and The Hero's Journey. These approaches enable individuals to reshape their perceptions, align their actions with their values, and find prosocial ways to achieve their goals.

WE CANNOT KEEP REACTING. More restrictions and reactive policies are not the answer. At some point, we must address the root causes, rethink our approach, and start *'fishing upstream'*.

Dr Logan emphasises this idea: *'If we pour more money and effort into children, and we spend the time and put the effort in with children, we can prevent a lot of what happens later in life ... "Fishing upstream" is, starting at age eight ... making sure the child is surrounded by people who are supporting them and moving them in the right direction ... Too often, we wait until they are aged 16 in a juvenile facility – or, worse yet, aged 18 in a correctional facility.'*

This shift requires more than just policies or programmes – it demands a change in how we view prevention. It's about asking the hard questions: *Why does this violence occur? What needs or struggles does it represent?* Prevention is about understanding people, getting to the heart of the *'why'* and *'how'*, and addressing those factors before they escalate into tragedy.

At their core, lone actors are human beings with the same fundamental needs for identity, belonging, and significance that we all share. Somewhere along the way, they become lost. Many never find their way back. Their violent acts, while horrific, arise from deeply human struggles. By addressing these struggles, we can disrupt the cycle of violence. We can create a society where fewer individuals feel so lost, so demoralised, so lonely, and so hopeless that harm becomes the answer.

When it all boils down, the power to change this lies with each of us. Every one of us has the capacity to influence others, to make a difference, and to play a role in ending the devastation caused by this violence.

It might involve learning more by gaining awareness and understanding of the warning behaviours and the motivations behind lone actor violence. It could be as straightforward as a phone call to report a critical piece of information that saves lives. It may even be something as simple, yet profound, as an act of kindness. Consider Aaron Stark's story – a conversation and a gesture of compassion saved not only his life but the lives of others who could have been his victims.

The ripple effects of one human connection can be immeasurable.

Prevention starts with each of us. It begins with how we treat others, how we notice those who are struggling, and how we respond in a time of need. A small action could change everything.

Lone actor violence is fundamentally a human problem and one that stems from unmet needs, disconnection, and societal shortcomings. And because it is a human problem, it demands a human response – one that prioritises connection, understanding, support, and guidance.

By working together, each of us playing our role, we can build a society where fewer individuals feel compelled to harm, and more find the connection and meaning they need to thrive.

Author's Note

I began writing this book in 2021 during the COVID-19 lockdown in New Zealand, but the journey that led me to this point started several years earlier. I had been closely following the rise of lone actor attacks across the globe, witnessing how these acts of violence were reshaping societies and security responses. Three attacks, in particular, stood out to me: the horrifying bombing and mass shooting in Norway in 2011, the 2014 Sydney Lindt Café siege which occurred while I was living in Australia, and the 2019 Christchurch terrorist attack in New Zealand. These events were devastating in their impact, and for me personally raised critical questions about how and why individuals commit such extreme acts of violence.

Before writing this book, much of my work had been focused on academic research exploring the role of grievances, fixations, and counterterrorism responses in lone actor violence. I spent several years researching, reading case studies, and analysing these incidents. At the same time, in my professional role as a forensic psychologist, I was seeing an increasing number of cases related to targeted violence and individuals exhibiting warning signs of lone actor tendencies. I had assessed and interviewed several offenders who had either carried out mass attacks or had been caught during the planning stages. The overlap between my academic research and my practical experiences led me to start compiling my notes and observations. What began as research and improving my own practices, gradually transformed into the foundation for this book.

I had no idea that completing this book would take several years of commitment and persistence. But for me, there was a strong motivation

– not just to analyse these cases, but to truly understand them. I wanted to explore how we arrived at this point in society, why we are seeing an increase in mass casualty attacks, and what is driving individuals towards violent ideologies. More specifically, I wanted to know:

- Why are grievances now being expressed through extreme violence
- What role does childhood upbringing play in the pathway to violence?
- How do beliefs and ideas develop into extreme and violent action?
- What role does the internet play in shaping and accelerating violent behaviour?
- How can we improve prevention efforts and identify individuals at risk before it's too late?

This book has been both an educational and personal journey – one that seeks to understand an unsettling trend of violence and also to explore potential solutions. Throughout the writing process, I was conscious of the ethical considerations involved in discussing cases. I debated whether to de-identify cases to avoid sensationalising these acts, but for the sake of clarity and accuracy, I have chosen to retain the names of offenders. My goal is not to give notoriety to these individuals but to provide clear examples of the many factors that contribute to violence and particularly how it can vary between perpetrators.

In writing this book, I have examined a wide range of cases – each of which has left behind a trail of trauma and devastation for victims, their families, and entire communities. I do not take that lightly. My hope is that by shedding light on these events, readers can gain a deeper understanding of the complexities and nuances of this form of violence. There are many misconceptions and myths surrounding lone actor attackers, and there is often a tendency to believe that there is little we can do to prevent these incidents. But that is not the case. We all play a role in prevention, whether through increasing our awareness, supporting individuals in crisis, or sharing information when concerns arise.

AUTHOR'S NOTE

The field has seen considerable growth in research and public awareness in recent years, which is encouraging. At the time of writing, I have drawn on the most up-to-date evidence and research, but as this topic continues to evolve, so too will our understanding.

I want to acknowledge several individuals who have significantly shaped my perspective on mass casualty violence and threat assessment through their pivotal work. I am especially grateful to criminal investigative psychologist Dr Matt Logan, forensic psychologist Dr Reid Meloy, and psychologist Dr Stephen White for their contributions to the field. Our ability to tackle mass violence is strengthened by collaboration, and organisations such as the Association of Threat Assessment Professionals (ATAP) have played a crucial role in connecting professionals and improving prevention efforts.

Through this book, I hope to contribute to this ongoing conversation to help bridge the gap between understanding and action, research and practice, and ultimately, to help prevent future tragedies.

Lastly, the views expressed in this book are my own and not representative of any organisations that I am affiliated with, including the New Zealand Police.

A Note On Sources

Writing a nonfiction book for general audiences presents different challenges compared to academic work, particularly when it comes to referencing and sourcing material. There is always a balance between readability and thoroughness. Pages full of citations and references can put off many readers and add significantly to publishing costs. At the same time, it remains essential to acknowledge and credit the work of others correctly.

I thought long and hard about the most suitable way to reference the many sources that have greatly influenced this book, and in the end, I decided to take two paths.

The first is a less formal bibliography included within the book itself. The second is a more detailed and comprehensive source list, outlining the specific articles and references used in each chapter and on particular pages. Transparency and appropriate credit are important to me, and I hope that through these two methods I can provide a book that is both appealing and accessible to general audiences, while also serving practitioners and academics who may seek more in-depth details and sourcing.

This approach means less page-flipping, fewer unappealing in-text citations, and reduced printing requirements. But for those who want the sources, details, and specifics, these can be found at: www.groundprooforensics.com/masscasualty.

Bibliography

Prologue

Brooks, N., Kupper, J., Thomas, R., Wilcoxson, R., & Blake, C. (in press). 'Interviewing Lone Actors: The Role of Grievances, Ideologies and Rapport in the Interview of the Toronto Van Attacker.' *Journal of Threat Assessment & Management.*

Collins, P. I. (2021). 'Incel: The Intersection of Misogyny and Extremism.' Presentation at the Asia Pacific of Association Threat Assessment Professionals Conference.

Healy, J., & Lovett, L. (2015, 2 October). 'Oregon Killer Described as Man of Few Words, Except on Topics of Guns.' The New York Times.

Kassam, A. (2018, 25 April). 'Woman Behind "Incel" Says Angry Men Hijacked Her Word "as a Weapon of War".' The Guardian.

Porter, C. (2021, 2 March). 'Toronto Van Attacker Found Guilty in City's Worst Mass Killing. The New York Times.

Thomas, R. (2022). 'The Incel Van Attack of Toronto, Canada – 23 April 2018.' *International Investigative Interviewing Research Group, 12*(1), 80–92.

Toronto Police Service. (2018). 'Electronic video interview of Alek Minassian and Detective Robert Thomas on April 23 2018.' Author.

White, S. G. (2017). 'Case Study: The Isla Vista Campus Community Mass Murder.' *Journal of Threat Assessment and Management, 4*(1), 20--47.

Introduction

Aamodt, M. G. (2016, 4 September). 'Serial Killer Statistics.'

Basu, N. (2021). 'Learning Lessons from Countering Terrorism: the UK Experience 2017–2020.' *Cambridge Journal of Evidence-Based Policing, 5,* 134–145.

Berkowitz, B., Blanco, A., Mayes, B. R., Auerbach, K., & Rindler, D. (2019, 5 August). 'More and More Deadlier: Mass Shooting Trends in America.' *The Washington Post*.

Brooks, N., & Shaw, R. (2022). 'Fixated and Grievance-Fuelled Persons: Considerations on the Dangers of Gaps, Silos and Disconnects.' *Psychiatry, Psychology, and Law, 29*(6), 854–870.

Calhoun, F., & Weston, S. (2003). *Contemporary Threat Management: A Practical Guide for Identifying, Assessing, and Managing Individuals of Violent Intent*. San Diego, CA: Specialized Training Services.

Capellan, J. A. (2015). 'Lone Wolf Terrorist or Deranged Shooter? A Study of Ideological Active Shooter Events in the United States, 1970–2014.' *Studies in Conflict & Terrorism, 38*(6), 395–413.

Corner, E., & Gill, P. (2015). 'A False Dichotomy? Mental Illness and Lone-Actor Terrorism.' *Law and Human Behavior, 39*(1), 23–34.

Densley, J., & Peterson, L. (2019, 1 September). 'Opinion: We Analyzed 53 years of Mass Shooting Data. Attacks Aren't Just Increasing, They're Getting More Deadlier.' *Los Angeles Times*.

Eby, C. A. (2012). *The Nation That Cried Lone Wolf: A Data-Driven Analysis of Individual Terrorists in the United States Since 9/11*. Naval Postgraduate School, Monterey CA Department of National Security Affairs.

Follman, M. (2022). *Trigger Points: Inside the Mission to Stop Mass Shootings in America*. Harper Collins.

Follman, M. (2022, 8 April). 'The Powerful Impact of Digital Media on Mass Shootings.' *Literary Hub*.

Gill, P., Horgan, J., & Deckert, P. (2014). 'Bombing Alone: Tracing the Motivations and Antecedent Behaviors of Lone-Actor Terrorists.' *Journal of Forensic Sciences, 59*(2), 425–435.

Gruenwald, J., Chermak, S., & Freilich, J. D. (2013). 'Distinguishing "loner" Attacks From Other Domestic Extremist Violence.' *Criminology & Public Policy, 12*(1) 65-91.

Hare, R. D. (1999). *Without Conscience: The Disturbing World of Psychopaths Among Us*. Guilford Press.

Hurlow, J., Wilson, S., & James, D. V. (2016). 'Protesting Loudly About

Prevent Is Popular but Is It Informed and Sensible?' *BJPsych Bulletin, 40*(3), 162–163.

Kelly, J. (2013, 16 February). 'Christopher Dorner: What made a police officer kill?' *BBC*.

Liem, M., van Buuren, J., de Roy van Zuijdewijn, J., Schonberger, H., & Bakker, E. (2018). 'European Lone Actor Terrorist Versus "Common" Homicide Offenders: An Empirical Analysis.' *Homicide Studies, 22*, 45–69.

Logan, M. H. (2015). 'Many Wear the Jersey but Few Play for the Team: Misfits Masquerading as Terrorists.' *Violence and Gender, 2*(1).

McCauley, C., Moskalenko, S., & Van Son, B. (2013). 'Characteristics of Lone-Wolf Violent Offenders: A Comparison of Assassins and School Attackers.' *Perspectives on Terrorism, 7*(1), 4–24.

Pathé, M. T., Haworth, D. J., Goodwin, T., Holman, A. G., Amos, S. J., Winterbourne, P., et al. (2018). 'Establishing a Joint Agency Response to the Threat of Lone-Actor Grievance-Fuelled Violence.' *The Journal of Forensic Psychiatry & Psychology, 29*, 37–52.

Petherick, W., Bose, S., McKinley, A., & Skrapec, C. (2021). 'A Rose by Any Other Name: Problems in Defining and Conceptualising Serial Murder with a New Proposed Definition.' *Journal of Mass Violence Research*.

Schuurman, B., Lindekilde, L., Malthaner, S., O'Connor, F., Gill, P., & Bouhana, N. (2018). 'End of the Lone Wolf: The Typology That Should Not Have Been.' *Studies in Conflict & Terrorism, 42*(8), 771–778.

Spaaij, R. (2010). 'The Enigma of Lone Wolf Terrorism: An Assessment.' *Studies in Conflict & Terrorism, 33*(9): 854–870.

Spaaij, R. (2012). *Understanding Lone Wolf Terrorism*. Springer Briefs in Criminology.

Stanley, E., & Lazaro, R. (2023, 19 October). 'Manchester Bomber Salman Abedi Murdered 22 in Suicide Attack, Coroner Rules.' *BBC*.

Subramanian, C. (2017, 7 October). 'Las Vegas Shooting: What was Stephen Paddock's Motive?' *BBC*.

Teich, S. (2013). *Trends and Developments in Lone Wolf Terrorism in the Western World: An Analysis of Terrorist Attacks and Attempted Attacks by Islamic Extremists*. Herzliya: International Institute for Counter-Terrorism.

Turner, N. D., Chermak, S. M., & Freilich, J. D. (2021). 'An Empirical Examination on the Severity of Lone-Actor Terrorist Attacks.' *Crime & Delinquency*, 1–28.

Winter, C., & Spaaij, R. (2018, 15 November). 'The Evolving Threat of Lone-Actor Terrorism.' *Inside Story*.

Worth, K. (2016, 14 July). 'Lone Wolf Attacks Are Becoming More Common – And More Deadly.' *Frontline*.

Yakeley, J., & Taylor, R. (2017). 'Terrorism and Mental Disorder, and the Role of Psychiatrists in Counter-Terrorism in the UK.' *Psychoanalytic Psychotherapy*, *31*(4), 378–392.

Chapter 1

Bowlby, J. (1960). 'Separation Anxiety.' *The International Journal of Psycho-Analysis*, *41*, 89–111.

Bowlby, J. (1969). *Attachment and Loss, Vol. 1: Attachment*. Basic Books.

Brooks, N., Honnavalli, V., & Jacobson-Lang, B. (2021). 'Children of ISIS: Considerations Regarding Trauma, Treatment and Risk.' *Psychiatry, Psychology, and Law*, *29*(1), 107–133.

Engel, P. (2013, 27 November). 'A 10-Year-Old Adam Lanza Created a Horrifying Book About Hurting Children.' *Business Insider*.

Heide, K. M., & Frei, A. (2010). 'Matricide: A Critique of the Literature.' *Trauma, Violence, & Abuse*, *11*(1), 3–17.

Ferris, T. (2018, 20 February). 'Dr Gabor Maté – New Paradigms, Ayahuasca, and Redefining Addiction'. Episode 298. *The Tim Ferris Show*.

Gazzaniga, M. S. (1995). 'Principles of Human Brain Organization Derived from Split Brain Studies.' *Neuron*, *14*, 217–228.

Maté, G., & Maté, D. (2022). *The Myth of Normal: Illness, Health and Healing in a Toxic Culture*. Penguin Books.

Perry, B. D. (2001). 'The Neurodevelopmental Impact of Violence in Childhood.' In D. Schetky & E. Benedek (Eds.), *Textbook of Child and Adolescent Forensic Psychiatry*. American Psychiatric Press.

Perry, B. D., & Szalavitz, M. (2008). *The Boy Who Was Raised as a Dog: And Other Stories from a Psychiatrist's Notebook. What Traumatized Children Can*

Teach Us About Loss, Love, and Healing. Basic Books.

Solomon, A. (2014, 10 March). 'The Reckoning. The Father of Sandy Hook Killer Searches for Answers.' *The New Yorker*.

Sonne, J. W. H., & Gash, D. M. (2018). 'Psychopathy to Altruism: Neurobiology of the Selfish-Selfless Spectrum.' *Frontiers in Psychology, 9*, 1–18.

Uhernik, J. A. (2017). *Using Neuroscience in Trauma Therapy: Creative and Compassionate Counseling*. Routledge.

van der Kolk, B. A. (2005). 'Developmental Trauma Disorder: Towards a Rational Diagnosis for Children with Complex Trauma Histories.' *Psychiatric Annals, 35*(5), 401–419.

Young, T. (2019, 13 May). 'Psychological Aspects of Adam Lanza.' LinkedIn Article.

Chapter 2

Baglivio, M. T., & Epps, N. (2016). 'The Interrelatedness of Adverse Childhood Experiences Among High-Risk Juvenile Offenders.' *Youth Violence and Juvenile Justice, 14*(3), 179-198.

Baglivio, M. T., Wolff, K. T. Piquero, A. R., & Epps, N. (2015). 'The Relationship Between Adverse Childhood Experiences (ACE) and Juvenile Offending Trajectories in a Juvenile Offender Sample.' *Journal of Criminal Justice, 43*, 229–241.

Blaskey, S., Cox, J. W., Natanson, H., Meckler, L., & Boburg, S. (2024, 3 October). 'The Making of an Alleged School Shooter: Missed Warning and Years of Neglect.' *The Washington Post*.

Brewer-Smyth, K. (2022). *Adverse Childhood Experiences: The Neuroscience of Trauma, Resilience and Healing Throughout the Life Course*. Springer

Costello, E. J., Erklani, A., Fairbank, J., & Angold, A. (2003). 'The Prevalence of Potentially Traumatic Events in Childhood and Adolescence.' *Journal of Child Psychology and Psychiatry, 54*, 402-422.

Craig, J. M., Malvaso, C., & Farrington, D. P. (2025). 'The Association Between Adverse Childhood Experiences and Different Types of Offending Behavior: An Examination Across Two Generations of British Males.'

International Journal of Offender Therapy and Comparative Criminology, 69(5), 611–629.

Craig, J. M., & Zettler, H. R. (2021). 'Are the Effects of Adverse Childhood Experiences on Violent Recidivism Offense-Specific?' *Youth Violence and Juvenile Justice, 19,* 27–44.

Centers for Disease Control and Prevention (2019, 2 October). *Preventing Adverse Experiences (ACEs): Leveraging the Best Available Evidence.* National Centre for Injury Prevention and Control, Centers for Disease Control and Prevention.

Dierkhising, C. B., Ko, S. J., Woods-Jager, B., Briggs, E. C., Lee, R., & Pynoos, R. S. (2013). 'Trauma Histories Among Justice-Involved Youth: Findings from The National Child Traumatic Stress Network.' *European Journal of Psychotraumatology, 4,* 20274.

Duke, N. N., Pettingell, S. L., McMorris, B. J., & Borowsky, I. W. (2010). 'Adolescent Violence Preparation: Associations with Multiple Types of Adverse Childhood Experiences.' *Paediatrics, 125*(4), 778-786.

Evans-Chase, M. (2014). 'Addressing Trauma and Psychosocial Development in Juvenile Justice-Involved Youth: A Synthesis of the Development of Neuroscience, Juvenile Justice and Trauma Literature.' *Laws, 3,* 744-758.

Jones, C. M., Merrick, M. T., & Houry, D. E. (2020). 'Identifying and Preventing Adverse Childhood Experiences: Implications for Clinical Practice.' *JAMA, 323,* 25–26.

Herrenkohl, T. I., Maguin, E., Hill, K. G., Hawkins, J. D., Abbott, R. D., & Catalano, R. F. (2000). 'Developmental Risk Factors for Youth Violence.' *Journal of Adolescent Health, 26*(3), 176–186

Matza, M. (2024, 6 September). 'Father of US School Shooting Suspect Charged with Murder.' *BBC.*

Perry, B. D., & Szalavitz, M. (2008). *The Boy Who Was Raised as a Dog: And Other Stories from a Psychiatrist's Notebook. What Traumatized Children Can Teach Us About Loss, Love, and Healing.* Basic Books

Reavis, J., Looman, J., Franco K., & Rojas, B. (2013). 'Adverse Childhood Experiences and Adult Criminality: How Long Must We Live Before We Possess Our Own Lives?' *The Permanente Journal, 17*(2), 44–48.

Rokach, A., & Clayton, S. (2023). 'The Consequences of Child Abuse.' *Healthcare, 11*(11), 1650.

Schecter, A., & Eggleston, J. (2024, 17 October). 'Alleged Georgia School Shooter and Father Indicted on Dozens of Charges by Grand Jury.' *CBS News*.

Schore, A. N. (2001). 'The Effects of Early Relational Trauma on Right Brain Development, Affect Regulation, and Infant Mental Health.' *Infant Mental Health Journal, 22*(1-2), 201-269.

Sonne, J. W. H., Gash, D. M. (2018). 'Psychopathy to Altruism: Neurobiology of the Selfish-Selfless Spectrum.' *Frontiers in Psychology, 9*, 1–18.

van der Kolk, B. A. (2005). 'Developmental Trauma Disorder: Towards a Rational Diagnosis for Children with Complex Trauma Histories.' *Psychiatric Annals, 35*(5), 401–419.

Yousif, N. (2024, 7 September). 'Boy, 14, and Father in Court Over Georgia School Shooting.' *BBC*.

Chapter 3

Alter, C. (2017, 27 May). 'Colorado Gunman's Notebook of Ramblings Becomes Evidence.' *Time Magazine*.

Center for Disease Control and Prevention. (2023, 10 August). *Provisional Suicide Deaths in United States, 2022*. CDC Newsroom.

Clifton, J. (2022). *Blind spot: The Global Rise of Unhappiness and How Leaders Missed it*. Gallup Press.

Deighton, J., Lereya, S. T., Casey, P., Patalay, P., Humphrey, N., & Wolpert, M. (2019). 'Prevalence of Mental Health Problems in Schools: Poverty and Other Risk Factors Among 28,000 Adolescents in England.' *The British Journal of Psychiatry, 215*(3), 565–567.

Dugan, A. (2024, 10 July). 'Over 1 in 5 People Worldwide Feel Lonely a Lot'. *Gallup*.

Dumas, T. M., Ellis, W. E., Van Hedger, S., Litt, D. M., & MacDonald, M. (2022). 'Lockdown, Bottoms Up? Changes in Adolescent Substance Use Across the COVID-19 Pandemic.' *Addictive Behaviors, 131*, 107326.

Federal Bureau of Investigation. (2002). *Crime in the United States, Uniform*

Crime Report 2002. Author.

Ferris, T. (2018, 20 February). 'Dr Gabor Maté – New Paradigms, Ayahuasca, and Redefining Addiction'. Episode 298. *The Tim Ferris Show*.

Holt-Lunstad, J., Smith, T. B., & Layton, J. B. (2010). 'Social Relationships and Mortality Risk: A Meta-Analytic Review.' *PLoS medicine, 7*(7), e1000316.

Holt-Lunstad, J., Smith, T. B., Baker, M., Harris, T., & Stephenson, D. (2015). 'Loneliness and Social Isolation as Risk Factors for Mortality: A Meta-Analytic Review.' *Perspectives on Psychological Science, 10*(2), 227–237.

Hunter, T. (2023, 11 April). 'Technology's Role in the Loneliness Epidemic.' *The Washington Post*.

Jofre, S. (2017, 26 July). 'The Batman Killer: A Prescription for Murder?' BBC.

Jones, H. E., Manze, M., Ngo, V., Lamberson, P., & Freudenberg, N. (2021). 'The Impact of the COVID-19 Pandemic on College Students' Health and Financial Stability in New York City: Findings from a Population-Based Sample of City University of New York (CUNY) Students.' *Journal of Urban Health, 98*(2), 187–196.

Liem, M., van Buuren, J., de Roy van Zuijdewijn, J., Schonberger, H., & Bakker, E. (2018). 'European Lone Actor Terrorist Versus "Common" Homicide Offenders: An Empirical Analysis.' *Homicide Studies, 22,* 45–69.

Maese, E. (2023, 24 October) 'Almost a Quarter of The World Feels Lonely'. *Gallup*.

Moniuszko, S. (2023, 29 November). 'Suicide Deaths Reached Record High in 2022, But Decreased for Kids and Young Adults, CDC Data Shows.' *CBS News*.

Mouzos, J. (2005). *Homicide in Australia: 2003-2004 National Homicide Monitoring Program (NHMP) Annual Report*. Australian Institute of Criminology.

Newberry, L. (2023, 10 October). More than 1 in 7 Men have No Close Friends: The Way we Socialize Boys is to Blame. *Los Angeles Times*.

Office of the Surgeon General (OSG). (2023). *Our Epidemic of Loneliness and Isolation: The U.S. Surgeon General's Advisory on the Healing Effects of Social Connection and Community*. US Department of Health and Human

Services.

Reid, W. (2018). *A Dark Night in Aurora: Inside James Holmes and the Colorado Mass Shootings*. Skyhorse Publishing.

RNZ. (2024, 11 July). 'Why Modern Boyhood Is a Lonely Place, Interview with Jesse Mulligan and Ruth Whippman.' *Radio New Zealand*.

Sadler, K., Vizard, T., Ford, T., Goodman, A., Goodman, R., & McManus, S. (2018). *Mental Health of Children and Young People in England, 2019, Trends and Characteristics*. NHS Digital, UK.

Schore A. N. (2017). 'All Our Sons: The Developmental Neurobiology and Neuroendocrinology of Boys at Risk.' *Infant Mental Health Journal, 38*(1), 15–52.

Siemaszko, C., & Blinder, R. (2018, 12 April). 'Chilling Notebook Shown Self-Professed 'Broken' Mind of Aurora Shooter James Holmes.' *New York Daily News*.

Wilson, M. J., Mansour, K., Seidler, Z. E., Oliffe, J. L., Rice, S. M., Sharp, P., Greenwood, C. J., & Macdonald, J. A. (2025). 'Intimate Partner Relationship Breakdown and Suicidal Ideation in a Large Representative Cohort of Australian Men.' *Journal of Affective Disorders, 372*, 618–626.

Witters, D. (2023, 4 April). 'Loneliness in U.S. Subsides From Pandemic High.' *Gallup*

World Health Organization. (2023, 31 March). *Depressive Disorder (Depression)*. WHO.

World Health Organization. (2023, 27 September). *Anxiety Disorders*. WHO.

Zhang, C., Ye, M., Fu, Y., Yang, M., Luo, F., Yuan, J., & Tao, Q. (2020). 'The Psychological Impact of the COVID-19 Pandemic on Teenagers in China.' *The Journal of Adolescent Health, 67*(6), 747–755.

Chapter 4

Bowles, N. (2018, 26 October). 'Silicon Valley Nannies Are Phone Police for Kids.' *The New York Times*.

Brooks, M. (2023, 1 October). 'How Much Screen Time Is Too Much?' *Psychology Today*.

Cutler, D. M., Glaeser, E. L., & Norberg, K. E. (2001). 'Explaining the Rise in Youth Suicide.' In J. Gruber (Ed.), *Risky Behavior Among Youths: An Economic Analysis* (pp. 219–269). The University of Chicago Press.

Dias, B. S. (2023). *A Dangerous Road Without Warning Signs: The Blurred Lanes of Technology and the Targeted Violence Pandemic.* Doctoral Dissertation. California School of Forensic Studies, Alliant International University.

Easter, M. (2021). *The Comfort Crisis: Embrace Discomfort to Reclaim Your Wild, Happy, Healthy Self.* Harmony/Rodale.

Fogg, B. J. (2021). *Tiny Habits: The Smart Changes That Change Everything.* Virgin.

Follman, M. (2022). *Trigger Points: Inside the Mission to Stop Mass Shootings in America.* Harper Collins.

Follman, M. (2022, 8 April). 'The Powerful Impact of Digital Media on Mass Shootings.' *Literary Hub.*

Gould, M. S., & Lake, A. M. (2103). 'The Contagion of Suicidal Behaviour.' In *Institute of Medicine and National Research Council, Contagion of Violence: Workshop Summary*, 68–72. Washington: National Academic Press.

Gould, M. S., Wallenstein, S., Kleinman M. H., O'Carroll, P., & Mercy. J. (1990). 'Suicide Clusters: An Examination of Age-Specific Effects.' *American Journal of Public Health, 80*(2), 211–212.

Keen, F. (2020, 4 December). *After 8 Chan.* Crest Research.

Kupper, J., Christensen, T. K., Wing, D., Hurt, M., Schumacher, M., & Meloy, R. (2022). 'The Contagion and Copycat Effect in Transnational Far-Right Terrorism: An Analysis of Language Evidence.' *Perspectives on Terrorism, 16*, 4–26.

Macklin, G. (2019, July). 'The Christchurch Attacks: Livestream Terror in the Viral Video Age.' *CTS Sentinel, 12* (6), 18–29.

Maté, G. (2010). *In the Realm of Hungry Ghosts: Close Encounters with Addiction.* North Atlantic Books.

Royal Commission of Inquiry (2021). *Volume 2, The Terrorist,* 165–243. Royal Commission of Inquiry into the Terrorist Attack on Christchurch Mosques on 15 March 2019.

Sohn, E. (2016, 10 February). 'Smartphones Are Like Slot Machines.' *Stuff.*

Tech Against Terrorism. (2022). *The Threat of Terrorist and Violent Extremist-Operated Websites*. January 2022 Report.

Twenge, J. M. (2020). 'Increases in Depression, Self-Harm, and Suicide Among US Adolescents After 2012 and Links to Technology Use: Possible Mechanisms.' *Psychiatric Research and Clinical Practice, 2*(1), 19–25.

Williamson, B. (2020). *Brenton Tarrant: The Processes Which Brought Him to Engage in Political Violence*. The Handa Centre for the Study of Terrorism and Political Violence. University of St Andrews.

Winnick, M. (2022, July). 'Putting a Finger on Our Phones Obsession.' *Dscout*

Chapter 5

Brick, M. (2010, 18 February). 'Man Crashes Plane into Texas I.R.S. Office.' *New York Times*.

Borum, R. (2015). 'Assessing Risk for Terrorism Involvement.' *Journal of Threat Assessment and Management, 2*, 63–87. Doi: 10.1037/tam0000043

Brooks, N., & Barry-Walsh, J. (2022). 'Understanding the Role of Grievance and Fixation in Lone Actor Violence.' *Frontiers in Psychology, 13*, 1045694.

Brooks, N., & Ebbrecht, C. K. (2025). 'Lone Actor Grievance-Fuelled Violence and the Elusiveness of Motivation.' *Journal of Threat Assessment and Management*. Advanced Online Publication.

Corner, E., Taylor, H., & Bragias, A. (2023). 'Modelling Drivers of Grievance-Fuelled Violence.' *Trends and Issues in Crime and Criminal Justice: Australian Institute of Criminology*. Canberra.

FBI Behavioural Analysis Unit 1. (2025). *Beyond Belief: Preventing and Countering Violent Extremism in America*. U.S Department of Justice.

Gibson, K. A., Craun, S. W., Ford, A. G., Solik, K., & Silver, J. M. (2020). 'Possible Attackers? A Comparison Between the Behaviors and Stressors of Persons of Concern and Active Shooters.' *Journal of Threat Assessment and Management, 7*, 1–12.

Katz, N. (2010, 18 February). 'Joe Stack Suicide Note Full Text: America Zombies Wake Up and Revolt.' *CBS News*.

Menger, R., Kalakoti, P., Hanif, R., Ahmed, O., Nanda, A., & Guthikonda, B. (2017). 'A Political Case of Penetrating Cranial Trauma: The Injury of James Scott Brady.' *Neurosurgery, 81*(3), 545–551.

Miller, L. (2017). 'The Man Who Shot Reagan is Out of the Mental Hospital and Living with His Mother.' *Daily Intelligencer*.

Mullen, P. E., James, D. V., Meloy, J. R., Pathé, M. T., Farnham, F. R., Preston, L., & Berman, J. (2009). 'The Fixated and the Pursuit of Public Figures.' *The Journal of Forensic Psychiatry & Psychology, 20*(1), 33–47.

Sallet, J. B. (1985). 'After Hinckley: The Insanity Defense Re-Examined. The Insanity Defense and the Trial of John W. Hinckley.' *Yale Law Journal, 94*, 1545–1855.

Silver, J., Simons, A., & Craun, S. (2018). *A Study of the Pre-Attack Behaviours of Active Shooters in the United States Between 2000 and 2013.* Federal Bureau of Investigation: US Department of Justice.

Treasury Inspector General for Tax Administration. (2012, 10 July). *Office of Audit – Accounting for the Austin Incident*. Author.

Chapter 6

Allely, C. S. (2020). *The Psychology of Extreme Violence: A Case Study Approach to Serial Homicide, Mass Shooting, School Shooting and Lone-Actor Terrorism.* Taylor & Francis Group, 192–193.

Associated Press. (2023, 10 June). 'Ted Kaczynski, Known as the Unabomber Has Died in Prison at Age 81.' *NPR*.

Borum, R. (2015). 'Assessing Risk for Terrorism Involvement.' *Journal of Threat Assessment and Management, 2*, 63–87. Doi: 10.1037/tam0000043

Campion, K. (2024). 'Right-Wing Extremism in Australia: Current Threats and Trends in a Diverse and Diffuse Threatscape.' *Counter Terrorist Trends and Analyses, 16*(3), 1–6.

Chermak, S., & Gruenewald, J. A. (2015). 'Laying a Foundation for the Criminological Examination of Right-Wing, Left-Wing, and Al-Qaeda-Inspired Extremism in the United States.' *Terrorism and Political Violence, 27*(1), 133–159.

Eagleton, T. (1991). *Ideology: An Introduction.* Verso Books.

Fox News (2016, 20 June). 'Friend of Dylann Roof Says Suspect Planned Attack on College of Charleston.' *FOX News*.

Gill, P., Horgan, J., & Deckert, P. (2014). 'Bombing Alone: Tracing the Motivations and Antecedent Behaviors of Lone-Actor Terrorists.' *Journal of Forensic Sciences*, 59(2), 425–435.

Hughes, T. (2016, 11 April). 'Planned Parenthood Shooter "Happy" with His Attack.' *USA Today*.

Lemos, G. (2021, 29 November). 'Dayton Mass Shooter Acted Alone in 2019 Attack and Was Fueled by an "Enduring Fascination with Mass Violence," FBI Says.' *CNN*.

McBride, J. (2019, 12 August). 'Connor Betts: 5 Fast Facts You Need to Know.' *Heavy*.

Meloy, J. R., & Rahman, T. (2021). 'Cognitive-Affective Drivers of Fixation in Threat Assessment.' *Behavioral Sciences & the Law*, 39(2), 170–189.

Merriam-Webster Dictionary. https://www.merriam-webster.com/dictionary/extremism

Neuman, S. (2015, 20 June). 'Photos of Dylann Roof, Racist Manifesto Surface on Website.' *NPR*.

New York Times. (2016, 14 January). 'Colorado: Man Says Clinic Killings Were Unplanned.' *The New York Times*.

Rahman, R. (2018). 'Extreme Overvalued Beliefs: How Violent Extremist Beliefs Become "Normalized".' *Behavioral Science*, 8, 10, 1–11.

Rahman, T., Meloy, R. J., & Bauer, R. (2019). 'Extremely Overvalued Belief and the Legacy of Carl Wernicke.' *The Journal of the American Academy of Psychiatry and the Law*, 47, 1–8.

Roucek, J. S. (1944). 'A History of the Concept of Ideology.' *Journal of the History of Ideas*, 5, 479–488. https://doi.org/10.2307/2707082

Safi, M. (2023, 19 June). 'His Ideas Resonate: How the Unabomber's Dangerous Manifesto Lives On.' *The Guardian*.

Silva (2022): 'Ideologically Motivated Mass Shootings: A Crime Script Analysis of Far-Right, Far-Left, and Jihadist-Inspired Attacks in the United States.' *Journal of Policing, Intelligence and Counter Terrorism*.

Silverstein, J. (2015, 20 June). 'Dylann Roof Was Obsessed with Trayvon

Martin, Wanted to Save the "White Race": Friend.' *NY Daily News*.

Suerth, J. (2020, 31 May). 'What Is Antifa?' *CNN*.

Tibby, C. & Bayly, C. (2023). 'Left-Wing Violent Extremism: Identifying Precursors and Growth in New Zealand.' *National Security Journal*.

Wernicke, C. (1892). 'Ueber Fixi Ideen.' *Deutsche Medicinische Wochenschrift, 25*, 2.

Young, C. (2019, 6 August). 'The Dayton Murderer Is Proof We Need to Take Left-Wing Violence Seriously.' *Forward*.

Chapter 7

Abdullah, A. (2024). 'The Impact of Technological Advancement on Culture and Society.' *Scientific Reports, 14*, 32140.

Benar News Staff (2019, 6 May). 'Australian Court Sentenced Bangladeshi Woman for IS-Inspired Attack.' *Benar News*.

Brooks, N., Honnavalli, V., & Jacobson-Lang, B. (2021). 'Children of ISIS: Considerations Regarding Trauma, Treatment and Risk.' *Psychiatry, Psychology, and Law, 29*(1), 107–133.

Department of Foreign Affairs and Trade. (2022, April). *Preventing and Countering Terrorism and Violent Extremism 2022-26: Australia's International Engagement Update and Way Ahead*. Australian Government.

Dodd, V., & Halliday, J. (2013, 19 December). 'Lee Rigby Murder: Michael Adebolajo and Michael Adebowale Found Guilty.' *The Guardian*.

FBI Behavioural Analysis Unit 1. (2025). *Beyond Belief: Preventing and Countering Violent Extremism in America*. US Department of Justice.

Horgan, J. G., Taylor, M., Bloom, M., & Winter, C. (2017). 'From Cubs to Lions: A Six Stage Model of Child Socialization into the Islamic State.' *Studies in Conflict & Terrorism, 40*(7), 645–664.

Hossain, I., & Reza, S. (2018, 30 March). 'Melbourne Student Had Contact with Nibras: Police.' *Prothomalo*.

Koehler, D. (2020). 'Violent Extremism, Mental Health and Substance Abuse Among Adolescents: Towards a Trauma Psychological Perspective on Violent Radicalization and Deradicalization.' *The Journal of Forensic Psychiatry & Psychology, 31*(3), 455–472.

Oxford Dictionary. https://www.lexico.com/definition/radicalization

Perez, E., Prokupecz, S., Shoichet, C. E., & Hume, T. (2016, 14 June). 'Omar Mateen: Angry, Violent 'Bigot" Who Pledged Allegiance to ISIS.' *CNN*.

Quaglio, G. (2019, 18 February). 'How the Internet Can Harm Us, and What We Can Do About It'. *Scientific Foresight*, European Parliament.

Silva (2022): 'Ideologically Motivated Mass Shootings: A Crime Script Analysis of Far-Right, Far-Left, and Jihadist-Inspired Attacks in the United States.' *Journal of Policing, Intelligence and Counter Terrorism*.

Storm, K. J., & Eyerman, J. 'Interagency Coordination: Lessons Learned from the 2004 London Train Bombings.' *NIJ Journal*, 28-32, Issue 260.

Todd, B. (2016, 14 June). 'Was the Orlando Shooter Gay?' Situation Room, *CNN*.

Tran, D. (2022, 6 May). 'Canadian Prisoner Attacked by Convicted Terrorist Now in Legal Fight with Victorian Government.' ABC News. https://www.abc.net.au/news/2022-05-06/momena-shoma-kailee-mitz-jihad-stabbing-prison/101039600

Chapter 8

BBC News. (2016, 23 November). 'Jo Cox Murder: Thomas Mair Given Whole-Life Sentence.' https://www.bbc.com/news/uk-37978582

Cobain, I., Parveen, N., & Taylor, M. (2016, 23 November). 'The Slow-Burning Hatred That Led Thomas Mair to Murder Jo Cox.' *The Guardian*.

Cobain, I., & Taylor, M. (2016, 23 November). 'Far-Right Terrorist Thomas Mair Jailed for Life for Jo Cox Murder.' *The Guardian*.

Drogin, B., & Fiore, F. (2009, 7 November). '*Retracing suspect's footsteps*.' Los Angeles Times.

FBI National Press Office (2012). 'Judge Webster Delivers Webster Commission Report on Fort Hood.' *FBI*.

Ferran, L., & Meek, J. G. (2018, 19 October). 'US Army Officer-Turned-Terrorist Thought Fort Hood Attack Would Save Mother's Soul, Letter Shows.' *ABC News*.

Ganor, B. (2021). 'Understanding the Motivations of "Lone Wolf" Terrorists: The "Bathtub" Model.' *Perspectives on Terrorism*, 15(2), 23–32.

Kenber, B. (2013, 28 August). 'Nadal Hasan Sentenced to Death for Fort Hood Shooting Rampage.' *The Washington Post*.

Meloy, J. R. (2021, 26 October), 'The Menu for an Extremist Ideology.' *Psychology Today*.

Meloy, J. R., & Rahman, T. (2021). Cognitive-Affective Drivers of Fixation in Threat Assessment. *Behavioral Sciences & the Law*, 39(2), 170–189.

Moghaddam, F. M. (2005). 'The Staircase to Terrorism: A Psychological Exploration.' *American Psychologist*, 60(2), 161–169.

Poppe, K. (2018). *Nidal Hasan: A Case Study in Lone-Actor Terrorism*. The George Washington University.

Silva (2022): 'Ideologically Motivated Mass Shootings: A Crime Script Analysis of Far-Right, Far-Left, and Jihadist-Inspired Attacks in the United States.' *Journal of Policing, Intelligence and Counter Terrorism*.

Chapter 9

American Psychiatric Association (2022). *Diagnostic and Statistical Manual of Mental Disorders, 5th ed.*, Text Revised; DSM-5-TR. American Psychiatric Publishing.

Capellan J. A., Silva J., Mills C., Schmuhl M. (2023). 'Who Lives, Who Dies, Who Decides: Differences Between Mass Public Shooters Who Survive, Are Killed, and Commit Suicide.' *Journal of Investigative Psychology and Offender Profiling*, 20(1), 80–96.

Corner, E., Bouhana, N., & Gill, P. (2019). 'The Multifinality of Vulnerability Indicators in Lone-Actor Terrorism.' *Psychology, Crime & Law*, 25(2), 111–132.

Corner, E., & Gill, P. (2015). 'A False Dichotomy? Mental Illness and Lone-Actor Terrorism.' *Law and Human Behavior*, 39(1), 23–34.

Corner, E., Gill, P., Schouten, R., & Farnham, F. (2018). 'Mental Disorders, Personality Traits, and Grievance-Fueled Targeted Violence: The Evidence Base and Implications for Research and Practice.' *Journal of Personality Assessment*, 100(5), 459–470.

Del-Monte, J., & Graziani, P. (2021). 'Anticipatory, Relief-Oriented and Permissive Beliefs in Patients with Suicidal Behaviors: An Exploratory Case-

Control Study.' *Archives of Suicide Research*, 25(3), 629–640.

Gilligan, J., & Richards, D. A. J. (2021). *Holding a Mirror up to Nature: Shame, Guilt, and Violence in Shakespeare*. Cambridge University Press.

Gill, P., Clemmow, C., Hetzel, F., Rottweiler, B., Salman, N., Van Der Vegt, I., Marchment, Z., Schumann, S., Zolghadriha, S., Schulten, N., Taylor, H., & Corner, E. (2021). 'Systematic Review of Mental Health Problems and Violent Extremism.' *The Journal of Forensic Psychiatry & Psychology*, 32(1), 51–78. https://doi.org/10.1080/14789949.2020.1820067

Horgan, J., Shortland, N., & Abbasciano, S. (2018). 'Towards a Typology of Terrorism Involvement: A Behavioral Differentiation of Violent Extremist Offenders.' *Journal of Threat Assessment and Management*, 5(2), 84–102.

Knoll, J. L., White, S. G., & Meloy, J. R. (2022). 'Envy and Extreme Violence.' *International Journal of Applied Psychoanalytic Studies*, 19(4), 462–482.

Lam, L. (2025, 30 May). 'How Bondi Mass Killer Slipped Through the Cracks in Australia.' *BBC News*.

Lankford A. (2016). 'Public Mass Shooters and Firearms: A Cross-National Study of 171 Countries.' *Violence and Victims*, 31(2), 187–199.

NZ Herald (2024, 17 April). 'Sydney Mall Attack: Joel Cauchi's Last Message to Parents Before Murderous Stabbing Spree.' *NZ Herald*.

Peterson, J. K., Densley, J. A., Hauf, M., & Moldenhauer, J. (2024). 'Epidemiology of Mass Shootings in the United States.' *Annual Review of Clinical Psychology*, 20(1), 125–148.

RNZ News (2025, 4 April). 'Bondi Junction Stabbing Offender Joel Cauchi Diagnosed with Schizophrenia at 17.' *Radio New Zealand*.

RNZ News (2025, 4 April). 'Joel Cauchi Was a Tormented Soul, Says His Tearful Father Andrew, After Bondi Junction Stabbing.' *Radio New Zealand*.

Silver, J. (2024). 'Public Mass Murder, Suicidality, and the "Final Act Mindset": A Research Note.' *Homicide Studies*.

White, S. G. (2017). 'Case Study: The Isla Vista Campus Community Mass Murder.' *Journal of Threat Assessment and Management*, 4(1), 20--47.

Chapter 10

Ferris, T. (2018, 20 February). 'Dr Gabor Maté – New Paradigms,

Ayahuasca, and Redefining Addiction'. Episode 298. *The Tim Ferris Show.*

Frank, J. D. (1961). *Persuasion and Healing.* Baltimore: John Hopkins Press.

Lazic, M. (2023, 20 May). '13 Saddening Children of Divorce Statistics of 2022'. *Legal Jobs.*

Maté, G., & Maté, D. (2022). *The Myth of Normal: Illness, Health and Healing in a Toxic Culture.* Penguin Books.

Miller, C. C. (2015, Nov 4). 'Stressed, Tired, Rushed: A Portrait of the Modern Family. *New York Times.*

Olito, F. (2019, 30 January). 'How the Divorce Rate has Changed Over the Last 150 Years.' *Business Insider.*

Ortiz-Ospina, E., & Roser, M. (2020, 25 July). *Marriages and Divorces.* Our World Data.

Perry, B. D. (2001). 'The Neurodevelopmental Impact of Violence in Childhood.' In D. Schetky & E. Benedek (Eds.), *Textbook of Child and Adolescent Forensic Psychiatry.* American Psychiatric Press.

Perry, B. D., & Szalavitz, M. (2008). *The Boy Who Was Raised as a Dog: And Other Stories from a Psychiatrist's Notebook. What Traumatized Children Can Teach Us About Loss, Love, and Healing.* Basic Books.

Perry, B. D., & Winfrey, O. (2022). *What Happened to You? Conversations on Trauma, Resilience, and Healing.* Bluebird.

Schmale, A. H. Jr., & Engel, H. L. (1967). 'The Giving Up-Given Up Complex Illustrated on Film.' *Archives of General Psychiatry, 17*(2), 135-145.

Woźniewicz, A., & Cosci, F. (2023). Clinical Utility of Demoralization: A Systematic Review of the Literature. *Clinical Psychology Review,* 99, 10227.

Chapter 11

Angvik, M. (2017, 15 May). *Security and Rights: The Development of Norwegian Counter-Terrorism Measures Post 9/11 and Their Impact on the Private Sphere.* Dissertation: University of Oslo.

Associated Press. (2021, 19 July). 'Norway's July 22, 2011, Terror Attack: A Timeline.' *AP News.*

Brooks, N. (2025, 12 May). 'Assessing Nickolas Cruz, with Professor Charles Scott.' Episode 3. *The Targeted Violence Podcast.*

Devine, C., & Pagliery, J. (2018, 27 February). 'Sheriff Says he Got 23 calls About Shooter's Family, but Records Show More.' *CNN*.

FBI National Press Office. (2018, 16 February). *Statement on the Shootings in Parkland, Florida*. FBI.

Brooks, N., & Shaw, R. (2022). 'Fixated and Grievance-Fuelled Persons: Considerations on the Dangers of Gaps, Silos and Disconnects.' *Psychiatry, Psychology, and Law, 29*(6), 854–870.

Izak, K. (2022). *Anders Behring Breivik. A Case Study of a Far-Right Terrorist - A Lone Wolf (Part I)*. In Terrorism – Studies, Analyses, Prevention (pp. 280-314).

Melle I. (2013). 'The Breivik Case and What Psychiatrists Can Learn From it.' *World Psychiatry, 12*(1), 16-21.

Pilkington, E. (2018, 17 February). 'Florida Shooting: FBI Admits it Failed to Investigate Nikolas Cruz Tipoff.' *The Guardian*.

Ranstorp, M. (2013). "Lone Wolf Terrorism". The Case of Anders Breivik. *Sicherheit Und Frieden (S+F) / Security and Peace, 31*(2), 87–92.

Rose, J., & Booker, B. (2018, 1 March). 'Parkland Shooting Suspect: A Story of Red Flags, Ignored.' *NPR*.

Shaw, R. (2020). *The First Preventers Playbook: How to Intervene, Disrupt, and Prevent Tragedy Before it Strikes*. Advantage.

Shugerman, E. (2018, 27 February). 'Sheriff's Office Received Almost 50 Calls About Florida Shooting Suspect and his Brother, Report Claims.' *Independent*.

Taleb, N. N. (2007, 22 April). The Black Swan: The Impact of the Highly Improbable. *New York Times*.

Taleb. N. N. (2011). *The Black Swan: The Impact of the Highly Improbable* (Second Edition). Random House.

Taylor, M. (2011, 26 July). 'Breivik Sent 'Manifesto' to 250 UK Contacts Hours Before Norway Killings.' *The Guardian*.

United Nations Office on Drugs and Crime. (2022). *Manual on Prevention of and Response to Terrorist Attacks: On the Basis of Xenophobia, Racism and Other Forms of Intolerance, or in the Name of Religion of Belief*. United Nations, Vienna.

Chapter 12

Barry-Walsh, J., James, D. V., & Mullen, P. E. (2020). 'Fixated Threat Assessment Centers: Preventing Harm and Facilitating Care in Public Figure Threat Cases and Those Thought to be at Risk of Lone-Actor Grievance Fueled Violence.' *CNS Spectrums*, 1-8.

Bourke, L. (2015, February 23). 'Sydney Siege: Man Haron Monis Was Not Considered a High-Priority Threat, Finds Report.' *The Sydney Morning Herald*.

Brooks, N. (2023, April). *Lone Actor Violence: Examining Threats, Lessons, and Learnings in a Complex and Developing Field*. Full-Day Workshop, Brisbane, Australia.

Brooks, N., & Shaw, R. (2022). 'Fixated and Grievance-Fuelled Persons: Considerations on the Dangers of Gaps, Silos and Disconnects.' *Psychiatry, Psychology, and Law, 29*(6), 854–870.

Calhoun, F. S., & Weston, S. W. (2015). 'Perspectives on Threat Management.' *Journal of Threat Assessment and Management, 2*(3-4), 258–267.

Commonwealth of Australia. (2015). *Martin Place Siege: Joint Commonwealths – New South Wales Review*. Canberra

Corwin, M. (2008, 3 November). 'Inside the LAPD's Threat Management Unit.' *Police 1*.

Counter Terrorism Policing. (2021, 24 February). 'Pilot App Launches to Help Public Report Terrorist Content Online.'

Dearden, L. (2021, 23 February). New App Launched for Reporting Terrorist Material as Extremists Exploit Pandemic.' *Independent*.

Drysdale, D. A., Modzeleski, W., & Simons, A. B. (2010, April). *Campus Attacks: Targeted Violence Affecting Institutions of Higher Education*. U.S. Secret Service, U.S. Department of
Homeland Security, Office of Safe and Drug-Free Schools, U.S. Department of Education, and Federal Bureau of Investigation, U.S. Department of Justice. Washington, D.C.

Europol. (2024). *European Union Terrorism Situation and Trend Report 2024*. Publications Office of the European Union, Luxenberg.

Europol. (2022). *European Union Terrorism Situation and Trend Report 2022*.

Publications Office of the European Union, Luxenberg.

Europol. (2021). *European Union Terrorism Situation and Trend Report 2021.* Publications Office of the European Union, Luxenberg.

FBI Behavioural Analysis Unit 1. (2025). *Beyond Belief: Preventing and Countering Violent Extremism in America.* U.S Department of Justice.

Follman, M. (2022). *Trigger Points: Inside the Mission to Stop Mass Shootings in America.* Harper Collins.

James, D.V., & Farnham, F. R. (2016). 'Outcome and Efficacy of Interventions by a Public Figure Threat Assessment and Management Unit: A Mirrored Study of Concerning Behaviors and Police Contacts Before and After Intervention.' *Behavioral Sciences & The Law, 34*(5), 660-680.

James, D. V., Kerrigan, T. R., Forfar, R., Farnham, F. R., & Preston, L. F. (2010). 'The Fixated Threat Assessment Centre: Preventing Harm and Facilitating Care.' *Journal of Forensic Psychiatry & Psychology, 21*(4), 521–536.

Kingston, B., & Goodrum, S. (2023, 4 March). '3 Ways to Prevent School Shootings, Based on Research.' *The Conversation.*

Mullen, P. E., Pathé, M., James, D., Meloy, R., & Farnham, F. (2025). *Fixated Research Group.* Website, Fixatedthreat.com

Muro, D., & Craciunas, O. (2025, 28 April). 'What We've Learnt About Lone-Actor Terrorism Over the Years Could Help Us Prevent Future Attacks.' *Policing Insight.*

National Police Foundation. (2021). *Averted School Violence (ASV) Database: 2021 Analysis Update.* Washington, DC: Office of Community Oriented Policing Services.

Office of the Director of National Intelligence. (2021). *Annual Threat Assessment of the US Intelligence Community.* United States of America

Payne, S. R. T., & Elliot, D. S. (2011). 'Safe2Tell: An Anonymous, 2/7 Reporting System for Preventing School Violence.' *New Directions for Youth Development,* 103-111.

Pathé, M. T., Haworth, D. J., Goodwin, T., Holman, A. G., Amos, S. J., Winterbourne, P., & Day, L. (2018). 'Establishing a Joint Agency Response to the Threat of Lone-Actor Grievance-Fuelled Violence.' *The Journal of Forensic Psychiatry & Psychology, 29*, 37-52.

Pool Resolutions (2024). *2024 Annual Threat Report*. Pool Reinsurance Company Limited.

Scott, R., & Shanahan, R. (2018). 'Man Haron Monis and the Sydney Lindt Café Siege - Not a Terrorist Attack.' *Psychiatry, Psychology and Law, 25*(6), 839–901.

Staniforth, A. (2021, 7 January). 'From Threat to Threat: UK Community Policing and Counter-Terrorism.' *Policing Insight.*

Staniforth, A. (2024, 5 July). 'The Golden Thread: Community Policing and Counter-Terrorism.' *Policing Insight.*

State Coroner of New South Wales.(2017). *Inquest into the deaths arising from the Lindt Café Siege: Findings and recommendations.* New South Wales Government.

The Threat Lab. (unknown). 'The Insider, The Threat Lab News Letter.' *The Threat Lab*, Volume 2, Issue 2.

United Nations Office on Drugs and Crime. (2022). *Manual on Prevention of and Response to Terrorist Attacks: On the Basis of Xenophobia, Racism and Other Forms of Intolerance, or in the Name of Religion of Belief.* United Nations, Vienna.

William, W. L., Lane, J., & Zona, M. A. (1996). 'Stalking: Successful Intervention Strategies.' *Police Chief, 63*(2), 24-26.

Wilson, S. P., Pathé, M. T., Farnham, F. R., & James, D. V. (2021). 'Fixated Threat Assessment Centers: The Joint Policing and Psychiatric Approach to Risk Assessment and Management in Cases of Public Figure Threat and Lone Actor Grievance-Fueled Violence.' In J. R. Meloy, & J. Hoffman (Eds.), *International Handbook of Threat Assessment*, Second Edition, (pp. 471-487). Oxford University Press.

Chapter 13

Adi, A., & Mathbout, M. (2018). 'The Duty to Protect: Four Decades After Tarasoff.' *American Journal of Psychiatry Residents' Journal, 13*, 6-8.

Anfang, S. A., & Appelbaum, P. S. (1996). 'Twenty Years After Tarasoff: Reviewing the Duty to Protect.' *Harvard Review of Psychiatry, 4*(2), 67–76.

Aron, N. R. (2017, 27 September). 'The murder of this 20-year-old Berkley coed changed the laws around psychology forever.' *Timeline*.

Borum, R. (2023). 'Mapping the Terrain: The Current State of Risk and Threat Assessment Practice in the Violent Extremism Field.' In C. Logan, R. Borum & P. Gill (Eds.), *Violent Extremism – A Handbook of Risk Assessment and Management* (pp. 43-78). London: UCL Press.

Borum, R., Scalora, M., Otto, R., Schneider, K., Kennedy, K., VanBerschot, J., Mix, E., & Jaros, S. (2021). *Strucutred Professional Judgement (SPJ) Tools: A Reference Guide for Counter-Insider Threat (C-InT) Hubs*. Defense Personnel and Security Research Center (PERSEREC).

Brooks, N. (2021). 'When Clients Harm Others: The Challenges Confronting the Psychology Profession.' *Psychology Aotearoa 13*(2), 106-111.

Connolly, A. R. (2016, 19 January). 'Report: Arapahoe High School Dismissed Warning Signs Before 2013 Colorado Shooting.' *UPI*.

Cook, A., Hart, S. D., & Kropp, P. R. (2021). *Multi-Level Guidelines (MLG V2): Structured professional judgment protocol for group-based violence, Workshop Manual*. Protect International.

Corner, E., & Pyszora, N. (2022). 'The Terrorist Radicalization Assessment Protocol-18 (TRAP-18) in Australia: Face Validity, Content Validity, and Utility in the Australian Context.' *Journal of Policing, Intelligence and Counter Terrorism, 17*(3), 246–268.

Davis, M. R., & Ogloff, J. R. P. (2008). 'Risk assessment.' In K. Fritzon & P. Wilson (Eds.), *Forensic Psychology and Criminology: An Australian Perspective* (pp. 141–164). McGraw-Hill Australia Pty Ltd.

Dietz, P., & Martell, D. A. (2010). 'Commentary: Approaching and Stalking Public Figures—A Prerequisite to Attack.' *Journal of the American Academy of Psychiatry and the Law, 38*(3), 341–348.

Elliott, I. A., Randhawa-Horne, K., Hambly, O. (2023). *The Extremism Risk Guidance 22+: An Exploratory Psychometric Analysis. Ministry of Justice Analytical Series*. London, U.K: Ministry of Justice. Report No.: 978-1-84099-985-3.

Fein, R. A., Vossekuil, B., Pollack, W. S., Borum, R., & Reddy, M. (2022). *Threat Assessment in Schools: A Guide to Managing Threatening Situations and to Creating Safe School Climates*. United States Secret Service and United

States Department of Education. Washington, D.C.

Gill, P., Horgan, J., & Deckert, P. (2014). 'Bombing Alone: Tracing the Motivations and Antecedent Behaviors of Lone-Actor Terrorists.' *Journal of Forensic Sciences, 59*(2), 425–435.

Goodrum, S., Thompson, A. J., Ward, K. C., Woodward, W. (2018). 'A Case Study on Threat Assessment: Learning Critical Lessons to Prevent School Violence'. *Journal of Threat Assessment and Management, 5*, 121-136.

Gawande, A. (2009). *The Checklist Manifesto: How to Get Things Right.* Profile Books.

Harris, G. T., & Rice, M. E. (2007). 'Characterizing the Value of Actuarial Violence Risk Assessments.' *Criminal Justice and Behavior, 34*(12), 1638–1658.

Heilbrun, K. (1997). 'Prediction Versus Management Models Relevant to Risk Assessment: The Importance of Legal Decision-Making Context.' *Law and Human Behavior, 21*(4), 347–359

Hempel, A. G., Meloy, J. R., & Richards, T. C. (1999). 'Offender and Offense Characteristics of a Nonrandom Sample of Mass Murderers.' *Journal of the American Academy of Psychiatry and the Law, 27*(2), 213–225.

Kenyon, J., Carter, A., Watson, S., & Farr, J. (2025). 'Adapting Risk Assessments to a Changing Terrorism Landscape: Revising the Extremism Risk Guidance.' *Psychiatry & Behavioral Science*. Online release.

Megargee, E. I. (1976). 'The Prediction of Dangerous Behavior.' *Correctional Psychologist, 3*(1), 3-22.

Meloy, J.R. (2017). *Terrorist Radicalization Assessment protocol-18 (TRAP-18) users' manual* (Vol. 1.0). Multi-Health Systems.

Meloy, J. R., Hoffman, J., Guldimann, A., & James, D. (2012). 'The Role of Warning Behaviour in Threat Assessment: An Exploration and Suggested Typology.' *Behavioral Sciences and the Law, 30*, 256-279.

Meloy, R. J., Hoffmna, J., Roshdi, K., & Guldimann, A. (2014). 'Some Warning Behaviors Discriminate Between School Shooters and Other Students of Concern.' *Journal of Threat Assessment and Management, 1*, 203-211.

Meloy, J.R., & Gill, P. (2016). 'The Lone-Actor Terrorist and the TRAP-18.'

Journal of Threat Assessment and Management, 3(1), 37–52.

Monahan, J. (1980). *The Clinical Prediction of Violent Behavior.* U.S. Dept. of Health and Human Services, Public Health Service, Alcohol, Drug Abuse, and Mental Health Administration, National Institute of Mental Health. Washington, D.C.

O'Toole, M. E. (2000). *The School Shooter: A Threat Assessment Perspective.* U.S. Department of Justice.

Petherick, W., Kannan, A., & Brooks, N. (2020). 'Victim Precipitation: An Outdated Construct or an Important Forensic Consideration?' *Journal of Forensic Psychology Research and Practice,* 21 (3), 214-229.

Pressman, E., Duits, N., Rinne, T., & Flockton, J. (2018). *Violent Extremism Risk Assessment—Version 2 Revised (VERA-2R).* Utrecht, Netherlands Institute of Forensic Psychiatry and Psychology.

Silver, J., Horgan, J., & Gill, P. (2018b). 'Foreshadowing Targeted violence: Assessing Leakage of Intent by Public Mass Murderers.' *Aggression and Violent Behaviour,* 39, 94-100.

Silver, J., Simons, A., & Craun, S. (2018). *A Study of the Pre-Attack Behaviours of Active Shooters in the United States Between 2000 and 2013.* Federal Bureau of Investigation: U.S. Department of Justice.

Supreme Court of California. (1976). *Tarasoff v Regents of the University of California, 17 Cal. 3d 425, 551 P.2d 334, 131 Cal. Rptr. 14.*

Vitelli, R. (2014, July 28). 'Revisiting Tarasoff: Should Therapists Breach Confidentiality Over a Patient's Violent Threat.' *Psychology Today.*

Vossekuil, B., Reddy, M., Fein, R., Borum, R., Modzeleski, W. (2002). *Final Report and Findings of the Safe School Initiative: Implication for the Prevention of School Attacks in the United States.* Washington, DC: U.S. Department of Education, Office of the Elementary and Secondary Education, Safe and Drug-Free School Program, and U.S. Secret Service, National Threat Assessment Center.

Warren, L. J. (2017, October). 'Recognising Clients Who May Pose a Risk of Violence.' *InPsych.*

White, S., & Meloy, R.J. (2016). *Workplace Assessment of Violence Risk – 21-item (WAVR-21): User's manual* (3rd ed.). Specialized Training Services.

Williams, M.M., Jones, N.T., Cilke, T.R.R., Gibson, K.A., Gray, A.E., & O'Shea, C.L. (2024, 7 March). 'Assessing the Reliability and Validity of the North Carolina BeTA Investigation Overview-25 (NCBIO-25) in a Sample of Active Shooters and Persons of Concern.' *Journal of Threat Assessment and Management*. Advance online publication.

Woodward, W., & Goodrum, S. (2016). *Report on the Arapahoe High School Shooting: Lessons Learned on information Sharing, Threat Assessment, and System Integrity*. Prepared for the Denver Foundation and Colorado SB 15-214: Committee on School Safety and Youth in Crisis.

Chapter 14

Baumeister, R. F., Campbell, J. D., Krueger, J. I., & Vohs, K. D. (2005, December), 'Exploding the Self-Esteem Myth.' *Scientific America*.

BBC News. (2019, 4 December). 'London Bridge: Usman Khan Completed Untested Rehabilitation Scheme.' *BBC News*.

BBC News. (2021, 27 April). Fishmongers' Hall: Usman Khan Influential Terrorist Prisoner.' *BBC News*.

Dodd, V., Sabbagh, D., & Syal, R. (2020, 2 February). 'Streatham Attacker Freed from Jail Days Ago After Terror Conviction.' *The Guardian*.

Dodd, V., & Sabbagh, D. (2020, 3March). 'Streatham Attacker was Released Amid Fears he Felt Terrorism 'Justified.' *The Guardian*.

FBI Behavioural Analysis Unit 1. (2025). *Beyond Belief: Preventing and Countering Violent Extremism in America*. U.S Department of Justice.

Halliday, J. (2016, 20 March). 'Almost 4,000 People Referred to Deradicalisation Scheme Last Year.' *The Guardian*.

Hiatte, B. (2010). 'School Terror Lessons to Kill Australians (25 August, 2010).' *The Western Australian*.

Krier, B. A. (1990, 5 June). 'California's Newest Export: Culture: The Self-Esteem Task Force Will Fold This Month None Too Soon for Some Critics. But its Message is Circulating Worldwide.' *Los Angeles Times*.

Quenzler, J. (2015, 2 October). 'Anzac Day Terror Plot: Blackburn Boy Sentenced to Life.' *BBC News*.

UK Parliament. (2020, 24 February). *Terrorist Offenders (Restriction of Early*

Release) Bill, Volume 802. Author.

Horgan, J., Meredith, K. and Papatheodorou, K. (2020). 'Does Deradicalization Work?' In D. M. D. Silva, & M. Deflem (Eds.), *Radicalization and Counter-Radicalization* (Sociology of Crime, Law and Deviance, Vol. 25), pp.9-20). Emerald Publishing Limited.

Sanchez, D. (2018, 5 October). 'What the Self-Esteem Movement Got Disastrously Wrong.' *Mercator.*

Smelser, N. J. (1989). 'Self-Esteem and Social Problems.' In A. M. Mecca, N. J. Smelser, & J. Vasconcellos (Eds.), *The Social Importance of Self-Esteem* (pp. 1-23). University of California Press.

Storr, W. (2017, 3 June). 'It was Quasi-Religious: The Great Self-Esteem Con.' *The Guardian.*

Weaver, M. (2021, 10 June). 'Fishmongers' Hall Terrorist Usman Khan was Lawfully Killed, Inquest Finds.' *The Guardian.*

Weeks, D. (2021, March). 'Lessons Learned from the U.K. Efforts to Deradicalize Terror Offenders.' *CTC Sentinel,* 33-39.

Chapter 15

Boyle, M., & Johnstone, L. (2020). *A Straight Talking Introduction to the Power Threat Meaning Framework: An alternative to psychiatric diagnosis* (The Straight Talking Introduction Series). PCCS Books.

Brooks, N., & Ebbrecht, C. K. (2025). 'Lone Actor Grievance-Fueled Violence and the Elusiveness of Motivation.' *Journal of Threat Assessment and Management.* Advance online publication.

Gibson, K. A., Craun, S. W., Ford, A. G., Solik, K., & Silver, J. M. (2020). 'Possible Attackers? A Comparison Between the Behaviors and Stressors of Persons of Concern and Active Shooters.' *Journal of Threat Assessment and Management, 7,* 1-12.

Gibson, K. Brubaker, L., & Simons, A. (2024, 1 May). 'Publicly Humiliating Events: A Precursor to Workplace Violence?' *Security Management, ASIS International.*

Johnstone, L., & Boyle, M. (2018). 'The Power Threat Meaning Framework:

An Alternative Nondiagnostic Conceptual System.' *Journal of Humanistic Psychology, 65*(4), 800-817.

Logan, C. (2023). 'From Behaviours to People: Formulation-Based Risk Management in Violent Extremism.' In C. Logan, R. Borum, & P. Gill (Eds.), *Violent Extremism: A Handbook of Risk Assessment and Management* (pp. 135–178). UCL Press.

Meloy, J. R., Amman, M., Guldimann, A., & Hoffmann, J. (2025). 'The Concept of Last Resort in Threat Assessment.' *Journal of Threat Assessment and Management, 12*(1), 45–63.

Peterson, J. (2023, 15 December). 'The Demons of Childhood Trauma with Aaron Stark.' Episode 405. *The Dr. Jordan B. Peterson Podcast*.

Stark, A. (2018, 8 March). 'I Would Have Been a School Shooter if I Could've Gotten a Gun.' *The Washington Post*.

Stark, A. (2018). *I Was Almost A School Shooter*. TEDx Talk. Boulder, Colorado.

Chapter 16

Angvik, M. (2017, 15 May). *Security and Rights: The Development of Norwegian Counter-Terrorism Measures Post 9/11 and Their Impact on the Private Sphere*. Dissertation: University of Oslo.

Australian Government. (2022). *Safeguarding Our Community Together: Australia's Counter-Terrorism Strategy 2022*. Commonwealth of Australia.

Beauchamp, Z. (2022, 26 May). 'Australia Confiscated 650,00 Guns. Murders and Suicides Plummeted.' *Vox*.

Brooks, N., & Shaw, R. (2022). 'Fixated and Grievance-Fuelled Persons: Considerations on the Dangers of Gaps, Silos and Disconnects.' *Psychiatry, Psychology, and Law, 29*(6), 854–870.

Grimson, M. (2015, 25 July). 'Port Arthur Massacre: The Shooting That Changes Australia's Gun Law. *NBC News*.

Home Office. (2018). *CONTEST: The United Kingdom's Strategy for Countering Terrorism*. HM Government.

Knaus, C. (2023, 20 January). 'Over 17,000 Weapons Surrendered in First Year of Australian Firearms Amnesty.' *The Guardian*.

Lozada, C. (2021, 3 September). 9/11 Was A test. The Books of the Last Two Decades Show How America Failed.' *The Washington Post.*

Ministers for The Department of Social Services. (2023, 25 October). *Helping Young Men to Have Healthy, Respectful Relationships.* The Hon Amanda Rishworth MP, Media Releases. Australian Government.

Ministry of Justice and Public Security (2016). *Prop. 68L (2015-2016), Amendments to the criminal procedure act etc. (Covert coercive measures).* Norwegian Government.

Taleb. N. N. (2011). *The Black Swan: The Impact of the Highly Improbable* (Second Edition). Random House.

The Queen v. Martin Bryant. (1996). *In the Criminal Sitting of The Supreme Court Held at Number 7, Salamanca Place, Hobart, Before His Honour The Chief Justice, on Tuesday the 19th Day of November, 1996.*

Roberts, S., & Westcott, S. (2023, 16 November). 'Tackling 'Toxic Masculinity' in Australia: We Can't Afford to Get This Wrong.' *Monash University.*

Royal Commission of Inquiry into the Terrorist Attack on Christchurch Mosques on 15 March 2019. (2020, December). *Summary of Recommendations.* Author.

Royal Commission of Inquiry into the Terrorist Attack on Christchurch Mosques on 15 March 2019. (2020, December). *Executive Summary.* Author.

United States Studies Centre. (2022, 1 June). *By the Numbers: Stark Contrast in Australian, US Gun Deaths.* USSC.

Chapter 17

Berg, M., & Gerstein, J. (2023, 7 April). 'Judge Limits Biden Administration Contact with Social Media Firms.' *Politico.*

Chang, A. (2021). 'TikTok's Youth Mode: China's Restrictions on Teen Users.' *Reuters.*

Clayton, A. (2023, 12 May). 'It isn't Helpful: How Media and Mass Shootings May Reinforce Each Other.' *The Guardian.*

Dias, B. S. (2023). *A Dangerous Road Without Warning Signs: The Blurred Lanes of Technology and the Targeted Violence Pandemic.* Doctoral Dissertation.

California School of Forensic Studies, Alliant International University.

Dwoskin, E. (2019, 7 November). 'Facebook Says it Removes the Vast Majority of Terrorism Content Automatically.' *The Washington Post*.

European Commission. (2022). *Digital Services Act: Ensuring a Safe and Accountable Online Environment*. European Union.

Fisher, M., & Taub, A. (2019, 14 June). 'On YouTube's Digital Playground, An Open Gate for Pedophiles.' *The New York Times*.

Fox, J. A., Sanders, N. E., Fridel, E. E., Duwe, G., & Rocque, M. (2021). 'The Contagion of Mass Shootings: The Interdependence of Large-Scale Massacres and Mass Media Coverage.' *Statistics and Public Policy, 8*, 53-66.

Follman, M. (2022). *Trigger Points: Inside the Mission to Stop Mass Shootings in America*. Harper Collins.

Green, A. (2018, 23 February). 'Parkland Survivors Call for No Notoriety for Mass Shooters.' *The Guardian*.

Kim, J. (2013). 'Understanding South Korea's "Cinderella Law" and its Implications.' *CNN*.

Kupper, J., Christensen, T. K., Wing, D., Hurt, M., Schumacher, M., & Meloy, R. (2022). 'The Contagion and Copycat Effect in Transnational Far-Right Terrorism: An Analysis of Language Evidence.' *Perspectives on Terrorism, 16*, 4–26.

Larkin, R. W. (2009). 'The Columbine Legacy: Rampage Shootings as Political Acts.' *American Behavioral Scientist, 52*(9), 1309–1326.

Lindzon, J. (2025, 2 January). 'Remarkable Girl, 12, Commits Suicide over Cyberbullying, Leaves Family Distraught: 'Children are Lost in Social Media.' *New York Post*.

McMinn, D. (2018, 2 March). 'Why the 'No Notoriety' Campaign Wants to Keep Shooters' Names out of the News.' *NPR*.

Middleton, K. (2024, 13 June). 'Albanese Follow Dutton's Lead with Tougher Position on Children's Social Media Ban.' *The Guardian*.

Ministry of Foreign Affairs and Trade New Zealand. (2023). *The Christchurch Call: New Zealand's fight against online extremism*. MFAT.

Oremus, W. (2024). 'Why We Shouldn't Ban Kids from Social Media.' *Vox*.

Oksanen, A., Hawdon, J., Holkeri, E., Näsi, M., & Räsänen, P. (2014).

'Exposure to Online Hate Among Young Social Media Users.' *Sociological Studies of Children and Youth, 18,* 253–273.

Pearson, A. (2024, November 28). 'Australian PM Albanese Says Social Media Firms Now Have Responsibility to Protect Minors.' *Reuters.*

Rothfeld, M. (2018, 22 February). 'Parkland Families Push for 'No Notoriety' in Mass Shootings.' *The New York Times.*

Schildkraut, J., Elsass, H. J., & Stafford, M. C. (2018). 'Could it Happen Here? Moral Panic, School Shootings, and Fear of Crime Among College Students.' *Crime & Delinquency, 64*(11), 1582–1606.

Solomon, A. (2014, 10 March). 'The Reckoning. The Father of Sandy Hook Killer Searches for Answers.' *The New Yorker.*

Suicide Prevention Australia. (2024, 27 November). 'Reckless Haste: Rushed Legislation on Social Media Ban Risks Harm to Young Australians.' Media Release. *Suicide Prevention Australia.*

Toh, A. (2023, 15 May). 'Christchurch Call: Seeking to Curb Online Extremism and Prevent Violence.' *Human Rights Watch.*

United Nations Counter-Terrorism Committee Executive Directorate. (2022). *The Christchurch Call and its Global Impact.* United Nations.

Wall Street Journal. (2023, 8 July): 'WJS Opinion: The Biden-Big Tech Censorship.' *Wall Street Journal.*

Wall Street Journal. (2023, 10 July). 'WJS Opinion: Big Tech Censorship Goes to Court.' *Wall Street Journal.*

Chapter 18

Deci, E. L., & Ryan, R. M. (2000). 'The "What" and "Why" of Goal Pursuits: Human Needs and the Self-Determination of Behavior.' *Psychological Inquiry, 11,* 227-268.

FBI Behavioural Analysis Unit 1. (2025). *Beyond Belief: Preventing and Countering Violent Extremism in America.* U.S Department of Justice.

Gove, W. R. (1985). 'The Effect of Age and Gender on Deviant Behaviour: A Biological Perspective.' In A. S. Rossi (Ed.), *Gender and the Life Course* (pp. 115-144). New York, American Sociological Association.

Leibrich, J. (1993). *Straight to the Point: Angles on Giving up Crime.*

University of Otago Press.

Maruna, S. (2004). 'Desistance from Crime and Explanatory Style: A New Direction in the Psychology of Reform.' *Journal of Contemporary Criminal Justice, 20*(2), 184-200.

Maruna, S. (2007). *Making Good: How Ex-Convicts Reform and Rebuild their Lives*. American Psychological Association. Kindle Edition.

Maruna, S., Porter, L., & Carvalho, I. (2004). 'The Liverpool Desistance Study and Probation Practice: Opening the Dialogue.' *Probation Journal, 51*(3), 221-232

McAdams. D. (1996). *The Stories We Live By: Personal Myths and the Making of The Self*. Guildford Press.

Stark, A. (2018). *I Was Almost A School Shooter*. TEDx Talk. Boulder, Colorado.

Ward, T. (2002). 'Good Lives and the Rehabilitation of Offenders: Promises and Problems.' *Aggression and Violent Behavior, 7*(5), 513–528.

Ward, T., Mann, R. E., & Gannon, T. A. (2007). 'The Good Lives Model of Offender Rehabilitation: Clinical Implications.' *Aggression and Violent Behavior, 12*, 87–107.

Ward, T., & Marshall, B. (2007). 'Narrative Identity and Offender Rehabilitation. *International Journal of Offender Therapy and Comparative Criminology, 51*, 279–297.

Ward, T., Rose, C., & Willis, G. M. (2012). 'Offender Rehabilitation: Good Lives, Desistance and Risk Reduction.' In G. Davies & A. Beech (Eds.), *Forensic Psychology: Crime, Justice, Law, Interventions* (2nd edition) (pp 407–424). Oxford, UK: Wiley Blackwell.

Yates, P. W., & Prescott, D. (2011). *Building a Better Life: A Good Lives and Self-regulation Workbook*. Safer Society Press.

Chapter 19

Campbell, J. (1949). *The Hero with A Thousand Faces*. Pantheon Books.

Maher, K. (2016, 13 August). 'The Villain's Journey.' *Medium*.

McAdams. D. (1996). *The Stories We Live By: Personal Myths and the Making of The Self*. Guildford Press.

Perlin, J.D., & McAdams, D.P. (2024). 'Redemption: Stories Heroes Live By.' In S. T. Allison., J. K. Beggan., & Goethals, G.R. (Eds.), *Encyclopedia of Heroism Studies*. Springer.

Rogers, B. A., Chicas, H., Kelly, J. M., Kubin, E., Christian, M. S., Kachanoff, F. J., Berger, J., Puryear, C., McAdams, D. P., & Gray, K. (2023). 'Seeing Your Life Story as a Hero's Journey Increases Meaning in Life.' *Journal of Personality and Social Psychology, 125*(4), 752–778.

Solomon, P. (2013). *What is the Hero's Journey?* TEDx Talk. Rock Creek Park, Washington D.C.

Werning, M. (2016, 1 October). *Become an Everyday Hero*. TEDx Talk. University of Groningen, Netherlands.

Chapter 20

Calhoun, F., & Weston, S. (2003). *Contemporary Threat Management: A Practical Guide for Identifying, Assessing, and Managing Individuals of Violent Intent*. San Diego, CA: Specialized Training Services.

Daily Herald Contributor. (2024, January 25). 'Fishing Upstream': What RCMP Psychologist Says Could Stop the Next Myles Sanderson. *Prince Albert Daily Herald*.

Heath, D. (2020). *Upstream: How to Solve Problems Before They Happen*. Penguin Random House.

Honderich, H., & Murphy, J. (2022, 8 September). 'Canada Stabbing Suspect Myles Sanderson Dies After Arrest.' *BBC*.

Murphy, J. (2024, 28 February). 'Canada's Mass Killer's Last Words Revealed at Coroner's Inquest.' *BBC*.

Perry, B. D., & Winfrey, O. (2022). *What Happened to You? Conversations on Trauma, Resilience, and Healing*. Bluebird.

Werning, M. (2016, 1 October). *Become an Everyday Hero*. TEDx Talk. University of Groningen, Netherlands.

www.ingramcontent.com/pod-product-compliance
Lightning Source LLC
Chambersburg PA
CBHW022047290426
44109CB00014B/1015